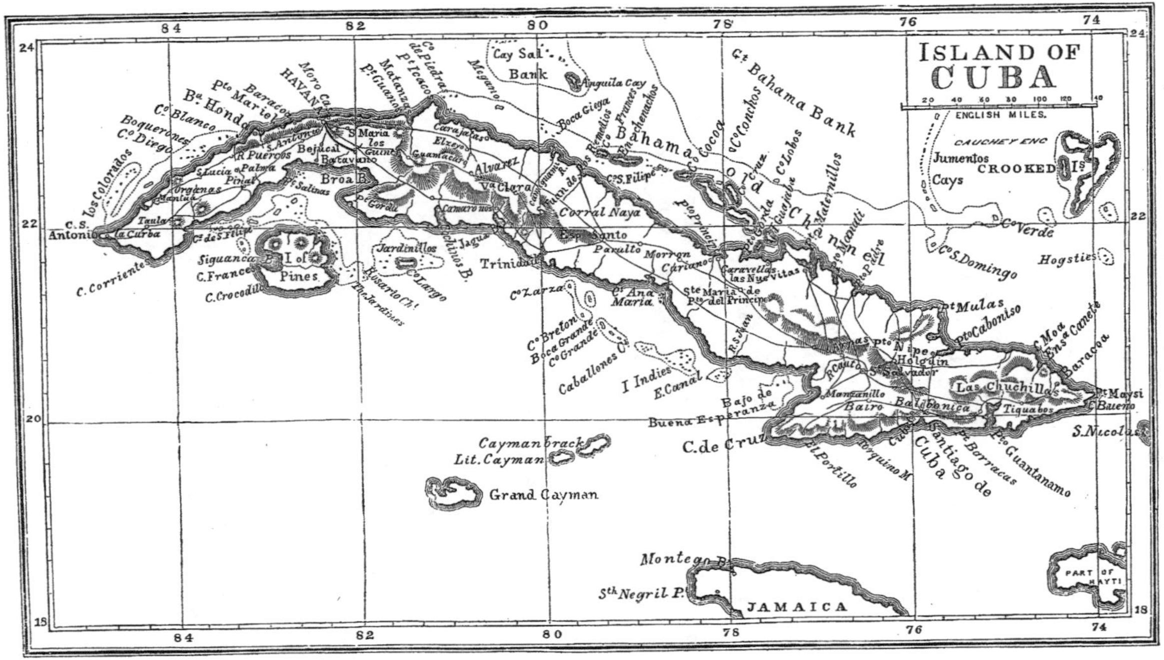

ISLAND OF CUBA
ENGLISH MILES.
CROOKED Is.
Jumentos Cays
Hogsties
Gt Bahama Bank
Old Channel
Cay Sal Bank
Anguila Cay
HAVANA
Moro Ca.
Matanzas
Pt. Guanos
Pt. Icacos
Co. de Piedras
Bahama
Cocoa
Bo. Honda
Co. Blanco
Boquerones
Co. Dirgo
los Colorados
C.S. Antonio
C. Corriente
Siguanca
C. Frances
C. Crocodile
I. of Pines
Broa B.
Jardinillos
Co. Largo
Rosario Ch.
The Jardines
Alvarez
Va. Clara
Corral Naya
Trinidad
Co. Zarza
Co. Breton
Boca Grande
Caballones C.
I. Indies
E. Canal
Bajo de Buena Esperanza
C. de Cruz
Manzanillo
Bairo
Holguin
Pto. Nipe
Pt. Mulas
Pto. Cabonico
Las Cuchillas
Santiago de Cuba
Pto. Guantanamo
Pt. Barracas
Baracoa
Pt. Maysi
S. Nicolas
Cayman Brack
Lit. Cayman
Grand Cayman
Montego B.
Sth. Negril P.
JAMAICA
PART OF HAYTI
Co. S. Domingo
Co. Verde
Tiquabos
Caravellas
las Nuevitas
Ste. Maria de Pto. del Principe
Cto. Ana Maria
Pto. Principe
Parulto
Morron
Cariano
Trinidad
Cochinos B.
Jagua
El Portillo
Turquino M.

CUBA,

AND

THE CUBANS;

COMPRISING

A HISTORY OF THE ISLAND OF CUBA,

ITS PRESENT SOCIAL, POLITICAL, AND DOMESTIC CONDITION; ALSO, ITS RELATION TO ENGLAND AND THE UNITED STATES.

BY THE AUTHOR OF "LETTERS FROM CUBA."

WITH AN APPENDIX,

CONTAINING IMPORTANT STATISTICS, AND A REPLY TO SENOR SACO ON ANNEXATION, TRANSLATED FROM THE SPANISH.

NEW YORK:
SAMUEL HUESTON, 139 NASSAU STREET.
GEORGE P. PUTNAM, 155 BROADWAY.
1850.

STEREOTYPED BY BANER AND PALMER,
201 William st., corner of Frankfort, N. Y.

PREFACE.

No excuse is deemed necessary for publishing a volume on Cuba, at a time when the attention both of England and the United States is directed toward that island with eager interest. Political events have transpired so rapidly within the last two years, that

> "That of an hour's age doth hiss the speaker."

We are borne onward by a force which seems hastening some great consummation. If all do not agree as to the result which these changes are to bring, no one can shut his eyes to the changes themselves. They have multiplied within the year; they are multiplying; they will continue to multiply. The conservative and the radical—the ultra whig and the ultra democrat—are all overwhelmed by the resistless course of things, if they stop even but a moment to contemplate it. What is to be done? Shall we attempt to stay this irresistible progression, and be swept away by it; or shall we rather do what we may to control and direct it?

As to Cuba, a word only need be said. With or without the United States, she will soon be free from Spanish dominion; and—which is of greater consequence to this country—if free without our aid or influence, she falls to England. How will the United States relish the possession by that nation of a point which commands the Gulf of Mexico and the mouth of the Mississippi?

The analysis of Cuban taxes in these pages is believed to be the first of the kind ever attempted; and it is hoped the chapters on the social and domestic manners of the Cubans, on religion and education, will interest the reader.

The Appendix contains much important statistical information, together with a translation of a pamphlet from the Spanish in reply to Don José Antonio Saco, on the subject of the annexation of Cuba to the United States. This last is given to illustrate the feeling among the Cubans themselves, and to show the opinions held by the leading Cuban planters.

It should be stated that the larger part of the first chapter of this work is abridged from the historical notice of Cuba in "Turnbull's Travels in Cuba."

New York, March 1st, 1850.

CUBA AND THE CUBANS.

CHAPTER I.

Cuba discovered by Columbus.—Names of the Island.—Character of the Natives.—Town of Baracoa.—Havana burnt in 1538.—Seat of Government transferred to Havana.—Succession of Governors. —Cultivation of Tobacco and Sugar introduced about 1580.—Slavery introduced at the same time.—Depredations of Pirates.—A Commissioner of the Inquisition comes from Carthagena to reside in Havana.—Jamaica taken by the English.—Apprehensions of the Cubans.—The English repulsed.—Walls commenced round the City of Havana in 1663.—City of Santiago destroyed by an Earthquake.—Invasion of the Island by the English in 1762.—Morro Castle taken by them July 30th, and the City of Havana on the 14th of August.—Distribution of the Spoils.—Peace concluded with England in 1763.—The Island restored to the Spaniards.—Results of the wise Policy of Las Casas.—Great Fire in 1802.—News of the Proceedings of Napoleon in Spain.—Its Effects in Cuba.—Negro Conspiracy.—Different Captains-General.

CUBA, the finest and largest of the West India Islands, was discovered by Columbus himself, on the 28th day of October, 1492, and was named by him Juana, in honor of Prince John, the son of Ferdinand and Isabella, the sovereigns of Aragon and Castile.

Upon the death of Ferdinand, the island was called Fernandina. It afterward received the name of Santiago, as a mark of reverence for the patron saint of Spain, and still later, the inhabitants, to illustrate their piety, gave it that of Ave Maria, in honor of the Holy Virgin.

Notwithstanding these several titles, the island is still principally known by its original Indian name of

Cuba; a name which it bore when the great navigator first landed on its shores, and which in all probability it is destined to retain.

* With regard to the character of the aboriginal inhabitants of the island, it is universally admitted by all the Spanish authors who have written on the subject, that they were disinterested and docile, gentle and generous, and that they received the first discoverer, as well as the conquerors, who followed in his track, with the most marked attention and courtesy. At the same time they are represented as being entirely given up to the enjoyment of those personal indulgences, and all the listlessness and love of ease, which the climate is supposed to provoke, and which is said to have amounted in the eyes of their European conquerors to positive cowardice and pusillanimity. They seldom spoke until first addressed by the strangers, and then with perfect modesty and respect. Their hospitality was unbounded; but they were unwilling to expose themselves to any personal fatigue beyond what was strictly necessary for their subsistence. The cultivation of the soil was confined, as Columbus had observed, to the raising of yams, garbanzos, and maize, or Indian corn, but as huntsmen and fishermen they were exceedingly expert. Their habiliments were on the most limited scale, and their laws and manners sanctioned the practice of polygamy. The use of iron was totally unknown to them, but they supplied the want of it with pointed shells, in constructing their weapons, and in fashioning their implements for fishing and the chase. Their almost total want of quadrupeds is worthy of notice.

Although the island was divided into nine principalities, under nine different caciques, all independent of each other, yet such was the pacific disposition of the inhabitants, that the most perfect tranquillity prevailed

* Turnbull's Travels in Cuba.

throughout the island at the time of the arrival of the invaders. The several governments were administered in the simplest form, the will of the cacique being received as law by his subjects, and the age he had attained being in general the measure of his influence and authority, and of the reverence and respect with which he was treated. Their religion was limited to a belief in the immortality of the soul, and to the existence of a beneficent Deity—*un Dios remunerador*. But their priests were cunning, superstitious, or fanatic, pretending to intelligence with malignant spirits, and maintaining their influence over the people by working on their fears, and practicing the grossest and most ridiculous extravagances. No sanguinary sacrifices were resorted to, however; still less could the gentle race be chargeable with the horrid practices of the savage anthropophagi; and, according to the earliest Spanish authorities, they distinguished themselves beyond any other Indian nation, by the readiness and docility with which they received the doctrines of Christianity.

The town of Baracoa, which was called *de la Asumpcion*, was the first that was founded, and was for some time considered the capital, until, in the year 1514, the whole of it had been overrun and examined. In that year, the towns of Santiago and Trinidad, on the southern side, were founded for the purpose of facilitating the communications of the new colonists with the Spanish inhabitants of Jamaica. Near the centre of the island also were established, soon after this period, the towns of Bayamo, Puerto Principe, and Santi-Espiritus, and that of Baracoa was considerably enlarged. In the sequel, as there was no town toward the north, that of San Juan de los Remedios was founded; and on the 25th of July, 1515, at the place now called Batabano, on the south side of the island, was planted a town with the name of San Cristobal de la Habana, in deference to the memory of the illustrious discoverer; but in the year 1519 this name was transferred to the place where the capital now stands. The leaning of the Spaniards toward the southern side of the island appears to have arisen from their previous possession of Jamaica and the Costa Firme; as till then they had no idea of the existence of the Floridas, or of New Spain; the expedition for the conquest of which, as well as the steps toward their first discovery, having been taken from the island of Cuba.

The town of Baracoa having first been raised to the dignity of a city and a bishopric, was declared the capital of the island in 1518, and remained so till 1522, when both were transferred to Santiago de Cuba. In 1538 the Havana, second city of the name, was surprised by a French privateer, who reduced it to ashes. This misfortune brought the governor of the island, Hernando de Soto, to the spot, who lost no time in laying the foundation of the *Castillo de la Fuerza*, one of the numerous fortresses which still exist for the defence of the city. With this protection, combined with the advantageous geographical position of the harbor, the ships already passing, charged with the riches of New Spain, on their way to the Peninsula, were induced to call there for supplies of water and provisions. In this way the Havana began to rise in importance by insensible degrees, insomuch that in 1549, on the arrival of a new governor, Gonzalez Perez de Angulo, he resolved on making it his place of residence. His example was followed by subsequent governors, and in this way the city, although without any royal or legal sanction, came to be silently regarded as the capital of the island, until in 1589 it was formally declared so by the peninsular government, at the time of the nomination of the first captain-general, *El Maestre de Campo*, Juan de Tejada, who was positively directed to take up his residence at the Havana.

In the annals of the island the names of the first governors and of their lieutenants have not been recorded with a degree of accuracy that can be altogether depended on. All that is known with certainty is, that the early chiefs resided at Santiago de Cuba, from its being the place where the largest population was collected, from its proximity to Jamaica and St. Domingo, and from its being the seat of the ecclesiastical jurisdiction. For the Havana and other towns of inferior importance, lieutenants were appointed. This system continued until the year 1538, when Hernando de Soto, who to the rank of *Adelantado* of the Floridas, added the office of governor of Cuba, having arrived at Santiago, passed a few days there, and then proceeded to the continent. In his absence he left the government of the island in the hands of a lady, Dona Isabel de Bobadilla, and gave her for a colleague, Don Juan de Rojas. This Rojas had previously resided at the Havana, in quality of lieutenant-governor; and it is from this date that the gradual transference of the seat of power from Santiago to the Havana may be said to have arisen. It was not till the year 1607 that the island was divided into two separate governments.

In 1545, Don Juan de Avila assumed the government, and to him in 1547 succeeded Don Antonio de Chavez, to whom the Havana is indebted for its first regular supply of water, bringing it from the river called by the aborigines Casiguaguas, and by the Spaniards Chorrera, a distance of two leagues from the city. At that period the trade of the place was limited. The largest and wealthiest proprietors were mere breeders of cattle; as yet agriculture was very little attended to, and any actual labor performed consisted in exploring the neighborhood in pursuit of the precious metals.

To this governor succeeded Dr. Gonzalo Perez de Angulo, who, according to the historian Urrutia, was the first who resided at the Havana during the greater part of his administration. At this period the number of cattle and the practice of agriculture had so much increased that the expeditions from the neighboring continent obtained their supplies at the Havana, and from thence also large quantities of provisions were sent to the *Terra Firma*. For some time large profits were made by means of these exports, more especially in the sale of horses for the troops; but the continental settlements, having at length been able to provide for themselves, this source of profit was dried up.

In the year 1554 the government was assumed by Don Diego de Mazariegos, and, during his administration, the Havana was again attacked and reduced to ashes by the French, notwithstanding the protection supposed to be afforded by the Castillo de la Fuerza. The other towns of the island were also insulted, insomuch that the bishop of the diocese was compelled to leave Santiago and take up his residence at Bayamo, causing a serious misunderstanding between the ecclesiastical authorities and the civil governor.

To Mazariegos, in 1565, succeeded Garcia Osorio, and to Osorio, two years afterward, Don Pedro Melendez de Avilez, who at the same time held the office of *Adelantado* of the Floridas, administering the affairs of the island for a number of years by means of a series of lieutenant-governors. At this period, the hospital of San Juan de Dios, and a church dedicated to San Cristobal, were erected at the Havana. This church was built on the spot now occupied by the residence of the captain-general. Don Gabriel Montalvo was the successor of Melendez, and assumed the government in 1576. In his time the Franciscan convent was erected, in spite of the opposition of the bishop; and preparations were made, by the building of suitable vessels, for the extirpation of the pirates by whom the coasts of the island were infested. Don Francisco Carreno, the successor of Montalvo, assumed the command in 1578. In his time the weights and measures of the island were regulated; and vast quantities of timber were shipped to the mother-country, to contribute toward the construction of the convent and palace of the Escorial.

During the administration of Don Gaspar de Torres, the successor of Carreno, who arrived in 1580, not only Cuba, but the neighboring islands of Jamaica and St. Domingo, were more than ever annoyed by piratical incursions. The expense occasioned by the attempts to suppress them was so great, that it became necessary to impose a special tax, called *la sisa de piragua*, to cover it.

At this period was begun the cultivation of tobacco and the sugar-cane, the labor of which was found to be too great for the indolent aborigines, whose numbers had already been materially diminished by the state of slavery to which they had been reduced. It was to promote the production of these new luxuries, that a royal license was first obtained for importing negroes from the coast of Africa.

The continued presence and increasing numbers of the pirates began to give a factitious importance to the castellanos of the fortress, which protected the harbor of the Havana, and sheltered the *lanchas* and *piraguas* and the *guardacostas* themselves. A military power thus insensibly arose, which, coming into collision with that of the civil governor, caused a great deal of disturbance and confusion. The next governor, Don Gabriel de Lujan, who arrived in 1584, came to such a serious rupture with Don Diego Fernandez de Quinones, the Castellano de la Fuerza, that the real audiencia of the district, at the instigation of Quinones, took it upon them to suspend Don Gabriel from his administration of the government, but some time afterward restored him. On the application of the *ayuntamiento*, the two offices were afterward combined and vested in the same individual. During Lujan's administration, several hostile demonstrations were made against the island; but none of them were seriously prosecuted. The attacks of a diminutive enemy, the ant, became so alarming, however, that it was thought necessary by the Cabildo, or chapter of the diocese, to elect a new patron saint, and to confer that dignity on San Marcial, the bishop agreeing to celebrate his fiesta, and keep his day yearly, on the condition of his interceding for the extermination of the hormigas and vivijaguas.

The successor of Lujan, Don Juan de Tejada, was the first governor who arrived with the rank of captain-general, in which was included the same powers and jurisdiction enjoyed by the *vireyes* of the continental possessions of the crown. Tejada was directed to commence the construction of the two fortresses now known as the Morro and the Punta, and for this purpose brought with him the Engineer Don Juan Bautista Antoneli; and he was authorized to negotiate with the provinces of New Spain for obtaining contributions, by which to support the garrison, which at that time was limited for all the three fortresses to 300 men. After the building of the Morro was begun, it is said that Antoneli having ascended the heights of the Cabana, remarked to those about him, that from that point the city and the Morro itself would be commanded. This opinion having been communicated to the government, the construction of the present fortress of the Cabanas was immediately determined on. During Tejada's government the Havana received the title of *Ciudad;* the ayuntamiento was increased to the number of twelve regidores; and a coat of arms was given to it by Philip the Second, bearing on a blue field three castles *argent*, in allusion to the Fuerza, the Morro, and the Punta, and a golden key to signify that it was the key of the Indies; the whole surmounted by a crown.

Tejada was succeeded as captain-general in 1602 by Don Pedro Valdes, who made strong representations to the court on the subject of the excesses committed by the pirates, by whose incursions Santiago had been almost depopulated. The bishop, on returning there from Bayamo on a temporary visit, was seized, tied, stripped, and carried off by the pirate Giron, and detained for eighty days on board his vessel, until he was ransomed by the payment of 200 ducats and five arrobas of beef by Don Gregorio Ramos, who, after rescuing the bishop, succeeded in destroying the pirate. From the insecurity of Santiago, this bishop attempted, but without success, to establish his cathedral at the Havana. The supreme government, however, to stay the progress of depopulation at Santiago, resolved on establishing there a subordinate governor with the rank of *capitan a guerra*, and appointed to the office Don Juan de Villaverde, the Castellano of the Morro, who was charged with the defence of his new jurisdiction against the pirates.

The successor of Valdes was Don Gaspar Ruiz de Pereda in 1608; and that of Pereda in 1616 was Don Sancho de Alquiza. This last had been previously the governor of Venezuela and Guiana, and he is recorded to have applied himself with energy to the working of the copper mines at Cobre in the neighborhood of Santiago; the superintendence of which was for some time annexed to the office of captain-general of the Havana, although it was afterward transferred to the lieutenant-governor at Santiago. The annual produce of that period was about 2000 quintals, and the copper extracted is represented to have been of a quality superior to any thing then known in the founderies of Europe. Alquiza died after having enjoyed his office only two years; and by a provision of the real audiencia, he was succeeded in the temporary command by Geronimo de Quero, the castellano of the Morro, whose military rank was that of *sargento mayor*. From this period till the year 1715 it appears that, in the nomination of captains-general, a declaration was constantly introduced to the effect that the castellanos of the Morro, on the death of the captain-general, should succeed to the military command of the island; but since the year 1715 an officer has been specially named with the rank of *teniente rey* or *cabo-subalterno*, whose functions acquire an active character only on the death or incapacity of his chief.

Doctor Damian Velasquez de Contreras succeeded Alquiza in 1620, and Don Lorenzo de Cabrera, the next captain-general, was appointed to the command in 1626. A charge was brought against Cabrera, that he had sold a cargo of negroes in the Havana without a royal license; which being backed by other complaints, the licenciado Don Francisco de Prada was sent out to inquire into them, and by him the captain-general was sent home to the Peninsula, when de Prada assumed the civil and political jurisdiction, and assigned the military command to Don Cristobal de Aranda, the alcaide of the Morro. During the joint administration of de Prada and Aranda it was resolved to shut up the entrance of the harbor by means of a chain drawn across it, a resolution which is described by the historians of the period as having been exceedingly extravagant and absurd.

The next captain-general was Don Juan Bitrian de Viamonte, who began his administration in 1630, and projected the construction of two strong towers, the one in Chorrera, and the other in Cojimar, but the plan was not carried into effect until the year 1646. At this period a certain good woman, known by the name of Magdalena de Jesus, established a sort of female sanctuary, called a *beaterio*, which gave rise to the establishment of the first female monastery of Santa Clara.

Fears of an invasion of the island by the Dutch now began to be entertained in the Peninsula; and as Viamonte's health was infirm, he was removed to the presidency of St. Domingo; and, in 1634, Don Francisco Riano y Gamboa was sent out to replace him. Gamboa introduced important reforms in the collection of the revenue. He established a court of accounts at the Havana, to which was afterward referred the examination of all public disbursements, not only for the island of Cuba, but for Porto Rico, the Floridas, and that portion of the Spanish navy called the windward fleet, *la Armada de Barlovento*. At first, a single accountant-general was named; but a second was afterward added, with instructions to visit alternately the various parts where the colonial revenue was collected or disbursed. During the government of Gamboa, also, a commissioner of the Inquisition came from Carthagena to reside in the Havana; to provide for whose support one of the canons of the cathedral of Santiago was suppressed. The bishops had for some time acquired a taste for residing in the capital, and other members of the ecclesiastical cabildo began to follow their example, soon degenerating into an abuse which loudly called for a remedy.

The successor of Gamboa was Don Alvaro di Luna y Sarmiento, who commenced his administration in 1639, and in the course of it completed the castle of Chorrera, two leagues to leeward of the Havana, and the Torreon de Cojimar, one league to windward.

In 1647, Sarmiento was succeeded by Don Diego de Villalva y Toledo, who, in 1650, was replaced by Don Francisco Gelder. During Gelder's administration, the establishment of the Commonwealth in England gave rise to serious apprehensions for the safety of the Spanish possessions in America; especially when it became known, that, in 1655, a squadron had sailed by order of the Protector, the ostensible object of which was the reconciliation of the English colonies to the new form of government, but with the real design of capturing Jamaica. It is scarcely necessary to add, that this design was successfully executed; that the Spanish defenders of Jamaica were dispersed, and the governor killed, and that many of the inhabitants removed in consequence to Cuba. An attempt on the Havana was also made by this expedition, but the assailants were successfully resisted. The failure is ascribed by the Spaniards to a sort of miracle performed in their favor. The invaders having landed on a very dark night, they became so terrified, according to the Spanish authorities, by the noise of the land-crabs and the flitting light of the fire-flies, which they took for an enemy in ambuscade, that they fled to their ships in the utmost disorder and confusion.

The next captain-general was Don Juan Montano, who arrived in 1656. During his time the Spaniards of Jamaica continued to defend themselves under two distinguished hacendados, Don Francisco Proenza, and Don Cristobal de Isasi; who, for their exertions in preserving the island to the Spanish crown, received thanks and honors from the court. Orders were also sent out to the other Spanish settlements in America to lend their assistance to the Jamaica loyalists; and a strong expedition was prepared in the Peninsula, having the same object in view. In the end, however, in consequence of the sickness which prevailed on board the ships, the expedition never sailed, and the Spaniards were compelled to evacuate the island.

Montano having died within a year after his arrival, was succeeded in the command, in 1658, by Don Juan de Salamanca, in whose time the incursions of the pirates became more troublesome than ever, on all the coasts of Spanish America. As many of them had the audacity to sail under the flags of France and England, the court of Spain addressed itself to these governments on the subject, and received for answer that, having no countenance or authority from either, the Spaniards were at liberty to deal with them as they thought fit. At this period the French, having established themselves in the island of Tortuga, began from thence by slow degrees, first on hunting parties, and afterward more permanently, to make encroachments on the neighboring coast of the island of St. Domingo; until, in the end, they had completely taken possession of the western part of it, and created there a respectable colony. According to the Spanish authorities, the French colonists of St. Domingo formed an alliance with the English in Jamaica, and, without the sanction of either of their governments in Europe, made piratical incursions in the Spanish territories, and at length became so formidable, that the Spaniards found it necessary to fortify their possessions, and to combine together for their mutual protection. The most remarkable of these piratical leaders was the Frenchman Lolonois and the celebrated Morgan.

In 1663, arrived as captain-general Don Rodrigo de Flores y Aldana, who in the following year was relieved by Don Francisco Orejon y Gaston, previously governor of Gibraltar and Venezuela. Fearing the neighborhood of the English in Jamaica, Gaston applied himself to the construction of the walls of the Havana; and to meet the expense he was authorized to levy half a real on each quarter of an arroba of wine, nearly equal to a gallon, which might be sold in the city; but this having given rise to complaints, the Spanish government by a royal cedula directed that $20,000 a year should be raised for the purpose in Mexico; and that as much more should be procured as the captain-general could extract by other means from the inhabitants of the Havana.

The next governor was Don Rodriguez de Ledesma, who assumed his functions in 1670, and prosecuted the work of fortification with the greatest ardor. He also prepared a naval armament for the protection of the coast. It was at this time that the working of the copper mines near Santiago was abandoned, and that the reconstruction of the cathedral in that city was begun; but the greater part of the slaves employed in the mines were sent to the Havana to work on the fortifications. During Ledesma's administration, a French party landed in the eastern part of the island, to the number of 800, under the command of one Franquinay, with the intention of plundering the city of Santiago, but they withdrew without doing any damage, alarmed, according to the Spanish accounts, by hearing the mere cry of "*al arma*." In 1675 the city of Santiago was destroyed by an earthquake, a calamity from which the Havana and the western parts of the island appear to be exempt. Ledesma complained bitterly to his government that the English authorities in Jamaica countenanced and encouraged the attacks of the pirates, and applied for leave to make reprisals. He was succeeded by Don Jose Fernandez de Cordoba Ponce de Leon, who began his administration in 1680, and continued the work of fortification with energy.

In 1687 Ponce de Leon was replaced by Don Diego de Viana e Hinojosa, and to him in 1689 succeeded Don Severino de Manzaneda y Salinas, during whose administration the city of Matanzas was founded, the first lines of it having been traced on the 10th of October, 1693, in presence of the captain-general, and many other persons of distinction. The etymology of the name Matanzas is much disputed by the antiquarians of Cuba, some ascribing it to the slaughter of Indians at the time of the conquest of the island, contending that the supposed Indian name Yumuri, that of one of the two rivers between which the city stands, is in fact a synonym in bad Spanish for this general massacre. Others contend, with equal pertinacity, that it was the natives who killed the Spaniards, while passing from one side of the bay to the other, having mutinied against their masters and used their oars successfully as weapons of offence. Seven of the Spaniards are said to have attempted to escape, but were carried prisoners to a neighboring Indian town, where they were all put to death except one, who escaped to tell the tale of the *Matanza.*

The next captain-general was Don Diego de Cordoba Lazo de la Vega; to him in 1702 succeeded Don Pedro Nicolas Benitez de Lugo, who died soon after his arrival. The next captain-general was Don Pedro Alvarez de Villarin, who arrived in 1706, and died the same year. After him, in 1708, came the Marques de Casa Torres, ex-governor of the Floridas, who having had some dispute with the auditor Don Jose Fernandez de Cordoba, was suspended from his office by the real audiencia.

The foundling hospital, or *Casa de Ninos Espositos,* vulgarly called *La Cuna,* was founded in 1711 by Don Fray Jeronimo de Valdes, an institution which still exists, and, like that of St. Pierre in the island of Martinique, is only resorted to by the white inhabitants, the presentation of a colored infant being a thing unknown. This fact, whether it arise from the sense of shame being stronger in the white mother, or from natural affection being stronger in the colored mother, is not unworthy of investigation.

Don Vicente Raja arrived as captain-general in the year 1716, bringing with him a royal *cedula,* declaring that in the event of his absence, illness, or death, the civil and military government should be transferred to the teniente rey; in case of his absence, illness, or death, to the castellano del Morro; and failing the castellano, to the sergeant-major of the garrison; and failing him, to the senior captain of infantry, so as that in no case the civil and military jurisdictions should ever afterward be divided.

In the following year Raja returned to Spain, and in 1718 Don Gregorio Guazo arrived as his successor. Nothing material occurred during his administration, and he was replaced in 1724 by Don Dionisio Martinez de la Vega. In his time a serious difference arose on the occasion of an appointment to the office of lieutenant-governor of Santiago. On the 10th of May, 1728, Lieutenant-Colonel Don Juan del Hoyo took possession of the local government, and a few months afterward a royal *cedula* arrived prohibiting his admission. On this the captain-general required his removal; but the ayuntamiento opposed it, saying it was one thing to remove an officer, and another not to admit him. Lawyers were consulted on the point; and the court of chancery of the district was referred to, who decided that the ayuntamiento were in the right, and the captain-general in the wrong. At this juncture the windward fleet, *la Armado de Barlovento*, arrived under the command of Don Antonio de Escudero, who, in his zeal for the royal service, and without any authority but that of force, laid hold of Del Hoyo, removed him from his employment, and carried him off to Vera Cruz. No sooner had he regained his liberty than he returned to the island; and having visited the town of Puerto Principe, which at that time formed part of his jurisdiction, the people rose against him, and having once more made him prisoner, sent him in irons to the Havana, from whence the captain-general had him carried to Madrid.

The next captain-general was Don Juan Francisco Guemes y Horcasitas, who arrived in the year 1734, and to him, in 1746, succeeded Don Juan Antonio Tineo y Fuertes, who died in the following year. He was the first captain-general who thought it necessary to establish a separate hospital for the reception of dissolute and incorrigible women; for which purpose the revenues of vacant ecclesiastical offices were to be applied. The date of the termination of the government of Martinez has not been very clearly defined: he was succeeded provisionally by Don Diego de Penalosa, as *teniente rey de la plaza*, and was replaced in 1747 by Don Francisco Cagigal de la Vega, who had previously been lieutenant-governor at Santiago. On leaving the command in 1760, the government was assumed provisionally by the Teniente Rey Don Pedro Alonzo; and he was relieved, in 1761, by Don Juan de Prado Porto Carrero, whose government was made so memorable by the capture of the city by the English.

The Habaneros themselves seem desirous to commemorate the event by retaining English names for the points of the coast where the landing of the expedition was effected, and for the fortresses which were occupied preparatory to the descent on the Morro. In the Memorias de la Real Sociedad Patriotica there are also some interesting notices of the event.

The captain-general, according to some accounts, was apprised of the fact that the English were preparing an expedition for the invasion of the island; but although he had made certain arrangements for the reception of the enemy, it is said that he never seriously believed that an invasion was about to take place. He made it his business, however, to ascertain what number of men might be relied on for the defence of the island; and even the proportion of slaves to whom arms might be safely intrusted. Juntas were frequently assembled for the discussion of these matters during the three months which intervened between the first rumor of the invasion and the actual descent of the enemy. At length, on the 6th of June, 1762, when a fleet of at least 250 sail had been reported as off the coast, the captain-general still refused to believe that this was the hostile expedition; insisting that it must be a homeward-bound convoy from Jamaica. On the morning of that day, he is said to have gone over to the Morro for the purpose of observing in person the movements of the fleet; and when he found that the garrison of the fortress had been called out under arms by the *teniente rey*, Don Dionisio Soler, he expressed his disapprobation of the proceeding—declaring it to be imprudent, and desiring that the troops might be sent back to their quarters.

After mid-day, however, he received notice from the Morro that the ships of war were approaching the coast, and appeared from their manœuvres to be preparing to effect a landing. Confounded by his own previous incredulity, the governor at length gave orders to prepare for a vigorous defence. The consternation produced by the ringing of alarm bells and the moving of artillery was extreme. Such of the inhabitants as possessed arms made haste to put them in order, and those who were not so provided presented themselves at the *sala real* to ask for them; but there were only 3500 muskets to be found, the greater part of them unfit for service, together with a few carabines, sabres, and bayonets. These were soon distributed; but in the end a great number of people remained unarmed for want of the needful supplies. The juntas were again assembled, consisting of the captain-general, the teniente rey, the marques del real transporte, general of marines, and the commissary-general, Don Lorenzo Montalvo, to whom were added the Conde de Superunda, as viceroy of Peru, and Major-General Don Diego Tabares, as governor of Carthagena, who happened to be then at the Havana on their return to Europe. Orders were issued by this junta to Colonel Don Carlos Caro to resist the landing of the enemy on the beach of Cogimar and Bacuranao, which they seemed to threaten; adding to his own regiment, De Edimburgo, the rest of the cavalry then in the city, together with several companies of the infantry of the line, and a few lancers, amounting altogether to about 3000 men.

The expedition sailed from Spithead on the 5th of March, 1762. Its chief object was, after seizing on the French possessions in the West Indies, to make a descent on the Havana, which was justly considered as the principal key to the vast possessions of the Spanish crown in the two great divisions of the American continent; the possession of which would effectually interrupt all communication between the Peninsula and the Gulf of Mexico, and thereby give the court of the Catholic king a distaste for the alliance with that of St. Cloud. The first rendezvous of the forces to be combined with the original expedition was at Martinique, and Sir James Douglas was ordered to unite his squadron, stationed at Port Royal, Jamaica, with that of Sir George Pocock, at the Cape of St. Nicholas, in the island of St. Domingo. From this point of union the expedition had the choice of two courses in proceeding toward the Havana. That which would have been the more easy of execution was to sail down the southern side of the island, and doubling the western cape, present itself before the Havana. But as this would have occupied more time, which the maintenance of secrecy rendered valuable, Sir George Pocock resolved on following the shorter and more difficult as well as dangerous course of the old Bahama channel, on the north side of the island. This resolution had the double effect of taking the enemy unprepared, and of obstructing the only course by which the French could send relief from St. Domingo. On the 27th of May the admiral hoisted his flag, and the whole convoys, consisting of 200 vessels of all classes, were soon under sail for the old Bahama passage. The Alarm and Echo frigates, sent in advance, discovered, on the 2d of June, five ships of the enemy, the frigate Tetis, the sloop of war Fenix, a brig, and two smaller vessels. An engagement immediately took place, in the issue of which one of the light vessels escaped, the other four being captured. On the evening of the 5th the Pan of Matanzas was visible; and on the morning of the 6th, being then five leagues to the eastward of the Havana, the necessary orders were issued for the commanders of the boats of the squadron and the captains of the transports, with regard to the debarkation of the troops. This duty was intrusted to the Honorable Commodore Keppel, at

2

whose disposal were placed six ships of the line, several frigates, and the large boats of the squadron. The admiral followed at two in the afternoon, with thirteen ships of the line, two frigates, the bomb vessels of the expedition, and thirty-six store boats. On presenting himself at the mouth of the harbor, for the double purpose of reconnoitering the enemy and making the feint of an attack to cover the operations of Commodore Keppel, he ascertained that twelve ships of the line and a number of merchant vessels were lying at anchor within it. On the following morning the admiral prepared his launches for landing a body of sailors and marines about four miles to the westward of the Havana. At the same time Lord Albemarle effected the landing of the whole of the troops, without opposition, between the rivers Bacuranao and Cogimar, about six miles from the Morro. A body of men having appeared on the beach, Commodore Keppel directed the Mercury and Bonnetta corvettes to disperse them; but a much greater number having soon afterward presented themselves with the evident intention of disputing the passage of the Rio Cogimar with the main body of the expedition, Captain Hervey in the Dragon was sent to bombard the fort, which afforded the enemy protection, but which very soon surrendered, leaving a free passage for the advance of the invaders.

From the prisoners taken on the 2d of June in the Tetis and Fenix, the presence of a naval force in the harbor became known to the English, together with the fact that most of the enemy's ships had completed their supplies of water, and were nearly ready for sea. Till then the governor, as has been stated, was almost wholly unprepared. The first notice he had of the actual approach of the expedition was obtained from the crew of the small schooner, which escaped from the pursuit of the Alarm and the Echo. As soon as he became convinced of the fact, the governor, as we have seen, assembled a council of war, composed of the chief officers under his command. At this junta de guerra the plan of defence was arranged, and a firm resolution was taken to resist the invasion to the last extremity. The defence of the Morro, on the possession of which the fate of the Havana in a great measure depended, was intrusted to Don Luis de Velasco, commander of the Reyna ship of the line, to whose gallantry and perseverance Sir George Pocock, in his subsequent report to the admiralty, pays a just tribute of commendation. His second in command, the Marques de Gonzales, commander of the Aquilon ship of the line, followed in all respects the example of Valesco, dying sword in hand in defence of his flag. The defence of the Punta Castle was in like manner assigned to a naval officer, Don Manuel Briseno, who had a friend in the same branch of the service for his second in command. This arrangement gave deadly offence to the officers of the army, who thought themselves unjustly superseded in the post of honor and of danger; but it was urged in excuse, that naval officers were better acquainted than those of the infantry or the cavalry with the use of artillery; and as the naval squadron had become useless by being locked up in the harbor, this was the only way in which they could be advantageously employed.

Before the governor could assemble the militia of the island under arms, he thought it necessary to declare war by proclamation against Great Britain. When his whole force was at length assembled, it was found in gross numbers greatly to exceed that of the invaders. It consisted of nine squadrons of cavalry, including in all 810 men; the regiment of the Havana 700; two battalions of the regiment de Espana 1400; two battalions of the regiment de Aragon 1400; three companies of artillery 300; seamen and marines of the squadron 9000; militia and people of color 14,000—making a grand total of 27,610. The greater part of the Spanish force was stationed in the town of Guanabacao, on the side of the bay opposite to the Havana, between the points where the invading forces had landed, in order to prevent them from turning the head of the harbor and attacking the city by land. The British force was divided into five brigades, amounting, with detachments from Jamaica and North America, to a total of 14,041 land forces. At daybreak, on the 7th, the troops were already on board the boats arranged in three divisions—the centre commanded by the Honorable Augustus Hervey; the right wing by Captains Barton and Drake; and the left, by Captains Arbuthnot and Jekyl. The first brigade was also the first to land; and as soon as the troops had formed on the beach, Lord Albemarle took the command, and marched in the direction of the city, which he did without further molestation as soon as the Cogimar batteries had been silenced. His excellency established his head quarters in Cogimar for the night; the troops were served with rations under arms; and several pickets were advanced to the eminences overlooking the Havana. After a succession of attacks on the part of Lord Albemarle, and a continued bombardment of the castle, the Morro surrendered on the 30th of July, and the town itself on the 14th of August, succeeding.

The spoils seized by the captors were of great value, and the distribution was a subject of much discontent; and it must be admitted that the partition, which gave three or four pounds to a soldier or a sailor, whose life was equally exposed with that of his superiors, and 100,000*l.* to an admiral or a commander-in-chief, was far from being impartial. In the distribution of the prize-money Sir George Pocock was placed on the same footing with Lord Albemarle, and Commodore Keppel with Lieutenant-General Elliot; the shares of the two former having amounted to 122,697*l.* 10*s.* 6*d.* each, and those of each of the two seconds in command to 24,539*l.* 10*s.* 1*d.* The whole spoil was, in fact, equally divided between the two services, having amounted altogether to 736,185*l.* 3*s.*, or 368,092*l.* 11*s.* 6*d.* each. But although the services and the chiefs were placed on an equality, the same rule could not be observed with the officers and privates. The share of a major-general was 6816*l.* 10*s.* 6½*d.*; that of a brigadier-general, 1947*l.* 11*s.* 7*d.*; that of an officer of the staff, 564*l.* 14*s.* 6*d.*; that of a captain, 184*l.* 4*s.* 7½*d.*; that of a subaltern, 116*l.* 3*s.* 0¼*d.*; that of a sergeant, 8*l.* 18*s.* 8*d.*; that of a corporal, 6*l.* 16*s.* 6*d.*, and that of a private soldier, 4*l.* 1*s.* 8½*d.* The share of a captain in the navy was 1600*l.* 10*s.* 10*d.*; of a lieutenant, 234*l.* 13*s.* 3¾*d.*; of other commissioned officers, 118*l.* 5*s.* 11½*d.*; of warrant officers, 17*l.* 5*s.* 3*d.*, and of ordinary seamen, 3*l.* 14*s.* 9¾*d.*

The peace having been concluded in 1763, the Conde de Ricla arrived at the Havana on the 30th of June, bringing the powers conferred by the treaty for the restoration of the British conquests in the island of Cuba, and accompanied by General O'Reilly, with four ships of the line, a number of transports, and 2000 men for the supply of the garrison. On their arrival they were received by the English with every demonstration of respect. On the 7th of July the keys of the city were formally delivered up to the Conde de Ricla, on whom the government had been conferred, and the English garrison was embarked on its return to Europe.

The restoration of the island to the Spaniards is regarded by the native writers as the true era from whence its aggrandizement and prosperity is to be dated. It was during the administration of the first governor that the new fortresses of San Carlos and Atares were erected, and the enlargement and rebuilding of the Morro and the Cabanas were begun. The old hospitals were placed on a better footing, and new ones were built. The court of accounts, and the whole department of finance, received a fresh impulse and a distinct form; and an intendant was named, who, among other arrangements, for the first time established the aduana, and created a custom-house revenue, the duties having been first levied on the 15th of October, 1764.

The Conde de O'Reilly, as inspector-general of the army, succeeded in organizing and placing on a respectable footing the regular troops, as well as the militia of the island. The city of the Havana having been divided into districts, the streets named, and the houses numbered, the truth came to be known, that the capital contained materials for the formation of a battalion of disciplined white militia. Beginning with the formation of a single company, the governor appointed lieutenants, sergeants, and corporals from the regular troops of the garrison, and, after a personal inspection, he followed the same course with the other companies. Adopting this principle in the other towns of the island, he soon succeeded in realizing his ideas, and creating a considerable force on which the government had every reason to rely. When the two white battalions of the Havana and Guanabacao were completed, it was still found that, with the addition of the stationary regiment of regulars and the other troops of the garrison, there would not be a sufficient force for the defence of the capital, so that the idea of forming two other battalions presented itself, the one of blacks, the other of people of color, and was immediately carried into effect.

Don Diego Manrique assumed the supreme command in 1765, but died within a few months after his arrival. He was succeeded in 1766 by Don Antonio Maria Bucarely, who prosecuted with energy the construction of the fortifications begun by the Conde de Ricla. Bucarely paid great attention to the due administration of justice, and was distinguished by the affability of his manners, the facility he afforded of access to his person, and the readiness with which he heard and redressed the grievances of the people; making it a boast that he had succeeded in adjusting differences and compromising lawsuits which had been pending for forty years. When afterward appointed viceroy of New Spain, the minister for the department of the Indies announced to him, by command of the king, as an unexampled occurrence, that during the whole period of his administration not a single complaint against him had reached the court of Madrid. Another of his merits with the people was the gentleness and address with which he effected the expulsion of the Jesuits, who had come to the island with Don Pedro Augustin Morel, and had acquired there large possessions. The church attached to their seminary is that which is now the cathedral of the Havana.

On the promotion of Bucarely in 1771, the Marques de la Torre was named his successor, and became one of the most popular captains-general who have ever administered the government. He was replaced in 1777 by Don Diego Jose Navarro, who introduced great improvements in the administration of justice, and the police of the tribunals, and in regulating the duties and functions of the *abogados*, *escribanos*, *procuradores*, *tasadores*, and other officers and dependents of the courts of law, in which the greatest abuses had previously, and have since prevailed. The base and deteriorated coin, which had been for some time in circulation was also called in and abolished in the time of Navarro. In the course of the war which had again broken out between England and Spain, an expedition was prepared at the Havana for the recovery of the Floridas, which produced the surrender of Pensacola, and the submission of the garrison. This gave rise to a belief that the English would make reprisals on Cuba or Porto Rico, and led to the dispatch of reinforcements on a large scale to the garrison of the Havana. The peace of 1783 soon followed, on which Lord Rodney prepared to return to England; and taking the Havana in his way, Prince William Henry, afterward William IV., having obtained leave from the admiral to go on shore, was so delighted with the city and the entertainments that were offered him, that he remained there three days, and did not return, if we may believe the Spanish writers, until Lord Rodney sent to his royal highness to say, that if he did not re-embark immediately, the squadron would set sail, and leave him behind. The Spanish general of marines, Solano, is said to have given the prince a breakfast which cost him $4000.

During the years which immediately succeeded the peace there appear to have been other changes in the colonial government besides those already noticed, beginning with Don Luis Gonzaga, followed by the Conde de Galves, Don Bernardo Troncoso, Don Jose Espeleta, and Don Domingo Cabello. In the time of this first Espeleta there was again a great outcry as to the number of lawyers in the colony, and particularly at the Havana, where there were already no less than eighty-five abogados with an equally liberal proportion of the inferior classes of the profession. Steps were taken to prevent their increase, and a regulation was enforced on the 19th of November, 1784, prohibiting the admission of candidates and the immigration of professors of jurisprudence from the other colonies; and no lawyer who had studied his profession in Spain was to be allowed to practice it in the courts of the island until six years at least after he had been called to the bar in the Peninsula.

Don Luis de las Casas arrived as captain-general in 1790, and the period of his administration is represented by all Spanish writers as a brilliant epoch in the history of the island. To him it is indebted for the institution of the *Sociedad Patriotica*, which has ever since done so much to stimulate the activity, and promote the improvement of education, agriculture, and trade, as well as literature, science, and the fine arts, combined with large and liberal views of public policy. To Las Casas, also, is the island indebted for the establishment of the *Casa de Beneficencia*, having been begun by a voluntary subscription amounting to $36,000. The female department was at first a separate institution, situated in the extramural portion of the city, but was added to the other on the completion of the buildings in 1794. In place of a monument to Las Casas, which he undoubtedly deserved as much as any of his predecessors, an inscription has been conspicuously engraved in the common hall of the school for boys, declaring that on its erection it had been expressly dedicated to the memory of the founder of the institution; reminding the young pupils that he had not only been the founder of the Casa de Beneficencia, but of the first public library, and the first newspaper which had existed in the island, and of the patriotic and economical society.

To increase the commercial prosperity of the island he had the sagacity to perceive that his object could not be better accomplished than by removing as far as his authority extended all the trammels imposed upon it by the old system of privilege and restriction. During his administration, also, large sums were expended in the construction of roads, especially the great Calzada del Horcon and the Calzada de Guadaloupe; but since then these highways have fallen so completely out of repair, as for the greater part of the year to have become next to impassable. It was Las Casas, also, who introduced the culture of indigo; and during his time the long arrear of causes on the rolls of the courts of justice was greatly reduced. The hurricane, which desolated the island on the 21st and 22d of June, 1791, afforded Las Casas a fresh opportunity for displaying the great resources of his mind in the promptitude with which he brought relief to the sufferers. In some districts the sudden rise of water in the rivers was most extraordinary, when the limited extent of land from sea to sea is considered. On the bridge then just finished across the Rio del Calabazal the water rose to the height of thirty-six feet above the parapets; and in the town of San Antonio, where the wells are sunk into the bed of a subterraneous river, the water rushed up through the artificial openings, and inundated the whole country.

The French revolution having communicated its irresistible impulse to the western parts of St. Domingo, the cabinet of Madrid took the alarm, and from the Havana and Santiago, Vera Cruz, the Caracas, Maracaybo, and Porto Rico, collected a force amounting altogether to 6000 men, the object of which was to suppress the insurrection. The sanguinary struggle which ensued, and the reverses which befell the Spanish troops, belong to another place. Suffice it here to say, by way of memorandum, that the interest of the Spanish government in the island of St. Domingo was definitely terminated by the treaty of Basle, soon afterward concluded with the French republic. It was to the energetic measures of Las Casas, at the time of this revolution in St. Domingo, that the island of Cuba was indebted for the uninterrupted maintenance of its tranquillity, in spite of the universal persuasion that a conspiracy had been formed at the instigation of the French, among the free people of color, to provoke a similar revolution in Cuba. On the occasion of his leaving the island in December, 1796, a formal eulogium on his merits as captain-general was recorded in the archives of the Ayuntamiento of the Havana, in which are enumerated the great benefits he had conferred on the community; among which, the most prominent are the discouragement of gambling; the arrest of vagrants and vagabonds; the clearing of the gaols of greater criminals, and the acceleration of the ends of justice in civil causes; the abandonment of a large portion of his own emoluments for the erection and support of the *Casa de Beneficencia* and other charitable institutions; the reduction and pacification of the maroons of Santiago; the suppression of the conspiracy among the people of color; the prohibition of the introduction of foreign negroes who had previously resided in other colonies, and the expulsion of those who had arrived from St. Domingo; the relief of the inhabitants from the clothing of the militia; the paving of the streets of the Havana; the making and mending of roads; the building of bridges, and the construction of public walks and alamedas; the erection of a convent, a coliseum, a primary school, a school of chemistry, natural philosophy, mathematics and botany; the improvement of the Plaza de Toros, and the rejection of the profit which his predecessors had derived from the supply of provisions for the troops. In this farewell eulogium he is also praised for the very questionable virtue of promoting the general prosperity, by the copious introduction of Bozal negroes from the coast of Africa, which is stated to have greatly extended the cultivation of the sugar-cane, the bread-fruit tree, the cinnamon-tree, and other exotic plants of inestimable value. It is more easy to sympathize in the praises bestowed upon him for the great hospitality he showed to the unfortunate refugees from St. Domingo, and for the exertions he made and the liberality he evinced in the institution of the Patriotic Society, the formation of a public library, the publication of the Diario, and of the *Guia de Forasteros*.

Las Casas, in 1796, was succeeded in the government by the Conde de Santa Clara, whose noble and generous disposition, and the affability of his manners, made the loss of his predecessor less sensibly felt. It is admitted, however, that he gave no encouragement to education, that he had no taste for letters, and that in his time the social emulation which had previously prevailed sunk rapidly into apathy and indifference.

It is a singular illustration of the dilatory habits of the people, and affords a sort of national characteristic, that for many years after the formal cession to the French of all interest in St. Domingo, the judges who exercised the supreme civil jurisdiction over the island of Cuba and other Spanish settlements continued to reside in the ceded territory, so that, in consequence of the recommencement of hostilities with England, all communication by sea was so interrupted as to interpose an insurmountable barrier to the exercise of the right of appeal, and to the ordinary administration of justice. The royal cedula, for the removal of this tribunal to Puerto Principe, is dated on the 22d of May, 1797; but it does not appear at what precise date the actual translation took place.

Santa Clara was succeeded, in 1799, by the Marques de Someruelos, whose administration continued for a much longer period than the five years to which, by the practice, if not by a formal regulation of the Spanish government, the term of service of the captains-general of the colonies has been usually limited. The public works which serve to commemorate the administration of Someruelos are the old theatre and the public cemetery; the execution of which last was confided to the bishop, who pursued the object with zeal, and the work was completed on the 2d of February, 1806. Its extent is not great, containing only 22,000 square yards; but the walls, the chapel, and the gateway, are on a scale which infers the outlay of a large sum of money. The chapel is ornamented with a painting in fresco representing the Resurrection, with the motto, "Ecce nunc in pulvere dormiam." Someruelos was thought by some to be stern and severe toward the poorer classes of society, and to reserve all his affability and condescension for the rich. On the occasion, however, of the great fire of 1802, which destroyed the populous suburb of Jesus Maria, leaving no less than 11,300 individuals without a roof to shelter them, the marques, moved by their distress, circumambulated the town, going actually from door to door to petition for their relief.

The belief again gained ground at the Havana, in 1807, that the English government contemplated a descent on the island; and measures were taken in consequence to put it in a more respectable state of defence, although, from want of funds in the treasury, and the scarcity of indispensable supplies, the prospect of an invasion was sufficiently gloomy. The militia and the troops of the garrison were carefully drilled, and companies of volunteers were formed wherever materials for them could be found. The French, also, not content with mere preparations, made an actual descent on the island, first threatening Santiago, and afterward landing at Batabano. The invaders consisted chiefly of refugees from St. Domingo; and their intention seems to have been to have taken possession with a view to colonize and cultivate a portion of the unappropriated, or at least unoccupied, territory on the south side of the island, as their countrymen had formerly done in St. Domingo. Without recurring to actual force, the captain-general prevailed on them to take their departure by a peaceful offer of the means of transit either to St. Domingo or to France.

The news of the abduction, by Napoleon, of the royal family of Spain reached the Havana by a private opportunity, at the moment when the cabildo was in session, when every member of it took a solemn oath to preserve the island for its lawful sovereign. The official intelligence did not reach the city till the 17th of July, 1808; when it was brought from Cadiz by the Intendant Don Juan de Aguilar y Amat, who arrived in the American ship Dispatch. The colonial government immediately declared war against Napoleon; and on the 20th, King Ferdinand VII. was proclaimed with general applause. The intelligence from Spain and the resolution of the captain-general were immediately communicated to all the colonial authorities in Spanish America. The events in the Peninsula soon began to be felt at the Havana; but the demands of the French intruders for the recognition of their authority were disregarded, and the public dispatches which came from them were destroyed. The Infanta Dona Carlota made similar pretensions, but these, like those of the French, were firmly resisted.

The foreign trade of the island was reduced to such an extremity by the events of the war, that the local authorities of the Havana, the ayuntamiento, and the consulado, began seriously to deliberate on the expediency of throwing the trade open, and admitting foreign supplies on the same terms with those from the Peninsula. There was some division of opinion; but the majority were for a free competition on an equal footing between the Spaniard and the foreigner, on the ground that Spain alone was unable to purchase or consume the enormous mass of produce then exported from the island; and so it was accordingly decided.

On the 21st and 22d of March, 1809, a serious disturbance arose, the object of which was to invite the return of the French to the island; but this popular movement, although considered dangerous at the time, and viewed with alarm by the captain-general, was speedily put down by the display of firmness and resolution on the part of all who had any thing to lose, and by the prompt offer of their personal services for its suppression. Proclamations were issued, a respectable force was collected, and the Marques de Someruelos presented himself in person to endeavor to pacify the discontented. Tranquillity was restored at the end of the second day, with the loss of only two or three lives; but not without the destruction of a great deal of property. The French settlers in the rural districts were, in this respcct, the greatest sufferers; and it had, in consequence, the effect of driving away several thousands of laborious and intelligent colonists, who were already deeply interested in the prosperity of the island.

Soon after these events a young man arrived from the United States, of whose proceedings and character, as an emissary of King Joseph, the colonial government had been previously informed. This unfortunate person, Don Manuel Aleman, was not even suffered to land. The alguazils went on board; took possession of his papers and his person; a council of war was immediately assembled: but his fate was determined beforehand; and on the following morning, the 13th of July, 1810, he was brought out to the Campo de la Punta, and hanged for his temerity.

The revolutionary proceedings in the continental provinces of Spain were now in full career toward that independence of the mother-country which they have since achieved. In the mean time, the island of Cuba enjoyed a degree of tranquillity quite remarkable under the circumstances of the sister colonies. This state of things was naturally, and not unjustly, ascribed to the political prudence and sagacity of the Marques de Someruelos. The colonial authorities petitioned the cabinet of Madrid for the farther prorogation of his government beyond the term to which it had been already extended. But the very fact of his having given so much satisfaction to the colonists, if we may judge from experience elsewhere, was not likely to operate with the government of the mother-country in deciding on a farther extension of his stay. Instead of acceding to the prayer of the municipal functionaries of the Havana, the government of Madrid thought fit to mark its sense of the interference by instantly recalling the title of "Excellencia," which, on a former occasion, had been granted to the ayuntamiento as a special mark of the royal favor, and of which they were not a little proud.

The western districts of the island were visited, in 1810, by another of those tremendous hurricanes, which sweep away so much life and property in these tropical regions. The city of the Havana was filled with consternation and dismay; the hopes of an abundant harvest were disappointed; in the harbor, so renowned for its security, the ships of war were driven from their anchors; and no less than sixty merchant vessels were destroyed.

In the time of Someruelos the Casa de Beneficencia was in danger of falling into decay; but in consequence of his earnest intervention, the Junta de Tabacos, which in Spain as in France is a royal monopoly, consented to purchase 100 slaves, whose labor or whose wages were to furnish funds for the benefit of the institution; thus by an extraordinary perversion making the practice of cruelty and injustice toward one portion of the human family contribute to a work of charity in favor of another. The slaves were at first employed in the manufacture of cigars, but have latterly been hired out for daily wages at whatever employment they could obtain.

A negro conspiracy broke out in 1812, which excited considerable alarm in the minds of the landed proprietors. That alarm was attended with its usual consequences: the negro leader Aponte and his associates were treated with unsparing severity, such as may be supposed to have been dictated much more by the fears of the *hacendados*, than by the strict justice of the case.

The successor of Someruelos was Don Juan Ruiz de Apodaca, afterward Conde de Benadito, who arrived on the 14th of April, 1812; and he, for the first time, combined the command of the naval force on the station with the office of captain-general of the island.

This unprecedented combination arose from the fear of the authors of the constitution of Cadiz, that their work and their representative would not be well received in this aristocratical colony. His first duty on his arrival was to proclaim the constitution; and although it doubtless excited an extraordinary sensation, it was not openly resisted.

The success of Apodaca in Cuba led to his promotion to the rank of viceroy of Mexico; and on the 1st of July, 1816, he was succeeded at the Havana by Lieutenant-General Don Jose Cienfuegos. In his time the third census of the island was accomplished. This captain-general made himself exceedingly unpopular at the Havana by the severe measures of police he proclaimed and enforced for the suppression of projects of sedition, and for the preservation of the public tranquillity. He resorted to an expedient which in other great cities would scarcely have become the subject of serious complaint—he caused the streets of the Havana to be lighted; but this was only a part of the proceeding to which the citizens objected. He insisted, also, on closing up the public thoroughfares immediately after the conclusion of the evening service in the churches; thus from that early hour confining the inhabitants to their own particular quarter of the city, and giving rise to clamorous representations and to the very disturbances which it was the object of the captain-general to prevent.

Senor Cienfuegos was for some time disabled by personal infirmity from the active administration of the government, and during that period his functions were performed by Don Juan Maria Echeverri, as cabo subalterno; but on the 29th of August, 1819, he was finally relieved by the arrival of his successor, Don Juan Manuel Cagigal, in the Spanish ship of war Sabina, with a convoy of troops for the supply of the garrison.

The following year, 1820, from the events which

took place in the Peninsula, was another period of trial and difficulty for a captain-general of the Havana; but it is admitted by all parties that Cagigal succeeded, by the prudence and delicacy of his conduct, in avoiding the evils which might have been expected to arise from the difficult and extraordinary circumstances in which he found himself placed. The extreme affability of his manners, and the perfect readiness with which he received and listened to all who desired to approach him, conciliated universal good will; and it appears that the high estimation in which he was held by the inhabitants excited in his breast a corresponding feeling, as, on the termination of his command, he applied for and obtained the special grace from the king of being permitted to take up his permanent abode in the island; and having retired to the town of Guanabacao, he died there some time afterward a simple but respected citizen.

The next captain-general was Don Nicolas Mahy, who arrived from Bordeaux in the French frigate Therese, on the 3d of March, 1821; but such was the turbulence which prevailed in these troublesome times that he proved unequal to the task of controlling the storm, and at length sunk under the difficulties which surrounded him. He died on the 18th of July, 1822, but retained to the last moment of his life the direct administration of the affairs of the government.

After his death the government was assumed provisionally by the *cabo subalterno*, Don Sebastian Kindelan; and on the 2d of May, 1823, the new captain-general arrived, Don Francisco Dionisio Vives, who was afterward raised to the dignity of Conde de Cuba. It was in his time that the fourth and last census of the island was accomplished. It was under Vives, also, that the rural militia was organized, and that the construction of the fortresses of Bahia-honda, Mariel, Jaruco, and the Cabanas was begun or completed. It was he who divided the island into three military departments; and it was under his auspices that the temple was erected on the Plaza de Armas of the Havana, on the very spot, where, if tradition is to be believed, the first Christian rite was performed in the New World. It is doubtless with the view of adding to the solemnity of the occasion that the temple is opened only once a year, on the anniversary of the day that mass was first said there, in the presence of Columbus, to return thanks to Heaven for the success which had attended his enterprise. It was also in the time of Vives that the two lunatic asylums, *el Departamento de Dementes*, were added to the *Casa de Beneficencia;* and it is recorded of him that he never failed to preside at the meetings of the institution, and to animate by his presence the drooping zeal of his colleagues in the direction.

On the 15th of May, 1832, Don Mariana Ricafort took possession of the government; and on the 1st of June, 1834, he was succeeded by Don Miguel Tacon, whose administration terminated on the 16th of April, 1838, when Don Joaquin de Espeleta, who had for some time resided at the Havana with the rank of sub-inspector-general of the troops, and second *cabo subalterno*, was promoted to the rank of captain-general, not provisionally, as had been usual on former occasions, but *como proprietario*, to use a form of expression in constant use, as applied to public offices in the language of Castile as well as in that of France.

General Espeleta marked his career by a straightforward course, strongly exemplified in his putting down all obnoxious and costly practices to obtain licenses and passports, which were favored, both by those preceding and succeeding him, from sordid and ignoble motives. His uprightness could not, however, wash out the political stain of his birth: for, by a mere chance, Espeleta was born at Havana. He was consequently soon removed, and before the regular term of five years, allotted to such offices in Spanish

America. The Prince of Anglona, the next captain-general in order of time, was a gentlemanly and courteous chief who, after one year's command in 1841, left the charge of the island to the noble-minded Don Geronimo Valdez, a man whose whole life had evinced a consistent love of liberty, scarcely ever met with in a Spanish soldier, for such he was. Being informed that there was a conspiracy on foot, and that many young men talked in a revolutionary strain, he answered: "I have a powerful army at my command; let the conspirators sally forth, and I shall destroy them, but not before." This liberality to the Cubans, and his conciliating course toward the abolitionist Turnbull, who had landed at an unfortified part of the island, for some sinister purpose, among the blacks; and more than all, his disinterested and faithful observance of the treaties condemning the African slave trade, brought on him the unrestrained attacks of those engaged or concerned in it as capitalists or officials of government. He was consequently hurried from his station in the most unceremonious manner, and the party who vainly endeavored to injure his name, charging him with motives treasonable to Spain, found in his successor a man better disposed to forward their selfish and sordid purposes, though for the same reason equally calculated to alienate the hearts of the inhabitants. Valdez had the courage and honesty to issue, during his short command, upward of a thousand grants of freedom illegally withheld by his predecessors from so many Africans who, according to the treaty, had become free. He left the palace of the captain-generals of Cuba in the same high-minded poverty in which he had entered it.

In 1843, General Leopold O'Donnell took the command of the island, and never was military despotism more successfully directed to destroy popular franchises, to establish individual oppression beyond the possibility of redress by altering existing institutions, and eminently to satisfy the avaricious thirst of the captain-general and his family and favorites. The bloody page of the negro insurrection, reported in another part of this work, was the most prominent feature of his governorship. At the close of one of General O'Donnell's balls, his wife sent for the baker who had supplied the entertainment, to come at 3 o'clock A. M., to take back the loaves not used! The baker refused, saying that he could not sell them except as stale bread, at a very reduced price. To this she replied that she had sent for him at so early an hour that he might have the chance of mixing it with the fresh bread he was to send around to his customers that morning. She was engaged in all kinds of profitable undertakings of the most obscure and common pursuits in life; monopolies of the most repugnant character were introduced for her advantage, based on the unbounded authority of a provincial tyrant. The cleansing of the sewers, and the locality fixed for the reception of the manure and dirt of the city were among the many sources of wealth which she did not scruple to turn to her advantage. But nothing was so fruitful to this family of dealers, as the slave trade which, it was publicly asserted, furnished emoluments even to the daughter of the captain-general. O'Donnell was part owner of the marble quarries of the Isle of Pines, whither he, by his sole authority, sent to labor a great number of suspected or accused persons, without judgment or sentence passed on them. The agency for obtaining passports, and other services connected with government, as published in the Havana papers, exhibits a degree of immorality and defiance of public opinion hardly to be found in any civilized country.

General Frederico Roncali, graced by one of the numerous titles which Queen Christina has so profusedly and undeservedly bestowed within a very recent period, took the command of the island in 1848. His ridiculous and perplexed action during the movement of the Round Island expedition, show how weak the strength of bayonets is, where it is unsupported either by the confidence of the soldiery, or by the love of the people for their rulers. The idea of marching out 4000 men, and stationing them in the central department of the island, and announcing to the soldiers that they were to receive double pay as soon as the enemy landed, merely because 400 Americans had taken their abode in an island 700 miles off, is a tacit acknowledgment of the impending termination of Spanish rule in Cuba—that tottering column of European despotism in America. General Roncali's incapacity was never made more manifest, however, than in his management of the Rey affair. Don Cirilo Villaverde, author of a novel entitled "Cecilia Valdez," and other literary works, being accused of corresponding with the editor of the Cuban paper called La Verdad, was confined to the Havana prison during his trial, which he had no reason to expect should be fair or favorable in its results to him. While there, a fraudulent bankrupt, by name Fernandez, being on the eve of escaping, through promises made to the jail-keeper Rey, of sharing with him the imaginary spoils of his bankruptcy, Mr. Villaverde succeeded in availing himself of the same opportunity to fly, and save himself, rather than trust to his innocence or the irregularity and corruption of Spanish military justice. The result, fully establishing the moral weakness of a government whose very agents turn against it, served to excite the anger and spiteful revenge of Roncali. He therefore succeeded, through the consul at New Orleans, Don Carlos Espana, in abducting the jail-keeper, who was thereby destined to be severely punished, or generously rewarded should he act as witness against such influential creoles as were suspected of dissatisfaction to the Spanish government. It is not necessary to add any thing further on this subject. The American public are sufficiently acquainted with the subsequent history of this ominous, sacrilegious, and insulting act of the authorized menial of a European monarch on the heretofore respected soil of America.

Whatever moral qualities and honest wishes some of the captain-generals may have possessed, they were compelled to follow out the restrictions and spoliations commenced by Tacon. The path of despotism, when justified by the national excuse of holding a distant colony, must always be one of inevitable and progressive oppression.

The historical sketch of Cuba is here concluded. The next chapter is designed to furnish an abstract of its political history, including a notice of the late insurrection, with an account of the remarkable policy which has brought the island to its present miserable condition.

CHAPTER II.

Political sketch previous to the XIXth century.—Indian population.—The Island a military post.—Commerce and Navigation.—Foreign trade.—Restrictions on trade.—Situation of Spain.—Political changes in 1812 and 1820.—The Constitution proclaimed.—Masonic Societies.—The old Spaniards.—Royal Order of 1825.—Count Villanueva.—Dangers of the Slave Trade.—Despotic Encroachments.—Rejection of the Cuban Deputies at Madrid.—General Tacon.—His Tyranny and Venality.—His Removal effected by a Compromise.—Fear of a servile Insurrection.—Cruel measures taken against the Creoles and free people of Color.—The work of the Countess of Merlin.—Anecdotes.—Insurrections in different parts of the Island. Enormities practiced by the officials of Government.—Their effect upon the native Cubans.—Present distressing Situation of the Island.

PREVIOUS to the eighteenth century, the history of the island of Cuba is mostly occupied with accounts of the settlements commenced by the first governor, Diego Velasquez; the noble defence of the Cazique Athuei, who was burned alive by order of the former; and the usual repartimientos or distribution of the territory and Indians among the Spanish settlers, which, through excess of labor, hastened the depopulation of the country. During that early period is also noticed the sailing of expeditions to more recently discovered and alluring regions; the beginning of the African slave trade; and the occasional descent and depredations of the buccaneers. The latter were so bold, from the scant population and absence of fortifications, that they carried off at one time the venerable Bishop Cabezas Altanurano, and at another, the very bells of the church and the cannons of the castle at St. Iago.

Soon after the royal decree of 1530, liberating the native Indians, the remnants of this unfortunate race appeared to have congregated in towns such as Guanabacoa, Guaisabana, Ovejas, and Caneyes-arriba, and to have applied their efforts to simple husbandry and grazing.

But the advance of Cuba must have been extremely limited or doubtful, since the Bishop Almendares estimated the population of all the towns and cities in 1612 at 6700 inhabitants.

The truth lies in the fact that, after having exhausted the Indian population, the island was only held as a military post on the way to the mines of Mexico, with little else to occupy its reduced population than the raising of cattle, on lands not appropriated. Till the latter years of the past century, commerce was not only confined to Spanish merchantmen, but to the periodical voyage of the fleet belonging to the privileged India Company. Foreign trade has only been authorized in the present century, when the European wars, forcing the Spanish flag from the seas, and the encroachment of contraband trade, made it impossible to oppose it.

In the laws and municipal rights of Cuba, we notice the same independent and liberal spirit which prevailed in all the settlements of Spain among the Moors, or elsewhere, as far as the Spanish settlers and their descendants were concerned. Thus in the sixteenth and seventeenth centuries, public assemblies of citizens were held to elect the members of the corporations; free and bold charges made and sustained against governors; and no taxation was permitted which was not sanctioned by these bodies, who exercised the same prerogatives in the Spanish peninsula, during the long suspension of representative government. As to the commercial restrictions which prevented the growth of this beautiful garden of America, they did not originate in any right, expressed or implied, to control the fate of Cuba, on the part of the European provinces, but in the peculiar notions of the age on matters of political economy. Equally injudicious was the system observed in the internal trade and relations between the several

Spanish provinces themselves, whose wealth and physical advance are to this day obstructed by antiquated prejudices. Aside, therefore, from the measures adopted to nationalize the commerce and trade of Cuba, or rather to direct their course by legislation, there was not, until the last twenty years, any serious precedent or open effort to justify a difference between the political rights of the Cubans and the Spaniards on the soil of Cuba. Were the conquest held as the foundation of such difference, the privilege should certainly attach to the descendants of those who shed their blood and used their means in the acquisition of the country—not to the recent emigration, much less to the salaried officers of the government.

The recognition of the popular principle in the Sociedad Patriotica and Consulado, established near the close of the eighteenth century, and the vast influence derived therefrom, and which, in after times, gave a liberal tinge to the local administration, is especially worthy of notice.

Struggling for her own independence, and boldly confronting the ambitious and mighty chieftain of the age, Spain, at the opening of the nineteenth century, appeared in a noble attitude. Actuated by the most sacred impulses of patriotism, and intensely engaged in the wars and policy of Europe, she could not and did not refuse whatever was requested by the Cuban assemblies. Cuba, on her part, repaid the liberality of the mother country by an unwavering loyalty. Unseduced by the alluring prospect of independence, and undismayed by repeated invasions from foreign powers, she shut her eyes to the former, and boldly resisted the latter, at the liberal expense of the treasures of the island and the lives of the inhabitants.

This brings us to a period marked by fluctuations in the political history of Spain and her dependencies, and it is now to be seen what were their effect upon Cuba.

The political changes adopted in Spain in 1812 and 1820 were productive of similar changes in the island; and when in both instances the constitution was proclaimed, the perpetual members of the municipalities were at once deprived of office, and their successors elected by the people. The provincial assembly was called, and held its sessions. The militia was organized; the press made entirely free, the verdict of a jury deciding actions for its abuses; and the same courts of justice were in no instance to decide a case a second time. But if the institution of the consulado was very beneficent during Ferdinand's absolute sway, the ultra-popular grants of the constitutional system, which could hardly be exercised with quiet in Spain, were ill-adapted to Cuba, though more advanced in civilization, stained with all those vices that are the legitimate curse of a country long under despotic sway. That system was so democratic, that the king was deprived of all political authority. No intermediate house of nobility or senators tempered the enactments of a single elective assembly. This sudden change from an absolute government, with its usual concomitant, a corrupt and debased public sentiment, to the full enjoyment of republican privileges, served only to loosen all the ties of decency and decorum throughout the Spanish community. Infidelity resulted from it; and that veil of respect for the religion of their fathers, which had covered the deformity of such a state of society, was imprudently thrown aside. As the natural consequence of placing the instruments of freedom in the hands of an ignorant multitude, their minds were filled with visions of that chimerical equality which the world is never to realize. The rich found themselves deprived of their accustomed influence, and felt that there was little chance of obtaining justice from the common people (in no place so formidable as in Cuba, from the heterogeneous nature of the population), and who were now, in a manner, arrayed against them throughout the land. They, of course, eagerly wished the return of the old system of absolute rule. But the proprietors only asked for the liberal policy which they had enjoyed at the hands of the Spanish monarch; not, most surely, that oppressive and nondescript government which, by separating the interest of the country from that of her nearest rulers, and destroying all means of redress or complaint, thrust the last offspring of Spain into an abyss of bloodshed and ruin, during the recent disgusting exercise of military rule, in punishing by the most arbitrary and cruel measures, persons suspected of engaging in an apprehended servile insurrection.

During the second period of democratic, or what was called constitutional government, which commenced in 1820, the masonic societies came into vogue as they did in the mother-country. They adopted different plausible pretexts, though to speak the truth, they were little more than clubs for amusement and revelry. One of them, called the "*Soles de Bolivar*," went so far as to discuss whether, in case of a Columbian invasion, it would be more expedient to avoid a collision in the presence of the slaves, by giving way peaceably before the invading army. Happily for Cuba, and certainly in consequence of the judicious interference of the United States, which foresaw in the preservation of its tranquillity the advantages of a fruitful commerce, the invasion did not take place. And if the island has since had to lament the gradual encroachments of the executive, in all the several branches of its politics and administration, it has also been preserved from the sanguinary results which the premature establishment of ultra free institutions has produced in all the numerous countries which once formed the dominion of Spain in America. For the difficulty of annexation, from the lesser influence the United States then possessed among nations and the controlling importance of the shipping interest in that country, made it unadvisable for Cuba to launch into a revolution unsustained, and in this way to experience a severe scourge, which, at that time, would have proved the principal if not the only fruits of independence to the first generation of its recipients. Under any circumstances the subsequent jealous policy of the Spanish government has been altogether unwarranted.

For the discussions of the "*Soles de Bolivar*" were owing to the countenance which the liberal government gave to those very societies; a thing entirely uncalled for among a people permitted to meet freely and name a portion of their rulers; and where, too, for political ends, no property qualification was required; a relinquishment which, however justified in a country like the United States, where constitutional rights have been exercised ever since colonial times, could not be safely overlooked in one just emerging from a despotic though beneficent government, and whose population comprehended such discordant elements.

A respectable portion of the old Spaniards residing in Cuba, were themselves desirous of upholding the constitutional system in the island which they saw tottering in Spain. General Vives, who commanded at that time, regarded the circumstance with anxious solicitude, and very reasonably inferred that, if the constitution of 1812 was sustained in Cuba after the king's absolute power was acknowledged in Spain, the consequences would be fatal to its dependence, however rational and honest the views of the constitutionalists might be considered. Hence his strenuous efforts in 1824, after the restoration of Ferdinand, to make the most of the wild and varying schemes which had been proposed in the "*Soles de Bolivar*," under the democratic institutions, and the relaxation of the reins of government before mentioned. The greatly reduced Spanish military force at that time in the island, and the fact that much of it consisted of regular regiments and native militia, are sufficient proof that to the solid good sense of the inhabitants, rather than any show of strength, should be attributed the immediate disappearance of those germs of disquietude. Not even the weakness of General Kindelan could induce the planters to lose sight of their chief interest. Though General Vives subsequently desired to impress the constitutional party with the idea that they might be carried farther than they meant to go, and with that view took especial care that a well-concerted scheme for throwing off the Spanish yoke should appear to have been devised, it must be acknowledged, that notwithstanding he caused the prosecution and imprisonment of many individuals, and occasionally the ruin and misery of their families, he oftentimes also interfered to mitigate the appalling and unavoidable excesses of those menials of government who are ever ready, under such circumstances, to exceed the wishes of the leading statesmen, and to make political difficulties subservient to the vilest purposes. That which should have warned the Spanish ministry of the inexpediency of establishing such inappropriate institutions, brought upon the island all its subsequent misfortunes; namely, the Royal Order of 1825, which is the existing law of the land, and which, translated, reads as follows:

War Department. The king our master, in whose royal mind great confidence has been inspired by your excellency's proved fidelity, indefatigable zeal in his majesty's service, judicious and well-concerted steps taken since Y. E. had charge of the government, in order to keep in quietude his faithful inhabitants, confine within the proper limits such as would deviate from the path of honor, and punish such as forgetting their duties would dare commit excesses in opposition to our wise laws; well convinced as H. M. feels, that at no time and under no circumstances whatever will the principles of rectitude and love toward H. M.

royal person be weakened which now distinguish Y. E.; and being at the same time desirous of preventing the embarrassments which under extraordinary circumstances might arise from a division in the command, and from the complicated authority and powers of the different officers of government, for the important end of maintaining in that island his sovereign authority and the public quiet, it has pleased H. M., in conformity with the advice of his council of ministers, to authorize your excellency, fully investing you with the whole extent of power which by the royal ordinances is granted to the governors of besieged towns. In consequence thereof H. M. most amply and unrestrictedly authorizes Y. E. not only to remove from that island such persons, holding offices from government or not, whatever their occupation, rank, class, or situation in life may be, whose residence there you may believe prejudicial, or whose public or private conduct may appear suspicious to you, employing in their stead faithful servants of H. M., who shall fully deserve your excellency's confidence; but also to suspend the execution of whatever royal orders or general decrees in all the different branches of the administration, or in any part of them, as Y. E. may think conducive to the royal service; it being in any case required that these measures be temporary, and that Y. E. make report of them for his majesty's sovereign approval.

In granting Y. E. this marked proof of his royal esteem, and of the high trust your proven loyalty deserves, H. M. expects that in due correspondence to the same, Y. E. will use the most wakeful prudence and reserve, joined to an indefatigable activity and unyielding firmness, in the exercise of your excellency's authority, and trusts that as your excellency shall by this very pleasure and graciousness of H. M. be held to a more strict responsibility, Y. E. will redouble his vigilance that the laws be observed, that justice be administered, that H. M. faithful vassals be protected and rewarded, and punishment without partiality or indulgence inflicted on those who, forgetful of their duty and their obligations to the best and most benevolent of monarchs, shall oppose those laws, decidedly abetting sinister plots, with infraction of them and disregard of the decrees from them issuing. And I therefore, by royal order, inform Y. E. of the same for Y. E.'s intelligence, satisfaction, and exact observance thereof. GOD preserve your excellency's life. Madrid, 28 May, 1825. AIMERICH.

By this it will be seen that Cuba has been, since 1825, and now is, under "martial law," the captain-general being invested "*with the whole extent of power* granted to the governors of *besieged towns.*"

The sad effects of this royal order, which the king only meant to be observed temporarily, and under a strict responsibility, "le mas estrecta responsibilidad," were not immediately felt. "Truth and justice compel me to assert," says one of the most enlightened Cubans, on being rejected from the Cortes, in common with all the deputies from the province, "that notwithstanding the terrible authority conferred on the captain-general by this royal order, Vives, who then held that office, far from putting it in execution during his long government, discovered that its application would be equally disadvantageous to Cuba and Spain. Under a mild and conciliatory policy this island became the refuge of many unhappy proscripts, who were expelled from the Peninsular territory by the arm of tyranny."

The judicious administration of the Count Villaneuva, as intendant, which had undoubtedly an influence materially advantageous to the country, was likewise calculated to make every one forget the depressed political condition to which the new law had reduced the inhabitants of Cuba. Under its fearful and comprehensive provisos, since become the scourge of the land, public bodies were respected. Some of them constantly consulted together on grave subjects, such as the rural and domestic police for the management of slaves, the imposition of taxes and judiciary reform, and enjoyed the privilege of printing their reports, without applying for the consent of the executive officers; and the press was moreover very far from being restricted as it now is.

As a proof that the political servitude created by the royal order of 1825 was not intended to be permanent, an extract is made from an article on the dangers of the slave trade, published in a periodical of Havana, in 1832, under the despotic government of Ferdinand, and seven years after issuing the royal order above referred to. Immediately following a very precise detail of facts, of the numbers of imported slaves, and of the relative position of the races, we read:

"Thus far we have only considered the power which has its origin in the numbers of the colored population that surrounds us. What a picture we might draw, if we were to portray this immense body acting under the influence of political and moral causes, and presenting a spectacle unknown in history! We surely shall not do it. But we should be guilty of moral treason to our country, if we were to forget the efforts now making to effect a change in the condition of the African race. Philanthropic laws, enacted by some of the European nations, associations of distinguished Englishmen, periodicals solely devoted to this subject, eloquent parliamentary debates whose echoes are constantly repeated on this side the Atlantic, bold exhortations from the pulpits of religious sects, political principles which with lightning rapidity are spreading in both hemispheres, and very recent commotions in several parts of the West Indies, every thing is calculated to awaken us from our profound slumber and remind us that we must save our country. And should this our beloved mother ask us what measures we have adopted to extricate her from her danger, what would those who boast themselves her dutiful sons, answer? The horrid traffic in human blood is carried on in defiance of the laws, and men who assume the name of patriots, being no other than parricides, cover the land with shackled victims. And as if this were not sufficiently fearful, with criminal apathy, Africans freed and brought to this country by English policy, are permitted to reside in our midst. How different the conduct of our neighbors the Americans! Notwithstanding the rapid increase of their country; notwithstanding the white has constantly been four fifths more numerous than the colored population, and have ten and a half millions to offset two millions; notwithstanding the importation of the latter is prohibited from one end of the republic to the other, while European immigration is immense; notwithstanding the countries lying upon their boundaries have no slaves to inspire dread, they organize associations, raise funds, purchase lands in Africa, establish colonies, favor the emigration of the colored population to them, increasing their exertions as the exigency may require, not faltering in their course, and leaving no expedient untried which shall prove them friends of humanity and their country. Not satisfied with these general measures, some states have adopted very thorough and efficient measures. In December, 1831, Louisiana passed a law prohibiting importation of slaves even from other states of the Union.

"Behold the movement of a great people, who would secure their safety! Behold the model you should imitate! But we are told 'Your efforts are vain. You cannot justly reproach us. Our plantations need hands, and if we cannot obtain negroes, what shall we do?' We are far from wishing to offend a class equally deserving respect and esteem, including many we are happy to call friends. We are habitually indulgent, and in no instance more so than in that before us. The notions and examples to which they have been accustomed justify in a great measure the part they act, and an immediate benefit and remote danger authorize in others a course of conduct which we wish may never be generally and permanently adopted. We would not rudely censure the motives of the planters. Our mission requires us only to remark, that it is necessary to adopt some other plan, since the change in politics is inconsistent with and hostile to the much longer continuance of the illicit traffic in slaves. We all know that England has, both with selfish and humane motives, made and is still making great efforts against it by means of treaties. She is no longer the only power thus engaged, since France is also taking her share in the enterprise. The United States will soon appear in the field to vindicate down-trodden humanity. They will adopt strong measures, and perseveringly pursue the pirate negro-dealer. Will he then escape the vigilance of enemies so active and powerful? And even should some be able to do so, how enormously expensive must their piracy be! It is demonstrable that the number of imported negroes being then small, and their introduction subject to uncommon risks, their cost would be so enhanced as to destroy the motive for preferring slave labor. A proper regard to our true interests will lead us to consider henceforth other means of supplying our wants, since our present mode will ultimately paralyze our resources and be attended with baneful consequences. The equal distribution of the two sexes in the country, and an improved treatment of them, would alone be sufficient, not merely to prevent a diminution of their number, but greatly to increase it. But the existing disproportion of the sexes forbids our indulging in so pleasing a hope. We shall, however, do much to effect our purposes by discontinuing certain practices, and adopting a system more consonant to the good principles that should be our guide.

"Would it not be advisable to try some experiments that we may be able to compare the results of cultivating cane by slaves, with such other method as we may find it expedient to adopt?

"If the planters could realize the importance of these propositions to their welfare, we should see them striving to promote the introduction of white and the exclusion of colored hands. By forming associations, raising funds, and in various ways exerting themselves vigorously in a cause so eminently patriotic, they would at once overcome the obstacles to the introduction of white foreigners, and induce their immigration by the guarantees of good laws and the assured tranquillity of the country.

"We may be told that these are imaginary plans, and never to be realized. We answer that they are essays, not difficult or expensive, if undertaken, as we suggest, by a whole community. If we are not disposed to make the voluntary trial now, the day is at hand when we shall be *obliged* to attempt it, or abandon the cultivation of sugar. The prudent mariner on a boisterous ocean prepares betimes for the tempest, and defies it. He who recklessly abandons himself to the fury of the elements is likely to perish in the rage of the storm.

"'How imprudent,' some may exclaim, 'how imprudent,' to propose a subject which should be forever buried in 'lasting oblivion!' Behold the general accusation raised against him who dares boldly avow new opinions respecting these matters. Unfortunately there is among us an opinion which insists that 'silence' is the true policy. All feel the evils which surround us, are acquainted with the dangers, and wish to avoid them. Let a remedy be suggested and a thousand confused voices be simultaneously raised; and a significant and imploring 'Hush!'—'hush!' is heard on every side. Such infatuation resembles his who conceals the disease which is hurrying him to speedy death, rather than hear its unpleasant history and mode of cure, from his only hope, the physician's saving science. Which betrays censurable apathy, he who obstinately rushes headlong to the brink of a mighty precipice, or he who gives the timely warning to beware? Who would not thus save a whole community perhaps from frightful destruction? If we knew most positively that the disease were beyond all hopes of cure, the knowledge of the fact would not stay the march of death, while it might serve but as a terrifying annunciation of his approach. If, however, the sick man is endowed with a strong constitution, that with timely prescription promises a probable return of health, it would be unpardonable to act the part of a passive spectator. We heed not that the selfish condemn, that the self-admiring wise censure, or the parricidal accuse us. Reflections of a higher nature guide us, and in the spirit of our responsible calling as a public writer, we will never cease to cry aloud, 'Let us save our country—let us save our country!'"

Nothing would more forcibly illustrate the rapid encroachment of despotism in the island than the publication, now, of a document like the above, or any thing discreditable, or disparaging to the slave-dealers. Whoever should dare make the experiment, would most certainly do it at the risk of his life. Further comment on the progress of tyranny is unnecessary.

Not to lose sight of the order of events, it must be borne in mind that immediately after the overthrow of the constitution, and precisely at the time the persecution for revolutionary opinions commenced under the order of 1825, the country was in its most flourishing and healthy period. The fruits of the several acts for promoting the country's welfare and the development of its resources, which owed their origin to corporations, before they had lost their vitality, had been gathered. Moreover, the judicious and liberal policy above described was continued by the intendant, who could then act with great independence. As chief of the financial department, the Count de Villanueva regulated the mode of keeping accounts, corrected abuses, introduced greater simplicity in the collection of taxes, and established several facilities beneficial to the merchants. By means of his great influence at Madrid, he was enabled to supersede the captain-general in the presidency of the consulado, and directing the labors of that body, he made them subserve the development and improvement of the country. Availing himself of the general wealth, and of the increasing agriculture of the island, he daringly taxed its products; and it is generally believed that it was during his administration, taxes of various kinds were imposed for the first time without the consent of those to be affected by them. He represented "de facto" the people of Cuba; was the chief fiscal agent; the friend and adviser of the captain-general; the favorite of Ferdinand's government. A skillful and mighty authority like his could, at such a period, draw abundant resources from the country for the metropolis, and promote at the same time the interests of the former by reforming abuses. To both these objects were his exertions successfully directed. To his discriminating judgment it was very evident that a vast territory, capable of great agricultural production, could not maintain its position, much less make progress, should its commerce be again limited to the mother-country. He was aware that the probable results of such limitation would be the total annihilation of the surplus revenue, of which they were so desirous at court; the immediate paralysis of agriculture, the fountain of the island's wealth; and a very extensive contraband trade.

Villanueva had the waters of the Husille brought

into the city by a well-devised though costly plan; the roads near Havana macadamized, and a mud-machine erected to clear the anchorage and preserve the wharves. He established the more modern and rational system of selling at auction to the lowest bidder the performance of various services, particularly for the government or the public. He enlarged the Spanish navy from the navy-yard of Havana; the regular intercourse between the two countries by mail packets was his suggestion, and the Guines railroad is a crowning, ever-memorable, and enduring monument of his enterprise and genius. Amidst these improvements, beneficial to Spain and the island, the count was enabled to make frequent and heavy remittances to the general treasury in Spain, which was so relieved by them that the demands were gradually augmented without any regard to the means of meeting them, and the inevitable consequence was, the sacrifice of the necessities of the island to the urgency of their payment. Thus it happened that the Bank of St. Ferdinand, the establishment of which was one of the acts which do honor to Villanueva, had no opportunity of doing any service to the public, as its capital was specially sent for from Madrid. In brief, Count Villanueva's administration can in no way be better appreciated than by bearing in mind that whatever liberal and enlightened views he carried into practical effect, he had nothing similar to guide him or excite his emulation, in all the Spanish territory. His power in Cuba was great, his influence in Madrid had no equal, and his credit abroad was such that his promise and acceptance was a source of revenue at court. The authority of the captain-general himself being eclipsed by his, it is certainly no matter of surprise that public bodies and individuals should have sunk into insignificance.

It was in such a state of political weakness and general prosperity, that the estatuto real, which was the first liberal act of Christina's regency, found Cuba. Under it the inhabitants of the island observed, as they always had done, the laws promulgated in the mother-country. A number of members were added to the municipalities, equal to the number of hereditary members, and the former were by express proviso to be individuals who were highest on the tax list. Thus formed, these corporations elected the deputies who represented the interests of the island at the Spanish congress. This slight political change, which enabled the corporations of Havana, Santiago de Cuba, and Puerto Principe, to name three deputies in the "estamentos" without other free institutions, was certainly not calculated to alarm the royal authority, however jealous it might be supposed. Three votes, more or less, could not of course cause any uneasiness; but it is ever the consequence of free institutions, in just proportion to their worth, to diminish the importance of individuals. Here, then, was one of the causes of that strenuous opposition so successfully exerted to deprive the island of deputies to Madrid. Such a refusal, where there is an immense amount of productive capital to be benefited or injured, or destroyed by the enactments of government, and where the colony is not even allowed delegates to represent its interests at court, has no parallel in any civilized country professing to approve of liberal institutions. The island was at that time governed by General Tacon, whose short-sighted, narrow views, and jealous and weak mind, were joined to an uncommon stubbornness of character. Never satiated with power, it was through his influence that the wealthy portion of the community was divested of the privileges conferred on them by the estatuto. He even deprived the old municipalities of Havana of the faculty of naming the under-commissaries of police. In his own immodest report of his reign, as it was justly termed, he enumerated the very extensive and costly buildings and public works he had constructed, and from the singular manner in which he accounts for procuring the ordinary means, we must suppose he had the power of working miracles. To sustain his absolute government by trampling on every institution, was the necessary consequence of his first violent and unjustifiable act. It was consequential upon his own and his followers' efforts. For any power, any institution, not dependent on the palace of the captain-general, might be the means of denouncing abuses, of exposing the real deformity of his and their pretended patriotism; and the numberless parasites whose interest ever was to blind the royal eyes, magnified the virtues of their hero, while they were rapidly accumulating fortunes at his side. In order to obtain credit in the management of the police, he displayed a despotic and even brutal activity in the mode of exacting from the under officers, distributed in the several wards of the city, under personal responsibility, the apprehension and summary prosecution of criminals. They soon found that there would be no complaint, provided they acted vigorously and brought up prisoners. So far from presuming their innocence, or requiring proof of their crimes, those who were once arrested were put to the negative and difficult task of proving their innocence. The more unwarrantable the acts of his subalterns the more acceptable to him, since they, in his opinion, exhibited the energy of his authority. They trembled in his presence, and left it to persecute, to invent accusations, to imprison, and spread terror and desolation among the families of the land! It is but just to add, that the banditti and thieves and professed gamblers were terrified by his sweeping scythe, and became much more modest than they had been during the brief government of the weak and infirm General Ricafort, the predecessor of Tacon. The timid and short-sighted merchant who perceived this reform, did not comprehend or appreciate the illegality of the system, nor its pernicious effects on the future destinies of the country, and was the first to justify the man who dared interpose himself between the Spanish monarchs and their subjects, to silence every complaint of the latter, and to say to the former, "You shall never hear the petitions of your American vassals contrary to my pleasure." The political servitude at that moment implanted in the country was new, and of course excited discontent, which was not unfrequently vented in the random conversation of young men.

The consequence of all this was, a regular system of espionage. The prisoners were distributed in the castles, because the jails were insufficient to contain them. In the dungeons were lodged nearly six hundred persons, the cause of whose detention nobody knew; a fact authentically proved by a casual circumstance. In the streets, in the highways and fortresses, under a scorching sun, and during the unhealthy season, the poor Carlist prisoners, having surrendered themselves, trusting to the faith of liberals, were suffered to sicken and sink miserably into a premature grave. Let it not be supposed, however, that his political persecution was confined to the enemies of the liberal institutions then existing in Madrid. The contrary may be adduced from the inconsiderate protection extended by him to the famous friar Cirilo Almeda, of whose machinations he appeared to approve, and from the fact that events favorable to the queen were at a certain period not permitted to appear in the distorted press of Havana. His creed was soon ascertained. He considered those whom he thought likely to tear the veil from his tyranny, the veritable traitors, the enemies of the throne, and the advocates of independence in Cuba. He destroyed all freedom of discussion in the municipal body, usurped its powers, and frightened away such members as he thought would not bend sufficiently to his will. He constructed an enormously high, massive, level road through the widest avenue of the city, which has since been removed, at the expense of the same suffering community who had to pay for its erection, and had to suffer its unhealthy effects while it remained. General Tacon moreover established a privileged market for selling meat and fish, to the detriment of the public and the public revenue, and for the profit of himself and his nearest friends. Those who doubt this statement, may find a clue to the facts in the "Expression de Agravios, ante el Tribunal Supremo de Justicia, por el Ayuntamiento de la Habana sobre cargos en residencia al General Tacon," printed in New York by Desueur and Company, in 1839. Among other things it will there be seen how a man living at the table and board of Tacon, was subsequently found to be interested in the contract for the meat and fish market, without its being absolutely binding on him to perform the condition of paying in his amount of stock in order to be entitled to his share of the profits, which he did nevertheless receive.

It will likewise be found that the party to that contract was illegally preferred to the more regular bidders. It may further be ascertained from that work that when the contractors obtained the grant and commenced exacting unauthorized fees, to the great injury of the public, a suit was instituted to investigate and reform the abuse at the tribunal of one of the alcaldes, and that the record was claimed and taken possession of by Tacon, who still lies under the charge of having caused it to disappear, as it is stated in his successor General Espeleta's official answer, that it is not to be found in the archives of the captain-generalship.

Notwithstanding General Tacon's efforts at the first election under the estatuto, the voice of his Excellency Don Juan Montalvo y Castillo was raised in Madrid at the Cortes, and the misconduct of the former partially exposed. As it continued, Messrs. Armas and Saco were named for the second congress during his government, both very enlightened and able men, well acquainted with the circumstances, and friendly to the welfare of the island, and as much opposed to the ultra-liberal or revolutionary ideas, as desirous of removing from the Spanish peninsular government the shame and discredit of such lawless proceedings on the part of the chief metropolitan authority. To discover imagined conspiracies, to commence suits blindly approved by his assessor, to expatriate, to vex, to imprison the citizens, these were Tacon's noble exploits. His artful reports found credit at court. He was therefore continued in his government, and the Spanish Cortes in 1836, by a majority exceeding thirteen votes, shut their doors, which had always been open to American representatives, against the deputies of the island, then elected and at Madrid. They were obliged to return without being allowed the privilege of uttering their grievances. This was the single but serious act of usurpation which robbed the descendants of the island's conquerors of all interference in its administration and tributary system. Some time after the oath to the constitution had been taken at Madrid in 1837, the Spanish General Lorenzo, commanding in St. Jago, encouraged by the encomiums and rewards conferred in former times and in similar instances, on such authorities as first followed the impulse given at the court of a political change, thought it his duty to conform to the plan most approved by all parties, royalist or liberal, viz.: to repeat the cry raised at the seat of government.

He therefore proclaimed the constitution. The wily old general who had so successfully deprived the country of all representative or delegate system, would not of course very quietly allow his fabric to be leveled to the ground. He made an ostentatious display of his authority, and though well satisfied of the pacific views of the eastern part of the island, insisted upon fitting out an expensive expedition, which cost the inhabitants more than $500,000, and would have it proceed, notwithstanding that the commissioners sent by Lorenzo made a formal promise that the eastern part of the island should preserve their system until the queen decided, or would obey at once Tacon's order to annul the constitution, provided an amnesty were granted for the single act of proclaiming the same, their sole offence. General Tacon again made use of his favorite weapon against the islanders, applying it to General Lorenzo and the intendant of Havana, by perfidious suggestions calculated to impair their well-proven loyalty to their sovereign. Such improbable stories, the ill-disguised animosity of his passionate language, the cognizance by some impartial Peninsular tribunals of some of his grossly-imagined plans of conspiracy, all had an influence to force the Spanish court to acknowledge, without, for reasons of policy, publicly avowing it, the irregular and disorderly course of Tacon's administration, and he was removed from office. The removal of General Tacon is said to have been effected by a compromise between the ministry and Olivar, acting as agent for Villanueva, in which the rights of the Cubans were sacrificed to the latter's personal ambition. It was then agreed that no political assembly, or any rights whatever, should be allowed the Cubans, but that Tacon should be removed. This discreditable compromise was the undoubted origin of the immediate discontent and subsequent rapid adoption of the principle of annexation through the island. Nothing was more efficient in drawing the mask from his face than the unskillfulness of Joaquin Valdez, his standing conspiracy-witness and confidential agent, who in framing one of his plans got into a strange dilemma by compromitting the intendant of Cadiz, and other respectable old Spaniards, supposed to be concerned in the plot.

It should be mentioned, to the honor of the Spanish name, that at the subsequent sittings of the Cortes, and before the removal of Tacon, as if the injuries which had been inflicted on Cuba called for immediate redress, it was generally admitted as a matter of course, what has since been artfully withdrawn from the sight of the congress, that the political condition of that distant colony should be attended to and ameliorated without delay. A generous and high-minded Spaniard, Don Antonio Benavide, equally loyal to his country and desirous of the welfare of its inhabitants, clearly and ably insisted upon the adoption of any system in lieu of the omnipotence of the captain-general. But the zeal and high sense of justice entertained by the congress could give no relief, where the agents of the local government were active, and the oppressed country had no delegates to maintain her rights. The only result was a royal order authorizing Tacon to call a junta, which he took care should be formed to his liking generally, composed of authorities named by government, in its pay, with three or four private individuals among the general's pliant tools. This junta was to propose special laws for the government of the island. The consequence was exactly what might have been expected. The chief soon perceived that, however yielding the members might be, they must draw up some rules ostensibly to restrain his untamed will, or excite the ridicule of even the Spanish court. After calling together and dispersing them instantly, under a show of separating them into committees, he rendered the whole attempt inefficient, and feigning fear of danger from the plots of the white population, caused every feeling of justice to Cuba to be forgotten in Spain. The only proposition which seems to have transpired from the sitting of that strange, transitory, and expensive junta, was to make the island a vice-royalty and Tacon vice-king. Ludicrous as it may appear, it is no less true.

Notwithstanding it was under free institutions that Spain granted the establishment of the mixed Anglo-

Spanish tribunal at Havana, for the cognizance of prizes taken from the African trade, it was when the public bodies of the island were without sufficient energy to raise their spontaneous protest on political questions, that the Castilian name was humbled by the floating fortress which the English anchored in the port of Havana, as a rallying signal for the blacks, openly and malignantly avowed, and sufficiently evident from the fact that it was manned by black men in British uniforms! These soldiers, distributed in the heart of the city, the greater number liberated from slave-ships by the tribunal, who both during and subsequently to their apprenticeship were left in the country in direct communication with their bond-brethren, were the first instruments of spreading discontent among the slave population. Very far from independent, and from representing the interest of the wealthy planters, must have been the public bodies of the island, who thus patiently saw the germs of violent insurrection sown broad-cast over the land, without most earnestly assailing the Spanish ministry with their complaints. It was not however until about the year 1835, that the disproportion of the races became alarming. In 1837, General Tacon received an official communication from Madrid, inclosing a copy of a note from the Spanish minister at Washington, containing a vivid picture of the dangers to Cuba from the abolitionary efforts making in the United States and generally all over the world. He who had heedlessly given new life and development to the policy which Vives had only partially unfolded, and which consisted in separating the old Spaniards from the natives, was now made to feel that the co-operation of the country's *bourgeoisie*, in all their united effort, was requisite to oppose the encroachments of the abolitionists.

The exposition of the minister at Washington, though abounding with contradictory opinions, was, in the main, exact. It predicted immediate danger. No public bodies existing which could be considered as emanating even indirectly from the people, rich or poor, he having discredited and crushed all such institutions, what could he do? He contrived to call a general meeting of the planters in the city of Matanzas, whose very judicious report provided for domestic and rural government, material defence, and funds to carry their plans into effect. The colonization of the island by white inhabitants, which had been unlawfully terminated, was demanded by this meeting of planters, who also insisted upon the establishment of a rural militia. In consequence of these requisitions, their resolutions on the first were not carried into execution. The immigration of whites has been materially obstructed by an influential party, who consider it hostile to the introduction of laborers more consonant to their taste and interest. General Valdez was latterly named captain-general, an honest and generous soldier, whose memory is still dear to the liberal party in Spain, wearing many honorable marks of worth, gray in the service of his country, but his capacity undoubtedly impaired by age, joined to a general ignorance of the colonies and of political affairs, common to all the military as a class. A person observing the progress of English pretensions respecting Cuba, would certainly conclude that Lord Palmerston had himself chosen such a man, who, though beyond the reach of bribery, and incapable of willful wrong to his country, was, from his weakness, a suitable and manageable instrument. Let it, however, be said in his praise, that he had occasion to show that when the captain-general chooses to put an end to the slave trade, it is in his power to do so.

Soon after his arrival, a series of by-laws made for the government of the slaves was published, wherein, instead of providing for the real circumstances of the occasion, the dominical rights of the master were suddenly attacked, yet not so much, perhaps, by their positive provisos, as by the appearance of interference at a period when the restlessness and uneasiness of the blacks required measures of an entirely contrary nature. The management of a slave country is always a difficult matter. To avoid the commission of great errors, in the condition of Cuba, would have been scarcely less than miraculous. The actual feelings of the blacks could not, with certainty, be ascertained by individuals who had either recently arrived from Spain, or never attended on the estates but for a few moments, or during excursions of pleasure. Thus it happened, that many judicious planters, judging from the small and gradual changes in the domestic life of the blacks, foresaw the coming storm for years, while the government agent could not comprehend, and resolutely refuted, such opinions as they thought unnecessarily alarming, and decidedly against their interest in the African trade.

Mr. Turnbull, the English consul, who, from his European reputation, would never have been allowed to occupy the post of consul at Cuba, had the Cuban proprietors had an organ of complaint, other than the government agents, concerted incendiary plots, and boldly followed them, notwithstanding the timely interference of Garcia, one of the governors of the city of Matanzas.

Several incidents might be named, evident precursors of an insurrection, which, for many years before the late repeated attempts, demanded a change in the system of the whole island; a change which would have taken place under a government having the means and disposition to ascertain the true state of things.

For the better understanding of the subject, it must be remembered that the ancient balance of influence established by the Spanish law between the military class and the judicial, or lettered part of the community, had been altogether lost; the former having been intrusted with every branch of the administration, even to the making of by-laws for the black slave population, which was submitted to the control of government agents, perhaps under the direction of their allies, the slave-dealers. At the same time an ominous policy commenced; the colored inhabitants were particularly favored; had numerous meetings, called *cabildos*, and enjoyed even greater privileges than the whites—being formed into military bodies for public defence, whereas the whites could not form a militia for their own safety, even in moments of pressing danger, and in those places where the disproportion of the races was most frightful.

Laws were enacted, purporting to alleviate the condition of the slaves; an apparent protection, calculated more to harass the owner than to realize the improvement of the former, without any attempt to instruct either. This was accompanied with the continuation of the slave trade, and the barbarous political oppression of the native creoles, whose every thought was looked upon with jealous suspicion. It seemed evident that the policy consisted in placing the lives and property of the inhabitants of Cuba in such imminent danger as to choke any feeling of resentment respecting the political changes which the Spanish government adopted for the exclusive advantage of the metropolitan part of the community. Thus was the dissatisfaction of the blacks fostered. How else can be explained the cause of the progress made in the island in that respect, and not in those slave-holding countries which surround it, and which, having a more frightful disproportion in numbers between the races, and greater freedom in the press and institutions, are withal enjoying comparative tranquillity?

The bonds between master and slave were gradually severed; the affections destroyed; the mutual relations of the races, for which the Spaniards had been always distinguished, were broken; and while every one deprecated the perilous situation of the Cubans, the latter continued unarmed; the slave trade augmented the causes of fear; and no moral reform was adopted to soften the harsh features and discordant views of the subjected or of the dominant race. It seemed as if occasional ruptures, which should awaken the natives to a sense of danger, were the most acceptable offering to the administration. Such did come to pass from time to time; what was the nature of these disturbances can, perhaps, be best understood by the following extract from the work of the Countess of Merlin, entitled "The Slaves in the Spanish Colonies;" who, though not a solid writer, has a style which savors of her sex, and is quite entertaining. She wrote some where about 1840:

"The suavity of manner of the Cuban toward his slave inspires the latter with a respectful feeling, which is akin to worship: there is no limit to this affection; he would murder his master's enemy publicly in the streets at mid-day, and would perish for his sake under torture, without giving a wink. To the slave, his master is his country and his family. The slave takes the family name of his lord; receives his children at their birth; shares with them the food which was prepared by nature in female breasts; serves them in humble adoration from earliest infancy. If the master is sick, the slave watches over him day and night; closes his eyes in death; and when this takes place, throws himself sorrowfully on the ground, cries wofully, and with his nails rends his own flesh in despair. But if a vindictive feeling is awakened in his bosom, he recovers his natural ferocity; he is equally ardent in his hatred and in his love; but very seldom does it happen that his master is the object of his revengeful fury. When an insurrection is not excited by foreigners (which, by the by, is not often the case), the cause of it may be traced to violent enmity toward the overseer. Here is a fact which proves the moral influence of the masters over the minds of these savages. A few months previous to my arrival, the blacks of the sugar estates of my cousin, Don Rafael, became insurrected. The slaves lately imported from Africa were mostly of the

Luccoomee tribe, and therefore excellent workmen, but of a violent, unwieldly temper, and always ready to hang themselves at the slightest opposition in their way.

"It was just after the bell had struck five, and the dawn of morning was scarcely visible. Don Rafael had gone over to another of his estates, within half an hour before, leaving behind him, and still in tranquil slumbers, his four children and his wife, who was in a state of pregnancy. Of a sudden the latter awakes, terrified by hideous cries, and the sound of hurried steps. She jumps affrighted from her bed, and observes that all the negroes of the estate are making their way to the house. She is instantly surrounded by her children, weeping and crying at her side. Being attended solely by slaves, she thought herself inevitably lost; but scarcely had she time to canvass these ideas in her distracted mind, when one of her negro girls came in, saying, 'Child, your bounty need have no fears; we have fastened all the doors, and Michael is gone for master.' Her companions placed themselves on all sides of their female owner, while the rebels advanced, tossing from hand to hand among themselves a bloody corse, with cries as awful as the hissing of the serpent in the desert. The negro girls exclaimed, 'That's the overseer's body!' The rebels were already at the door, when Pepilla (this is the name of the lady), saw the carriage of her husband coming at full speed. That sweet soul, who, until that moment, had valiantly awaited death, was now overpowered at the sight of her husband coming unarmed toward the infuriated mob, and she fainted. In the mean time, Rafael descends from the vehicle, places himself in front of them, and with only one severe look, and a single sign of the hand, designates the purging house for them to go to. The slaves suddenly become silent, abandon the dead body of their overseer, and, with downcast faces, still holding their field-swords in their hands, they turn round and enter where they had been ordered. Well might it be said, that they beheld in the man who stood before them the exterminating angel."

It should be observed, with regard to this moral influence, which can always be more or less preserved, that it is the source of safety for every slave country as long as slavery is sustained, and the guarantee of order when it is abolished. Painful is it, therefore, to see it fast declining in the island, since the military menials of government in the interior take pleasure in, and extort scandalous profit by, debasing and robbing the degraded, uninstructed white population.

Where a free white man can be carried publicly through the country with his arms tied behind him (the American citizens, Christopher Boone and others, were thus ignominiously exposed), merely on suspicion, or through the malignant avarice of an illiterate, ignorant soldier, acting as sole authority in the land, the white race cannot command that respect, and exercise the influence, which saves the southern states from continued insurrections.

"Although the movement," the countess continues, "had for a moment subsided, Rafael, who was not aware of its cause, and feared the results, selected the opportunity to hurry his family away from the danger. The *quitrin*, or vehicle of the country, could not hold more than two persons, and it would have been imprudent to wait till more conveyances were in readiness. Pepilla and the children were placed in it in the best possible manner; and they were on the point of starting, when a man, covered with wounds, with a haggard, deathlike look, approached the wheels of the quitrin, as if he meant to climb by them. In his pale face the marks of despair and the symptoms of death could be traced, and fear and bitter anguish were the feelings which agitated his soul in the last moments of his life. He was the white accountant, who had been nearly murdered by the blacks, and having escaped from their ferocious hold, was making the last efforts to save a mere breath of life. His cries, his prayers, were calculated to make the heart faint. Rafael found himself in the cruel alternative of being deaf to the request of a dying man, or throwing his bloody and expiring corse over his children: his pity conquered; the accountant was placed in the carriage as well as might be, and it moved away from the spot.

"While this was passing on the estate of Rafael, the Marquis of Cardenas, Pepilla's brother, whose plantations were two leagues off, who had been apprised through a slave of the danger with which his sister was threatened, hastened to her aid. On reaching the spot, he noticed a number of the rebels, who, impelled by a remnant of rage, or the fear of punishment, were directing their course to the Sabanas,* searching for safety among runaway slaves. The Marquis of Cardenas, whose sense of the danger of his sister had induced him to fly to her help, had brought with him, in the hurry of the moment, no one to guard his person except a single slave. Scarcely had the fugitive band perceived a white man, when they went toward him. The marquis stopped his course and prepared to meet them; it was a useless temerity in him against such odds. Turning his master's horse by the bridle, his own slave addressed him thus: 'My master, let your bounty get away from here; let me come to an understanding with them.' And he then whipped his master's horse, which went off at a gallop.

"The valiant 'Jose,' for his name is as worthy of being remembered as that of a hero, went on toward the savage mob, so as to gain time for his master to fly, and fell a victim to his devotedness, after receiving thirty-six sword-blows. This rising, which had not been premeditated, had no other consequences. It had originated in a severe chastisement inflicted by the over-

* The Sabanas are large open and barren plains, the last abodes resorted to by runaway slaves.

seer, which had prompted the rebels to march toward the owner's dwelling, to expound their complaint. They begged Rafael's pardon, which was granted, with the exception of two or three, who were delivered over to the tribunals. A remarkable truth of the love of the slaves toward their lord, is the fact of their stopping in the outset the engine which was at the time grinding, and preventing the explosion which would otherwise have taken place. Not only do the inhabitants of Cuba forward the emancipation of their slaves by procuring for them the means of gaining money, but they often make the grant without any retribution. A service of importance, a mark of attachment, the act of nursing the master's child, assiduous care during the last illness, or the priority of services of an old member of the family, are all acts rewarded by the gift of liberty. Sometimes the slave considers this benefit as a punishment, and receives it weeping."

These are very charming ideas. It is a pity that the countess should, by entering continually in the field of romance, get so far from the regions of truth. This remark, however, applies, in the paragraphs quoted, only to the assertion that the slaves in any case object to being made free, or that such gifts are so common. There are facts both pleasing to the philanthropist and worthy of credit. The following, from the touching pen of the lady of Merlin, afford a happy illustration of them:

"Though the slave enjoys the right of holding property, at his death it passes to the master; but if he leaves children, the proprietor never deprives them of the inheritance. It sometimes happens that the free negro makes his will in favor of his former master. Here is an example. During the scourge of the cholera, an old woman was attending the sick negroes of my brother. She had continued in his service, although she had freed herself many years before. Being taken with the disease, she called my brother and said to him:

'My master, I am going to die. These eighteen ounces of gold are for your bounty; this piece of money for my comrades; and this good old man, my husband, also, if your bounty will let him have an ounce to help him on through life, it is well.' The poor old woman did not die, but had a most miraculous escape.

"I will refer to another anecdote, showing the lofty and delicate feeling in the heart of a slave. The Count of Gibacoa owned a slave, who, being desirous of ransoming himself, asked his master 'how much he asked for him?' The answer was, 'Nothing; thou art free henceforth.' The negro was silent, looked at his master, wept, and went off. A few hours afterward he returned, bringing with him a fine *bozal*, or newly-imported African, whom he had purchased with the sum intended for his freedom; and he said to the count: 'My master, your bounty had one slave before; it has now two.'

"The blacks become identified with the affairs of their masters, and take part in their quarrels. The captain-general, Tacon, who, during the time of his government in Cuba, performed some few beneficent acts in this colony, but from his harsh and inflexible temper excited much ill-feeling, and took pleasure in humbling the nobility by his despotism, had persecuted the Marquis of Casa Calvo, who died while exiled. Some time afterward, and for the purpose of a magnificent banquet, which Tacon was to give the latter, he solicited the more renowned cooks of the city; but the best of them was a slave to the Marchioness of Arcos, a daughter of the unfortunate Casa Calvo. Dazzled by the very height of his station, the general imagined that nothing would oppose his will; and he asked the lady to allow him the services of the cook; but she, as might be expected, refused. Mortified with the failure, the general offered the negro not only his freedom, but an additional and abundant gift, should he choose to enter his service; but the negro answered: 'Tell the governor that I prefer slavery and poverty with my master to wealth and liberty with him.' "

These acts, however, of devoted fidelity on the part of the slaves are descriptive of a period in the history of the slavery of Cuba long since passed. Though the romantic and very youthful heart of the countess would prolong the dream, every one must be awakened to the sad reality which now covers this land.

Not very far apart, in time, from the insurrection of Montalvo, another took place, some where near Aguacate. In 1842, there was one in Martiaro, for the second time. On the last occasion, the slaves were made bold by the impunity which, through the deranged system of justice, and the influence of their owner, had been obtained for them previously. In the same year, the captain of the district of Lagunillas found an incendiary proclamation, which had fallen from the pocket of a foreign mulatto, who was employed as mason. A monk appeared on an estate near Limonar,* under pretence of requesting alms for the Virgin, whose image he carried with him, and went on prophesying to the blacks, that on St. John's day they would become free. In July of the same year, the slaves of an estate near Bemba committed several acts of insubordination, and murdered a neighbor. An Italian hair-dresser was imprisoned in 1841 for receiving proclamations of an incendiary nature. The negroes of Aldama, under the very walls of Havana, refused to work, and claimed the right of freedom. In January, 1843, a colored man, suspected by his companions of having revealed the particulars of the murder of an officer of government, by the name of Becerra, was assassinated by one of his own class, who, being afterward taken, committed suicide in gaol. In March, 1843, there happened at Bemba an insurrection of five hundred negroes, belonging to the railroad company and others. Very soon after, there was another movement on a large estate;

* The Triangulo.

and before that year closed, it occurred a second time. Soon after, the insurgents made a formal rally, doing many bloody deeds, and murdering numbers of the whites of different ages and sexes.

The above brief retrospective view of a few only of the principal signs which were indicative of disquietude among the slave population is very important at the present day, when the irregularity of the proceedings in the discovery of the plot has been the origin of an absolute disbelief of all charges against every one of the slave population. The information received officially at Havana from the Spanish minister at Washington, and through the court of Madrid, as far back as 1834, in which the dangers which threatened the island were fully shown, had been altogether slighted. So also were these events, though marked with blood, and showing unequivocal symptoms of a coming storm. It gathered not in a single day, but came gradually on; and the humbled landholder was doomed to see the clouds of destruction hanging over his property, amid the general apathy of the officers of government, who alone were intrusted with the care of that in which they felt no interest.

A rich planter, having obtained, subsequently to the last bloody insurrection of November, 1843, by means of a negro woman, and by hiding himself during the night in the room where she slept with her husband, the particulars of a plan of devastation and bloodshed so extended as to make him shudder with horror, the local government seemed at length to awake from a sleep fraught with such imminent danger. One of the immediate results was a meeting of the planters called in the city of Matanzas for the third of December. The meeting was held; a committee named to propose, on the seventeenth, a report, which report being unfavorable to the slave trade, the planters were not allowed to meet again, and the military administration went through those difficult circumstances, guided by its own incompetent intelligence, or by the suggestions of the ignorant.

How did they act? What system did they adopt to quell the general commotion among the colored population, which was so visible to every eye? The answer to these questions will be found in the ungrateful task which it is here necessary to perform.

Under the impression derived from some testimony obtained by the military tribunals, established for the occasion, and composed of officers of inferior grade, it was supposed that the conspiracy framed by the blacks comprehended every individual of that unfortunate class. No one was excepted: every one must be guilty; and those who would or could reveal nothing, were marked as the most criminal. Acting upon this ground, a general investigation, or what was called "*expurgo*," was ordered throughout the whole land, and intrusted to the most ignorant officers, whose system of inquiry was reduced to questions implying the answers required, and accompanied by the most violent chastisement, often inflicted in such a manner as sooner or later to produce death. Suggestions were made of the utility of employing lawyers of eminent standing, whose ingenuity and capacity would have advanced the proceedings efficiently; but nothing of the kind met a hearing. The following are a few of the atrocious acts which resulted from conferring judicial powers upon military officers of an inferior class.

Under date of March 6th, 1844, the captain-general addressed a letter to General Salas, who presided over the military tribunal stationed in the interior, in answer to the dispatches of the latter, consulting him as to the necessity of using violent means in the prosecution of those *free* colored persons under indictment, who should refuse to discover their associates, and setting forth the good effects which those means had produced among the slaves. In this letter his excellency authorized these same means to be employed with the free colored population, and manifested his approbation of their chastisement in the country where they should be taken, and of the attendance of the officer, in order to certify the testimony!

These officers, thus raised by a power above the laws, and above the dominical rights of the owners of slaves, with very few exceptions, exercised their authority in a manner the most sordid, brutal, and sanguinary. Under the universal alarm raised, and extending to every hut, whoever was bold enough to insinuate a doubt respecting facts revealed under the most atrocious tortures, was deemed an abolitionist; although his interests and previous conduct presented a much safer guarantee of his opinions than the trust which should be placed in uneducated and hungry officers of the army. It was quite common for the latter to demand and obtain money from the accused, in order to save their lives, or their bodies from barbarous lashing.

One of these prosecuting attorneys, judges, and executioners, at one and the same time, namely, Don Ramon Gonzales, ordered his victims to be taken to a room which had been whitewashed, and the walls of which were besmeared with blood and small pieces of flesh, from the wretches who had preceded them in this cruel treatment. There stood a bloody ladder, where the accused were tied, with their heads downward, and whether free or slave, if they would not avow what the fiscal officer insinuated, were whipped to death by two stout mulattoes selected for this purpose. They were scourged with leather straps, having at the end a small destructive button, made of fine wire. At the spot called the farm of Soto, were butchered in this manner M. Ruiz, C. Tolon, George Blakely, and other freemen; and their deaths were made to appear, by certificates from physicians, as having been caused by diarrhœa. This new minister of the law had been formerly prosecuted for theft, extortion, and even deeper crimes, committed while he commanded the criminal's depot.

Don Mariano F—— brought on himself the execration and odium of the whole city of Matanzas for his barbarous treatment of Andrew Dodge, a colored man, born free, who was generally beloved and esteemed, and was the owner of a considerable property. He was tied to the ladder and flogged on three different occasions, but never avowed what he was accused of; and finally he was executed, in defiance even of those sanguinary laws of old, which instituted the ordeal of torture in ages called barbarous. He also caused a free negro, Pedro Nunez, to be tied hand-and-foot and hung to the ceiling of the house, keeping him in this painful position through the night, his body having been previously lacerated by the whip. Again, by threatening to inflict punishment, he obtained from the mulatto, Thomas Vargas, an affidavit against a man of the same class, called Fonten. He used to visit Vargas at his dungeon every day after sentence had been passed on him, to assure him sportingly that he would not fail to receive four bullets through his body. The prophecy was of course fulfilled.

Don Juan Costa, another of the acting officers, had likewise his share in this work of accusation; and there were, in the process of his making, ninety-six certificates of an equal number of deaths of the indicted during the investigation. Of these, forty-two were freemen and fifty-four slaves. They all had died under the lash; and that you may judge of the intensity of their sufferings, I will record what appears from the process, viz.: "Lorenzo Sanchez, imprisoned on the first of April, died on the fourth; Joseph Cevallero, imprisoned on the fourth, died on the sixth; John Austin Molino, imprisoned on the ninth, died on the twelfth: and so on through an infinite number.

Don Jose del Peso punished a negro one hundred and ten years old, who died at the Matanzas jail.

Don Francisco Illas, the enlightened and humane fiscal officer, who appears among those of his class as if to redeem the Spanish name from the dark stain brought upon it by his associate, was called to certify to the death of this old man; but he drew back horror-struck from the spot when he beheld a man so worn by age, having his body cut into pieces by the pitiless lash. The unfortunate victim had complained of the fiscal Peso, accusing him of stealing from him forty-five dollars. Del Peso, after inflicting severe punishment, found sport in hanging the accused victims on a tree, and then cutting the ropes to see them fall to the ground in bunches. He had been a journeyman tailor at Havana.

Don Ferdinand Percher presented his process, having seventy-two certificates of deaths of prisoners during the prosecution; twenty-nine freemen and forty-three slaves. "I have one hundred prisoners in souse," said he once, before a number of respectable citizens, "and if one escapes I am willing to have him nailed to my forehead."

Don Leon Dulzaides, in July, 1844, had a free negro placed in the jail in what is called "campaign-stocks," which is a most distressing position of the body, the arms being arranged so as to hold the legs; and thus placed, ordered him to be whipped unmercifully, until he should confess. Another of the fiscals, who was acting in his official character in the next room, was called by the cries of the victim, and obtained for him a suspension of punishment. Dulzaides demanded the punishment of death for twenty-seven prisoners, but the council sentenced only two. During the reading of the sentence, he used to ask money of such as were saved from death. Seventy prisoners of Don Jyacinth —— died during the prosecution, of whom thirty-five were freemen. This fiscal was suspended from office.

Don Miguel Ballo de la Rore, being on the estate

of Oviedo, extorted from the negroes affidavits accusing their master, who being absent, was apprised through his administrator or *econome*, that he was a lost man, but that the fiscal would save him, provided he paid two hundred ounces of gold. The administrator wrote several letters on the subject, which were handed to General Salas, president of the tribune, who wrote to the fiscal, ordering him not to continue the prosecution on that estate.

Don Manuel Siburu, fiscal of the prosecution against the English and American machinists, had demanded in his accusation the sentence of death upon an Englishman named Elkins. The members of the military tribunals, however, being intimidated by the consequences that might follow, and at the same time well aware that the testimony had been extorted by the lash, consulted respecting the case with General O'Donnell. The latter answered, that they should proceed from what they found in the process, and look well to what they did; which, as there was no mention of the torture in the proceedings, meant that they should crown by their sentence the system of barbarous cruelty commenced by the fiscals. The consultation was repeated, and a similar answer obtained. At the same time, Mr. Crawford, the English consul at Havana, officially informed the captain-general that he was aware that the British Majesty's subjects were being indicted and judged at Matanzas in a manner different from that adopted toward Spanish subjects; that as the testimony had been obtained by forcible means, whatever had been done was null; that there existed a treaty between the two nations, wherein it was stipulated that no Englishman should be judged in the Spanish dominions by special tribunals or committees, but by the regular order of the Spanish laws for Spaniards. The consul was persevering in his demand, and the captain-general, embarrassed also by the consultations aforesaid, was obliged to give up; and he consequently ordered that the prosecution against foreigners should be placed in the hands of Don Francisco Illas, to be made anew. This able officer soon perceived that nothing was to be met with in what had been done but falsehood, infamy, and calumny, disconnectedly thrown together by the stupid Siburu. Within two months afterward the prisoners were declared innocent, and liberated. It was in the presence of this same Siburu, that another of his prisoners, the aged and respectable mulatto, Ceballos, well known and esteemed by the merchants of Havana, suddenly expired on being shown the place of torture.

Don Pedro Linares had three old Indians whipped in Cardenas, two of whom died, who lived in that neighborhood, and had resided on the island since the acquisition of Florida by the United States, whence they had come, from their attachment to the Spanish nation. Don Pedro Acevedo, fiscal of the proceedings against the negroes on the coffee estate of Domech, who had been accused of possessing poison (which, by the by, was never found) for the purpose of killing their master, so contrived it as to throw the guilt on a young white man, a native of the Canary Islands, aged between nineteen and twenty-one, who was executed, declaring his innocence to the last moment of his life. On being exhorted by the priest to pardon his enemies, he complied with the request, excepting the fiscal, Acevedo, whom he could not pardon.

Don Pedro Llanes, another of the fiscals, filled up the measure of his crimes, which cried so loudly for punishment, that he was at length accused of numberless robberies, extortions of money, and all kinds of wickedness, and at last was stopped in his dark career, and imprisoned in the Havana jail. There, under the stingings of conscience, he placed in the hands of General O'Donnell two hundred and fifty ounces of gold, which had been the fruits of his rapacity; and soon after committed suicide by cutting his throat. Don Manuel

Mata, lieutenant-colonel of the Carlist ranks in 1834, another of the fiscals, was imprisoned at Havana for excesses and robberies committed in his official character during these disgraceful proceedings.

The remaining fiscals, Gala, Gherci, Flores Apodaca, Cruces, Custardoz, Marcotegui, Maso, Llorens, Sanchez, Rosquin, Baltanas, Alvarez Murillo, and Dominich, traversed the country in every direction, and strictly obeyed the orders they had received; some whipping or torturing free colored or slave individuals, and extorting false testimony and accusations, and others seizing horses, cattle, furniture, and whatever was owned by the free colored persons, all which they sold and converted into cash. It is hardly necessary to say, that the fiscals took from their victims every cent which they possessed.

It is but justice to add, that the fiscals named Mendoza, Arango, and Illas are honorable exceptions to this host of miscreants. Signor Illas, above all, has called forth the approbation of all the feeling part of the community, and of the friends of justice and humanity, for his able, judicious, disinterested, and impartial conduct and deportment in the cases of the French coffee-planters and the English and American machinists, as well as of all who fell under his control. In the cases under the direction of the fiscal Ballo, this officer did not demand that sentence of death should be pronounced on any of his prisoners; the tribunal nevertheless sentenced two. The fiscal Lara demanded death for only one, and the tribunal sentenced four. The sergeant intrusted with the custody of the prisoners in the military jail at Matanzas is said to have collected twenty thousand dollars in cash for prison-fees and other arbitrary charges exacted from the prisoners.

In the city of Matanzas, the general persecution of the colored race was converted by the fiscals into means of gratifying their lewd passions upon the distracted daughters, wives, and sisters of their male victims. So far did they carry their barefaced impudence, that a ball was given by several of the fiscals, and attended by the consulting lawyer of the military tribunal, where none but women of color appeared. At a late hour of the night, the doors were closed; and all the inmates being in a state of disgraceful nudity, one can imagine what scenes of revelry and debauch followed. Acts of such low and stupid infamy serve to show how the several channels of civilization are interwoven, and how easy it is for man, when once authorized to trample on any of the salutary restraints of society, to mock and despise whatever comes in the way of his most sensual appetites.

And now, in order justly to estimate the trust placed in the hands of these agents of military justice, the nature of their duties should be stated. They had separately the jurisdiction of a tribunal, with power to imprison and call before them whomsoever they would interrogate. The testimony which they obtained was received privately, no one being present except the fiscal and the witness. The fiscal would write down and sign the declaration, the blacks and the majority of witnesses knowing neither how to read nor write. Not even the notary, who is required to be present at the affidavits before the ordinary tribunals, appeared on these occasions to check the arbitrary, malicious, or blind impressions of the fiscal. Officers of the army were named to act as counsel for the individuals indicted, whether colored or white, free or bondsmen. These counselors, incapable through lack of talent or learning, were not allowed to read the proceedings regarding the persons whom they were to defend. All the instruction they had must be derived from a hasty and general abstract of facts made by the same fiscal, whose last duty was to demand the sentence which, in his opinion, should be imposed on the criminal.

Too much blame should not be attributed to the chief who, commanding the island at this delicate period, could not be approached by the wisdom and intelligence of the land. The invariable and jealous policy which, for many years, has directed the administration of Cuba, drew away from the absolute military authority whatever was enlightened and spirited. Men of vulgar habits and little education were the natural upholders of a barbarous system; and it was not easy to find officers of superior worth to act under a cruel impulse, and to execute sanguinary orders; so that this strange course was unavoidably placed in the most incapable or polluted hands. It is, therefore, manifestly unjust to charge upon the chief authority of the island the faults which were due to the political jealousy, or the institutions, if such a name can be applied to the despotism established. But on the other hand, it would be an embarrassing question for those who have professedly enhanced acts of the same high functionary, to analyze and point out minutely the measures by which the island has been saved, and wherein the high capacity of the chief magistrate has been made manifest.

With regard to the truth of the conspiracy, and whatever ground it originally had, it has been so much embroiled and connected with incoherent, false, and improbable testimony, adduced by the fear of punishment, that a general opinion is fast gaining ground at the present day, that it never existed, and that the few reports and conversations of a rebellious nature, mentioned with some plausibility in the course of the investigations, are the constant and latent workings of the slaves, which, in all ages, have accompanied the institution of slavery. This would be a difficult matter to decide. The events which preceded the general and scourging inquisition lately gone through with, together with the simultaneous and visible impudence of the free colored race, are certain indications of a disturbed state of mind in at least some sections of the country. On the other hand, the indictments followed up by different fiscals, and the use of the torture without obtaining satisfactory evidence to dispel all manner of doubt as to the existence of a plot, speak against its credibility. It can also be alleged that the very ignorance of the prosecutors, and the irregularity of their mode of procedure, were calculated to hinder the discovery of a plot, without deciding that it had positively no foundation. It is more likely that the conspiracy was in its infancy; and that when the avenging storm which swept over the land was heard from afar, it increased the number of the discontented, who, through despair, prepared for some last acts of devastation and blood. There is one painful reflection, which fixes itself upon the considerate observer of events. While foreigners, after long delay, obtained a hearing of their cases, and after being paraded through the country, tied hand-and-foot on horseback, and kept in a filthy dungeon, were declared innócent, the white creoles, who had been imprisoned with equal injustice, remained still incarcerated, and their cases undecided, because they had no consul to claim for them the rights of civilized man!

CHAPTER III.

Geographical Situation of Cuba.—Its Beauty and Fertility.—Different Names of the Island in illustration.—Notice of "Notes on Cuba, by a Physician."—Trip to Guines.—Beautiful Farms.—Hedges of Aloes.—Plantain Fields.—Sugar and Coffee Estates.—Tropical Trees.—Singular way of distributing Milk.—Life in Guines.—The Valley of the Yumuri.—The Bay of Matanzas.—The Ceiba and Jaguey-marcho.—Subterraneous River.—Robbers.—Storm in the Rainy Season.—Errors in the "Notes on Cuba."—The Author's ludicrous Mistakes.—False Notions of Slavery.—Oppressive Acts of the Officers of the Law.—Bad Influence of the Slave-Trade Party.

In the two preceding chapters have been given a short historical and political sketch of Cuba, in which it will be seen that the island is at present in a most degraded and oppressed condition, and apparently without prospect of any favorable change on the part of its rulers. Before going into a detail of the wrongs which Cuba now endures, and the grievances of which her inhabitants complain, and before considering her present position with Spain, and her prospects for the future, it is advisable to give some idea of the island itself, and the character—social and domestic—of its inhabitants.

Cuba is about 780 miles in length by 52 in mean breadth, and has a superficial area of 43,500 square miles, being nearly equal in extent to all the other islands taken together. It is traversed throughout its whole extent by chains of mountains, whose highest peaks, Potullo and Cobre, attain an elevation of more than 8500 feet; and the plains beneath are copiously watered, and rendered fit for producing in the highest perfection all the objects of tropical culture. The climate, particularly in the western part, although tropical, is marked by an unequal distribution of heat at different seasons, indicating a transition to the temperate zone. The mean temperature is 70°, but in the interior and eastern part 73°. The hottest months do not average more than 84°–85°, and the coldest present a mean temperature of about 70°. Ice sometimes forms at night after a long continuance of the northers, but snow never falls. Hurricanes are of much less frequent occurrence than in the other islands. The situation of Cuba, commanding the entrance of the Gulf of Mexico and the communication between North and South America, gives it a high commercial and political importance. Indeed, such designations as, "The Queen of the Antilles," "The Key of the Gulf," "The Sentinel of the Mississippi," "The Beautiful Antille," "The Gem of the American Seas," indiscriminately bestowed upon this enchanting island, are sufficiently significant of its advantageous commercial position, and its remarkable natural beauty and fertility.

A work published some four or five years since, entitled "Notes on Cuba, by a Physician," contains such correct descriptions of the country, and such faithful delineations of the landscape and the several phenomena of nature, while in other respects it abounds with mistakes, that it is thought best to make some use of its contents in this work, both to afford very interesting descriptions of the island, and to point out the errors of the author in more important points.

The following is from the account of his trip to Guines, on the railroad:

"We were thus carried by well-stocked farms, surrounded by hedges of aloes, their dagger-pointed and stiff long leaves closely interlaced, bidding defiance to either ingress or egress, while from the centre of these clustered lances, erect flowering stems, with twined branchlets and cup-like blossoms, raised their candelabra forms a score of feet high, in their primness looking more like the work of art than nature. Then came the square-trimmed lime hedge, with its small clusters of white flowers yielding their perfume to the air, equally impenetrable to man or beast; and next long lines of uncemented stone fences, built of the jagged honey-comb coral rock that abounds throughout the country. These often inclosed whole acres of luscious fragrant pines, each sustained by a short footstalk above the circle of thorny leaves compassing the plants that were spread low over the ground; some were still small and blue with the half-withered flowerets that blossom all over the fruit; others were ripe, large, and of a golden hue, while a few of the hardier kind, but less esteemed, were of a reddish green tint.

"Now we passed by fields of plantains growing thickly together, bearing above their frail trunks heavy bunches of green fruit, with their terminating cones of unfructified flowers, their long, tender fan-like leaves, torn in shreds by the winds and drooping around, ragged and bruised, giving them the appearance of a crowd of slatterns in dishabille. Surrounding us on every side, many other valued treasures of our hot-houses springing from the rich soil, arrested the attention by their foliage, or flowers not wearing moreover the sickly look of pampered care, but fresh and vigorous, tended by nature's skillful hand.

"But the trees of the tropics alone are an inexhaustible source of admiration and wonder to the stranger. We were soon beyond the immediate neighborhood of the city (Havana), its gardens, its farms and its hamlets; and their places were supplied by extensive sugar and coffee estates, with their large potreros and woodlands. Here the royal palm, queen of the forest, met the eye on every side. Sometimes isolated and irregularly scattered over fields of sugarcane with their tall straight trunks and their tufted crowns of long, branch-like fringed leaves, waving and trembling in every breeze, and glistening in the rays of the sun, they stood like so many guardian spirits of the land keeping watch over the rich verdure, stretching far in the distance beneath them. Now in long avenues of turned Corinthian columns, their long leaves, reaching across and intermingling, forming one continuous high-sprung arch, and their trunks glossed with white lichen as with paint, they led the eye to the country mansion of the planter with its cool *verandahs* and its back-ground of neatly-thatched negro-houses, while in the adjoining potreros large clumps of them sheltered with their shade the cattle grazing peacefully at their feet."

And again when in Guines: "Slowly promenading under the porches of the houses, I could not refrain from occasionally peeping into the parlors and chambers as I passed their large iron-grated windows. But the inmates were all up, and although now and then a fair senora might be seen in dishabille, the whole household was generally engaged in the duties of the day, for the creole is always an early riser. Several were engaged in sweeping the pavements; others were clustered around the milkman's cow, which had been brought to their doors, and were waiting their turn to have their pitchers filled from the slow stream; while a calf tied just without tasting distance looked piteously on, and at times showed signs of impatience, as he saw his morning meal borne off. When all had been supplied he was muzzled, and his halter tied to the extremity of the cow's tail. One rush to the bag was tried but the cruel netting frustrated all attempts to taste the bland fluid, and the poor animal quietly followed in the rear as the man drove his cow to the houses of his other customers.

"At other doors the malojero was counting out his small bundles of green fodder, each containing a dozen stalks of Indian corn, with the leaves and tassels attached, the common daily food of the horse. On their pack-horses were bundles of small-sized sugar-cane, neatly trimmed and cut into short pieces, and selected small on account of their superior richness, offering to the creole a grateful refreshment during the heat of the noon. Others carried large matted panniers slung over their clumsy straw saddles, filled with fine ripe oranges, the favorite and healthy morning repast of the native and the stranger, the well and the invalid. As the day progressed, mounted monteros were seen galloping through the streets, just arrived from their farms; each with his loose shirt worn over his pantaloons, its tail fluttering in the breeze, while his long sword, lashed to his waist by a handkerchief, dangled at his back. Then there was the heavy cart laden with sugar, for the railroad depot, drawn by eight strong oxen, the front pair some twenty feet in advance of the rest, its freight of boxes bound down firmly with cords, and covered with raw hides. By its side the driver stalked, dressed in a loose shirt and trowsers, which once may have been white, but now closely resembled the soil in their hue, and a high-peaked straw hat, with a wide rim, on his head. He held in his hand a long pole, armed with a goad, with which he urged forward his slow-moving team, often striking the sharp nail at its extremity repeatedly into the flank of an ox, until the poor animal, in his endeavors to escape, seemed to drag the whole load by his sole strength. Other carts were returning to their distant sugar estates, laden with planks cut into proper sizes and fastened in packages, each containing all the sides to make a sugar box; thus put up by our ingenious northern friends for the Cuba market.

"The arriero with his pack-horses, eight or a dozen in number, was also urging them on by his voice and the occasional crack of his whip, while they staggered under their heavy loads of charcoal, kegs of molasses, or aguardiente (rum), and the halter of each being tied to the extremity of the tail of the horse before, moved in single files, carefully picking their way. Suddenly one of the hindmost would stop to survey the path, when there would be such a general stretching of tails that bid fair to leave some of them in the state of Tam O'Shanter's mare after her hard-won race. The whip of the arriero would, however, soon remove the difficulty, and the long line would again move forward."

The pictures of the country in the vicinity of Guines; the negro pranks on Twelfth-day, and their dances; the cock-pit and cock-fighting; the madruga baths and scenery; and above all, the detailed accounts of the Carlota coffee estate, are accurate, and leave true and vivid impressions.

"There are several beautiful drives near Matanzas," says the author; "but those which no stranger should neglect are that to the Cumbre, the ridge of the high hill rising north of the city, and that to the valley of the Yumuri, which it separates from the sea. Accompanied by a friend at whose house I was staying, I left the city in a volante before sunrise, and following a road of the roughest kind, which, passing behind the handsome barracks and the airy, large hospital situated on the slope of the hill, wound up its steep acclivity, I gained the narrow ridge of the Cumbre. Here, as I walked along the level road, I knew not on which side to fix my eye, so beautiful were the landscapes that surrounded me. Seaward, the widely-extended ocean, with numerous vessels on its great highway, the Gulf Stream, and more than thirty miles of the shores were included in a single view. Then there was the long, broad bay of Matanzas, dwindled in size, and looking like a majestic river with its fleet of vessels riding at anchor, and the city at its head covering the level plain and creeping up the hill beyond it. On the other side of the ridge, far down below our very feet, lay the lovely valley of the Yumuri, with its grounds now broken into sharp peaks, now gently undulating; its cane-fields, with their pea-green verdure, and the dark green foliage of the tall palms scattered irregularly over them; its orange groves and luxuriant plantations with broad waving leaves; its cocoas, its almonds, and its coffee, with here and there a gigantic ceiba spreading out its massive arms high in air. As the mist, which in different parts hung over the scene, rose in fleecy masses, or gradually dissolved in the increasing heat of day, and farm after farm, and cottage after cottage, became lit by the bright sun's rays, throwing into bold relief the illuminated portions, while the rest still lay in the deep shade of the Cumbre, a landscape was presented that I had never seen rivaled even amid the picturesque scenery of Switzerland.

"The valley is very small, which, indeed, adds to its beauty, and is so completely hemmed in on every side by high precipices, that it seems entirely cut off from the rest of the world; while the oriental and quiet air it presents is in strong contrast with the busy city just by it, and the long extent of mountainous region stretching far in the distance beyond. At the foot of the height on which I stood, a small cottage was perched, on the very summit of a small conical hill, and with all the appurtenances of a farm-yard, lay like a picture below me; the objects were much diminished in size, but the crowing of the cock and the bleating of the kids came distinctly on the ear, and heightened the interest of the scene. The whole formed a lovely, secluded nook, and one could not refrain from envy of the happy lot of the montero whose home it was. But the heart was pained on recurring to the past history of the vale; and while fancy sketched the scenes of murder and carnage which this place had witnessed, of its once peaceful people, it seemed well that the name of the neighboring city should be so significant of the event. It was here that, in 1511, numbers of the aborigines were cruelly massacred by the Spaniards, and the remnant, driven by bloodhounds to the surrounding heights, were forced in despair to throw themselves over their brinks into the river below, crying out '*Yo moir*,' I die; whence the name of the vale and river.

"On the ridge were several private residences, into one of which we were invited by its owner, who gave us that scarce article on a Cuba farm, a glass of fresh milk. In our descent to the city, several varied and beautiful views of it, and of the harbor and shipping, were presented; and when we reached the base of the hill, a short but rapid drive brought us into the gap, through which the Yumuri escapes from the valley. High precipices rose on each side, their summits crowned with a luxuriant growth, while, from the overhanging walls of the southern side, immense stalactites of various hues hung in irregular and grand festoons, amid which the entrance to a large cave was plainly visible. At its base the little river had expanded into a placid miniature lake, and beyond, through the cleft mountain, was seen the vale itself."

The following is a very picturesque description of the ceiba and the jaguey: "Soon after entering a coffee estate, I passed by one of those giants of a tropical forest, a powerful ceiba, with its large, tall trunk fixed to the soil by huge braces projecting from it in different directions, and rising branchless and erect sixty feet, where it threw out immense horizontal arms of massive timber. The extremities of these only were subdivided into branches and twigs, which, covered by foliage, formed an umbrella-shaped canopy over the whole. But although themselves free from leaves, these stout arms supported on their broad surfaces a luxuriant garden of air-plants. There were the wild-pines in close set hedges, with gutter-shaped leaves and cup-like cavities filled with the condensed dews of night, serving as cisterns for the winged tribes during the long drought of winter. Other species in branches of strings hung pendent, or in fan-like shapes spread close to their foster-parent; while some, as the night-blooming ceres, with hairy coats, like long creeping insects, clung to the sides and under surfaces of the branches, or wound around the trunk itself. Nor was this garden devoid of beauty. A partial glimpse could here and there be had of flowers of the brightest scarlet, of the richest brown, and of a delicate pink, exciting vain longings in the beholder to explore their aerial beds. Not far from this tree was another as large, inclosed in the deadly embraces of the *jaguey-marcho;* it was a mortal struggle for mastery between the two giants; but how powerful soever had been the *ceiba,* it was evident from the size of the other, the multiplied folds of its arms around the trunk of its foster-parent, and its luxuriant branches and foliage already overtopping it, that the victory would soon belong to the parasite. Near was a jaguey-marcho standing alone; the death of its victim had long been effected; and it pompously raised its distorted trunk, and spread its irregular foliage, where once before its noble-looking parent had stood in all its beauty."

The writer should have mentioned that the poets of Cuba have adopted the jaguey as the emblem of ingratitude. Equally true is the following: "I had now gained the foot of the hill, and commenced ascending its winding path amid irregular masses of jagged coral rock, of which the whole range seemed composed, and which, from the sharp points it presents over its whole surface, has received the very significant name of 'dog's teeth.' It was every where perforated by round holes of various sizes, traversing in every direction, the whole looking like some thick paste that had been suddenly petrified while in a state of violent ebullition. Here the ingenious Liebig could see his theory verified in forests of heavy timber springing from beds of barren rock, their roots penetrating into the holes and fissures, fixing the trunk firmly to the earth; while on the soilless bed rank air-plants, covered with their interlaced roots the petreous surface, or in clumps suspended in the air, clung to every tree.

"The foliage above was so thick that the rays of the sun penetrated only here and there through the almost twilight-shade that shed a softness on all below, where the dews of night hung in pearly drops on every leaf. Nothing could exceed the air of solitude reigning throughout this primeval forest. Scarcely a bird was seen amid its foliage, or a sound heard, save the faint murmur of the east wind through the thick canopy over head, and the boring of the worm penetrating the fallen timber. Even the solitary whistle of the small day-owl, and the occasional and distant clacking of the arriero, tended only to increase the sense of loneliness. It is in forests like this that the hutia loves to dwell, the wild-cat to hide her young, and the wild-dog to build his lair. Amid its deep recesses the runaway negro also seeks a home in some secret cave, spending his days in sleep and his nights in prowling about the borders of the neighboring estates."

"The creole," the author remarks in another part of his work, alluding to the countrymen "or monteros, is a finished orator, graceful in his actions and in his expressions. While talking, his whole frame is in motion; and one ignorant of the Spanish, could almost guess the drift of the conversation by his pantomime. I once listened to a most graphic description of William Tell's shooting the apple off his son's head by a mayoral (overseer) of a sugar estate. In one of my excursions I dined at the same table with him, and had been relating some anecdotes of courage, when he in his turn told that story. He was seated when he commenced, but warming with the subject, he arose from his chair, and, as the story proceeded, presented in succession the anxious crowd of spectators, the patient, unconscious child, the firm father, and the stern tyrant, in tableaux vivants that I had never seen excelled. At the moment when he had shot the arrow, and placed his hand on the other, ready to send it to the heart of the tyrant if the first pierced his son, the intense agony of the father, more intense because half-subdued and mingled with his deadly resolve, was so well depicted, that I gazed with unfeigned astonishment at the actor, when the cries of the crowd, joyful at his success, burst from them. Then came the daring response to the tyrant, that the second shaft was for his own heart, at which point his story closed, and I was revolving in my mind how a stranger to liberal institutions could depict the indomitable spirit of liberty dwelling in the bosom of the Swiss, when he said that all this happened to an Indian and his king in Mexico."

The description of the subterraneous river in the village of San Antonio is worthy of perusal: "On reaching the spot, I found the deep ravine, leading into the cave, dry; but the river which in the winter season disappears close by the town, would be heard rushing in its underground course near the opening. The ceiba, nearly a hundred feet high, rested the base of its immense trunk on the very edge of the rock overhanging the entrance; the huge braces common to this tree projecting a score of feet from it on the land, and firmly fixing it to the soil. It stood like some giant guard over the yawning cavern below, which seemed well suited to be the fabled residence of the terrible Ceme, worshiped by the Cuban Indian. The moon-beams lit up every object without, making the dark cavern still more dreary; numerous tree-frogs were piping their bird-like notes from the bushes covering the sides of the ravine, and bats were flitting down into it, while ever and anon a large wild owl swept across the chasm, hastily beating the bushes on its margin, and emitting his grinding cries. The whole spot was extremely picturesque; but one could not help fancying the stream, when swollen by the rains, thundering down into the wide mouth of this cave, and carrying with it whatever it bore throughout its subterranean course, depositing bones of animals, perhaps of men, of birds, reptiles, and land shells; and at its submarine outlet, ejecting some amid those of the finny tribes of the ocean and its shells; and when these shall have been upraised by the heaving earthquake, puzzling the future geologist by the incongruous mingling. The river is again seen deep down, through an opening in the rock about half a mile from the cavern, and pieces of wood thrown into the stream have appeared on the coast several leagues distant."

As a specimen of the once distracted state of the country, the "Notes on Cuba" contain the following story: "The short road of six miles between this place (Havana) and Regla, now so safe, was during the days of piracy much infested by robbers, bands of whom then roamed with impunity through all the surrounding country. A smart little Frenchman, who practiced the healing art in this city, was one night waited on by one of them, with a command to accompany him to a wounded man. Fearing the result of a refusal, he mounted a horse that the robber had brought with him, and rode some distance from the city under his guidance, when the two were suddenly surrounded by a band of armed men. The doctor now repented of his journey; nor were his fears lessened on their blindfolding him and leading him off on foot, although they assured him that no harm should come to him. After a long walk they reached a hut, where, the bandage having been removed from his eyes, he beheld a strongly-built man covered with wounds and exhausted by loss of blood. He was told to attend on him; and having dressed his wounds, and informed them that they were not necessarily fatal, his eyes were again blindfolded, and he was given in charge of his guide; a double handful of doubloons having been first offered to him as a fee, which he positively declined accepting. He was conducted safely home, and on the days appointed for his future visits the man and horse were found each night at his door. His patient got well, but the doctor would accept of no pecuniary recompense. In several of his rides afterward he was stopped on the road, but on being recognized was not molested; and on some occasions he was even accompanied by some of his robber friends to his home, when other bands, who did not know his worth, were prowling about the place."

The next extract is a picture of the daily storm during the rainy season: "For several consecutive days was the whole canopy of the heavens each noon hid by the heavy masses of clouds rapidly formed on the horizon, and over head presenting in their storm-like appearance a strong contrast by the clear blue of the noon's unclouded sky. About two o'clock began the gathering to one broad focus: and the black thunder-cloud, condensing in its frigid bosom the ascending vapors, and blending with its own immense mass the smaller ones in its course, with gathered and still increasing power, rose majestically against the opposing verge; its jagged edges apparently resting on the hills, and its pendent centre threatening destruction to all beneath. Then came the deep calm; and each leaf was motionless, while the scuds above rushed madly together, and curled and intermingled as if in fierce contest. And now the sudden blast burst through the still air, and the stout tree groaned, and the tender plant lay prostrate beneath its power. The long, pliant leaves of the tall palm, like streamers, fluttered in the rushing wind; the frail plantain's broad, tender foliage was lashed into shreds; the umbrageous alleys of mangoes waved their long lines of dense verdure, and all nature did homage to the storm-spirit; all but the powerful ceiba, whose giant trunk bended not, and whose massive arms and close-set foliage defied its utmost wrath; amid the turmoil it stood unmoved, a perfect picture of conscious strength. But the whole scene was soon hid by the torrents of rain that fell from the overcharged clouds. The atmosphere seemed converted into a mass of rushing waters; and mingled with its rattling gusts, was the lengthened crash and reverberating roar of the more distant thunder and the sharp shot-like report of that close by; while vivid streams and broad flashes of lightning played rapidly through the aqueous shroud. In less than an hour the storm had passed by, but fresh masses of clouds rose from different quarters, and their circumscribed showers often fell heavily within a few hundred yards, while near by not a drop descended."

Thus was the rainy season ushered in: "In the afternoon the clouds separated into banks, which hung about the horizon; and before evening the sun shone brightly through the transparent ether, and at length sunk into a gorgeously-colored and golden bed. A refreshing coolness pervaded the evening calm; the tolling of the different estate bells sounding the oracion, came sweetly on the ear; and when the shades of night set in, myriads of *cocullos* left their hiding places, and darting through the air, lit up the gloom with a thousand streams of lurid light, while the stars shone with a brilliancy not surpassed in the frigid zone."

And now, after enjoying these animated and vivid sketches, from the pencil of a correct, although at times a careless painter, would not one expect a similar excellence in his moral pictures? Would not one at least suppose his information to be judiciously obtained from reliable sources? It has always been supposed there was a near relation between a clear understanding and an artistical talent. It would seem natural that whoever is able to describe the beauties of the material world, must feel their harmony, and by *consequence*, possess superior intellectual faculties. How happens it, then, that the author of the "Notes on Cuba" should so incessantly err, when economical disquisitions take the place of his graphic representations of the external world? When the country's moral condition is the topic, he at once shows himself to be badly informed, and his judgment so partially and disparagingly exercised, that he constantly contradicts himself. His hasty views upon the gravest subjects indicate a weak intellect, easily led astray, even in opposition to the nobler and better feelings of his nature. Not to impute to the author, however, any unworthy motive, as the cause of the very serious and unaccountable mistakes in his work; for the ingenious acknowledgment of his inconsistencies at the close of the volume, excludes so severe an inference. It is both more charitable and reasonable to find their true cause in that inconsiderate manner of pronouncing on facts imperfectly known, so common to travelers, who, not wishing to appear deficient in their researches, are prone to adopt the most extravagant statements and opinions. Giving to the author's case the kindest construction, it must have been by mere chance, and certainly not from choice, that he generally happened to be thrown into company not the most select, and did not sufficiently test his opinions by inquiries among the better and more enlightened class of the community. How else could he have so exaggerated the devotion of the attendants at church, compared with the observance of sacred things in the United States? How could he have lavished enthusiastic praises on the disorderly habit of the country curates, whose vow of celibacy, voluntarily given only as a means of obtaining a livelihood, is perpetually broken, to the discredit of all Christian belief? The priests in Cuba are not respected; on the contrary, they are despised; and as their conduct belies the doctrines they have sworn to propagate, they set themselves quietly down to enjoy the bodily comforts of this life, without troubling themselves at all about their own or their flock's spiritual welfare. The superstitious credulity and faith in miracles of the monteros, or country people, is another of the subjects on which the author of the "Notes on Cuba" indulged his fruitful fancy. Just so also as to the fact that the Bible was zealously and devoutly studied. Would to God it were so! as it would evidence a concern for a future state, no where to be met with in the island. The tracts distributed with impunity, which the physician "notes" with exceeding pleasure, will certainly not excite wonder, when the reader is given to understand that the most celebrated works against Christianity are publicly and unrestrictedly sold throughout the country.

How far it can be said, consistently with truth, that the learned and enlightened Bishop of Havana was a perfect Tacon, let any inhabitant of the island decide, whatever political opinions he may entertain. Their actions did not evince any similarity of character; and it was reserved for the author to discover it in men who always created very different impressions. Bishop Espada and General Tacon, in times far removed from each other, owed their nomination to the liberal party of Spain. When absolute sway was re-established in the mother-country, the former continued to profess liberal views, and made successful efforts to extend the sphere of learning and education. The latter was ever active in crushing public spirit, in organizing a military government, and ruining public institutions, as far as lay in his power. The former was persecuted as an insurgent. The latter persecuted those who disapproved his omnipotence, and charged them with treason. It was of this same man that the author of the "Notes on Cuba" says, "he was a noble instance of the power of mind over brute force," and asserts with an air of triumph, that on his condemnation "he referred his judges to the records of the court as a proof of his mild administration." The records of the tribunals under his control, with none to publish the most common facts without his approbation, like the criminal statistics, are of little value. But the several processes against the objects of his hatred in Spain and Cuba, wherein his real character is revealed, and the sentence, which from motives of policy was not published in Havana by his successor, as the law required, might illustrate the point. "Men were sometimes taken suddenly from the midst of their families, where they lived in fancied security," (see the "Notes on Cuba,") "were shown the indisputable proofs of their guilt, and at once exiled from the island, as inimical to its government." What manner of procedure is this, by which Tacon was enabled to obtain proofs of guilt, and to sentence the accused without his knowledge? That such a panegyric, in itself revolting, should be volunteered by an American writer, is the only apology for such acts on the part of those who had not, like himself, enjoyed the advantages of a free country. So intent was he on exalting the moral reformer, as he is pleased to term him, that he mentions Tacon's macadamizing the streets of Havana, and candidly avows that the side-walks were buried by the structure, so that, he adds, "it is no wonder the ladies are not inclined to walk."

It is amusing, to those acquainted with the habits and customs of Cuba, to read of wonders in the country which no one except the honest doctor has had the good fortune to discover. Young ladies visiting burying-grounds to enjoy the sight of a funeral, as a matter of amusement; Indian agents, monteros, riding with muskets, or taking their sweethearts before them on the same saddle; a sacristan, or sexton, becoming a prominent character through his knowledge of the law, in a village where no law business is transacted; a country officer of justice chanting the church service at his wife's funeral; a marquis winning and exacting a dollar from his own slave at a cock-fight; another young lady riding sixty miles on horseback, in a day, to dance all the evening; the stare of women, whose total freedom from prudery did not prevent them from throwing a *furtive* glance at this wandering Esculapius, who might be sadly and undignifiedly confounded with the "barber-surgeon practitioners" of the land; the celebrated and favorite "olla podrida," a dish so rare and exquisite, and of which Spain may well boast, freely served in the lunatic asylum of Havana; and one of the patients of the institution handing a petition to the learned traveler, which the latter, from his knowledge of the Spanish (of which there are abundant specimens in his book), is pleased to commend for its pure Castilian. Happily though, in his wanderings through the island (which by the way, it may be observed, was made to widen for his comfort), he was not very difficult to please: he was tossed about in rather a shabby accoutrement, judging from the horses which dragged him along; and he actually began to relish the dinners in the country shops, or what he styles Spanish condiments. Rather than do violence to the customs of the land, he gayly joined in a drink of water with a porter; and probably from the same motive, accepted and did honor to the delicate morsels furnished by an unknown creole, a fellow-passenger on the railroad to Guines, who, an accident having detained the cars, generously provided him and others with an abundant luncheon. It is therefore singular that the author should be the first to observe, that the creole was not only economical, but parsimonious to an uncommon degree. "The Irishman," he says, "will empty his purse when the creole will hesitate to spend a medio."

When among country inn-keepers of the lower class of Catalonians, and their associates, and the captains of the partido, who, according to his own account, do not wash till noon, hearing himself called a Jew (which, even as a practical joke, is no sign of good-breeding), and animated by *practical jokes*, it is no wonder that the writer should have formed strange notions, and acquired a very imperfect knowledge of many important facts. He is made to understand that Guines has been increased by the construction of the railroad, and that foreigners are looked upon with envy.

He mistakes some of the above described class for the lofty Castilian hidalgo, a true specimen of whom he probably never met; and the unmeaning look of ignorance for an expression of contempt of the creoles. The ward of Puebla Nuevo, in the city of Matanzas, which has been stationary for many years, he cites as an instance of rapid advancement. He is made to believe in the existence of a young men's debating society, where subjects are discussed which in old Spain would not be named. The ludicrous kings of the negro tribes, who preside at their dances, he imagines to be engaged in directing their moral habits. He gives a glowing account of the products of a coffee and of a sugar-plantation, asserting that in common times the profits of the molasses produced on the latter would cover its current expenses. Unacquainted with the frauds committed in the reports manufactured for private purposes, and with the carelessness with which the statistics of the country are taken, by reason of the indolence or incapacity of the agents, he wonders at the marvelous results in the reports of mortality on the estates, and which are almost sufficient to make one wish himself a slave.

In fact, there seems to lurk about the author of the "Notes" a decided partiality for slavery, an evil which, in this age, is lamented even by those whose interest and safety require them to uphold it. He describes the slave as gay and happy; enumerates the laws in his favor, acknowledging at the same time that they are not enforced; attributes this mismanagement to the planters, whom he knows exert no influence in public enactments; and states that baptism and burial is all the negro receives in the way of moral and religious government; still maintaining that his condition is better than that of the European peasant and the manufacturing and mining class of England.

The author of the "Notes on Cuba," whose opinion appears vacillating, says that the slave trade is a source of wealth to the island, as it formerly was to Liverpool and Boston; that only two thousand blacks are imported annually; and that the whole country is in favor of its continuation. As the author in these particulars seems to have blindly adopted the slave-dealers' cant, it may not be amiss to show the gross delusion under which he labored. That Cuba has acquired her vast agricultural importance by means of imported negroes, is an undeniable fact. That by following another course, she would have attained her present extensive though precarious production, remains to be proved. To insist, however, at this late period, that her wealth is increased by the traffic, is more than absurd; it is absolutely false. It is well known that her real estate is, and had been for some time before the "Notes on Cuba" were written, fast declining in price, notwithstanding his report of its high value. It is also well known that the continuation of the slave trade has a direct tendency to jeopardize every kind of property, and to depreciate more especially the value of slaves in the island. It is, moreover, a most pernicious calumny to assert that the country is in favor of its continuation, and is as little to be relied on as his statement of the number of the imported, which he greatly underrates. Neither are the rich and enlightened planters, who see the fabric of their fortunes tottering before them, desirous of sustaining it, however the voice of public opinion may be assumed to be in favor of the selfish views of the few. An estate which eight years ago might be sold for $100,000 would not at this day command $25,000. A negro who could then have been purchased for $500, is at the present time to be had for $300. What, then, can be the sentiment of an intelligent community, had they the means of expressing it (which the author of the "Notes" grants they have not), other than in opposition to an economical and political error fraught with incessant danger? The Cuban planter is aware that while a stream of barbarians continually rushes in and mingles with their more civilized brethren, the work of civilization must be much obstructed, and that a restless race will ever be ready to second the machinations of wily plotters. The increase of the race by marriage is not feasible, and the warfare of the abolitionists will be most perseveringly prosecuted. They will not be deluded by the pretended humanity of the trade, such as we find on page 263 and others. The conviction of this truth has driven the more enlightened class from the markets, and lessened the price of a commodity, unfortunately so abundantly profitable, that it can bear great depression in price. The pretence that the slave trade betters the condition of the bondmen, by rescuing them from the hands of cruel African masters, who enslave their conquered enemies, is an argument which the author was taught by slave-dealers, and is too barefaced to receive countenance from reflecting men, even in Cuba. If there were no purchasers and no demand, the object of making prisoners of war among a barbarous people would be removed. Nay, the wars themselves, without their tempting and profitable pecuniary results, would cease, and the missionary be enabled to proclaim the gospel in the wilds of Africa.

Had the learned physician consulted the more respectable class of inhabitants, whom he certainly would not meet where practical jokes are allowed, and who, long before his excursion to the island, had presented petitions to government, together with statements of the perilous crisis which awaited the country, he never would have ventured the following singular prophecy: "Cuba has now nothing to fear from her slaves, whatever influence her increasing free colored population may hereafter exercise on her safety." He would not have been forced to add an appendix, even before the publication of his work, wherein his superficial view of the most serious matters is clearly exhibited. So unlucky was he, that he presumed to foretell that the free blacks would in any movement join the whites. And it is reasonable to suppose that while he wrote, the machinations of the free-colored of all shades, which have since come to light, were actually in progress. Had he drank at purer fountains, his blunders would, nevertheless, have been amusing; among which, his discovery of two represented classes is not the least—a veritable enigma. For it would be impossible to name any class of Cubans which is represented in the land.

The town of Cardenas has been denied direct commerce with foreign or even Spanish European ports. The production of sugar and the maintenance of all classes, so dependent on imports for most articles, were made to bear the additional expenses of a forced coasting shipment, because the administration considered it both expensive and favorable to contraband. The author of the "Notes on Cuba," though confessing at times the absolute nullity of the inhabitants as to all public measures, boldly asserts, in relation to removing the burdens imposed on the Cardenas trade, that "the merchants of Havana and Matanzas, who now export all its produce, have as yet had influence to defeat every movement for that object." It was in order to do away the alleged objections to this arrangement that the population of Cardenas built the custom-house, and not as an evidence of their readiness to pay its dues, as the author would have it. The convenience of the bay, the distances to other towns, the vision of the drunken Irishman charging the insurgents, and, in fact, all the information he obtained in the neighborhood of Cardenas, may be classed among the numberless fancies of his book. He erroneously estimates the duty on sales of real estate, called Alcabala, at $4,000,000, and, perhaps inconsiderately, and certainly with injustice, stigmatizes *all* the predecessors of General Valdez, by asserting, without an exception, that it was usual for captain-generals to receive a doubloon for every negro landed in Cuba. On the other hand, he draws an uncouth picture of the police, as much at variance with itself as with truth. When in a flattering mood he represents it as so active and excellent, that if it had any system, or were any thing else than a perpetual miracle, and could be described, he would surely propose its adoption in the United States.

Let the work speak for itself: "A country store had been broken open, and two or three men had been eased of their purses on the public road. The whole partido was aroused like a hive of bees against which a mischievous urchin had thrown a stone. The hitherto quiet inhabitants went about armed to the teeth, and there was great danger of their killing each other through mistake. The captain of the partido meanwhile was not idle. Visiting every dwelling in his jurisdiction, he compelled those who could not give a good account of themselves, and had not domiciliary passports, to quit the partido. Others on whom suspicion rested he sent as prisoners to Matanzas, there to prove their innocence; a mode of administering justice quite in vogue here, but which would depopulate many a section in other countries, and, I would add, that must have perfectly satisfied those robbed on the highway.

"These petty judges," he adds, with great truth, "are with very few exceptions, from Spain, a creole being scarcely ever intrusted with the office, and being without salaries, like so many vultures they prey upon the unprotected within their jurisdiction."

Is it credible that it is of the same country we read elsewhere in his work:

"Intoxication is very rare; the dormant passions are not aroused by it, and the laws are enforced. With all the corruption of the bench in Cuba, the murderer very seldom escapes from punishment; and so well is justice administered, in *certain cases*, that that foul excrescence on civilization, and most deliberate defier of the laws of God, the duellist, receives no mercy, and the crime is now unknown on the island."

Make a law to expel every person who cannot give a good account of himself, on the commission of a crime; name vultures for police agents; place corrupt judges on the bench, and a country will probably be free from excrescence, i. e., murder and duelling!

Even in the appendix, written after the recent insurrection, which would never have extended so far had the island not been ruled without the concurrence of the landholders, the author of the "Notes," seeing that his prophecies had wholly failed, still adheres to the dark banner under which he had enlisted, and still seeks the means of palliating what has and can have no excuse among civilized nations. In extenuation of the acts committed in Cuba during the judicial proceedings, he cites the punishments inflicted by the English in Dublin half a century ago, and adds, that if greater excesses were committed in the Antille, it was because they could be committed with greater impunity. Whatever horrors it has been the fate of the latter to witness, let not the abolitionist ascribe them to slavery. The author has his answer: "Abandoned to the caprice of the sub-commissions that visited the plantations, the whole population, afraid to utter one word against their acts, in despair saw their property sacrificed, and were compelled to witness the most revolting scenes of cruelty."

To the violent and powerful slave-trade party must, nevertheless, be ascribed, in a great measure, the errors and excesses committed in the investigation of the negro plots. This fruitful source of future danger, like all the other evils which threaten Cuba, must be attributed to that sordid class who, regardless of the welfare of the country, are wholly intent upon the acquisition of wealth.

CHAPTER IV.

Habits and Customs of the Island.—"Letters from Cuba."—Visit to the Estate of Don Santiago.—The Quitrin.—The Calesero.—Roads.—The Tavern of "La Perfecta."—Hard Fare.—Manuel's Distress.—Interesting Account of Himself.—Sugar Estate.—Don Santiago's Patriotism.—The Sugar Master.—Anecdotes.—Musical taste of the Cubans.—The Cuban Press.—Story of Maria del Rosario.—Evils and Abuses of the Administration of Justice.

PURSUING the plan first to give a correct idea of the creole inhabitants of Cuba, in the several relations of life, before setting forth an account of the grievances and oppressions under which they now groan, several extracts are here made from a series of papers entitled "Letters from Cuba," which first appeared in the Knickerbocker Magazine, about 1845. The first contains an account of a visit to a sugar estate, including the incidents of the journey.

I told you in my last, that I was just starting for Don Santiago's estate, and in his company. Our conveyance was a two-wheeled vehicle, very much like our "gigs," although larger, and set upon leather straps, which make it quite easy over the uneven roads of the country. It was drawn by three horses harnessed abreast; the one on the right side guided by my friend from his seat next to me in the "*quitrin*," the middle one tackled in the shafts, and the left one for the "*calesero*," or driver, to mount. The calesero had on well-polished leather boots, buckled all the way from the feet to the knee, thence open and stiff to the hip; a straw hat about nine inches high, with a moderate brim, and handsome colored ribbon, a black cravat, and a livery with silver ornaments. His knee buckles, his large heavy spurs, and the handle of his long whip, were of fine silver. After three hours' swift travel in the vicinity of the city (where the turnpike roads, which are kept in fine condition at a great expense, by the careful attention of the junto de fomento, presented an easy path), we gradually began to notice the uneven and broken way, which appeared to have received its improvement rather from continual travel than from any intended human agency. In some of these irregular avenues the soil, which is very soft and black, and rendered pliable by the heavy rains, would sink beneath the wheels of the "quitrin," while the heavy carts, with wheels seven feet in diameter, which we occasionally met on the way, cut deep and continuous trenches all along the road. My friend made me notice particularly that the peculiar ability of a calesero consisted in driving rapidly along the margin of these trenches, sometimes more than three feet deep, and extending several miles, without ever allowing the carriage-wheels to drop into them on either side. He likewise shows his skill in avoiding the stones, loose and fixed, which are scattered in the road. As I beheld the monstrous carts, loaded with two hogsheads of nearly two hundred gallons each, or eight boxes of sugar, constantly destroying by their large thin wheels the few repairs occasionally attempted, in addition to the several obstacles that require the ever-vigilant eye of the driver to avoid collision or excessive jolting, I was convinced that no other mode of conveyance would be better adapted to the condition of things.

Travelers are very much disposed to find fault with whatever may differ from their preconceived notions, or the standard to which habit has fashioned their opinions. It often happens, however, that further consideration furnishes some very good reason for not adopting what, in other circumstances, would be the height of perfection. I will give you an instance. You may frequently have heard that manuring land is not practiced in Cuba. In the staple production, sugar, the price of land is but an inferior item of the heavy capital to be invested; and so long as the distance of the new lands from market does not make the transportation of cane by carts too inconvenient, it will be more advantageous to work the new soil and obtain its virgin growth, than to manure the old fields, where manual labor is the most expensive. The ready market for vegetables raised near the city of Havana, affords great encouragement to the farmer's assiduity; and you will accordingly perceive that the soil is subjected to a very elaborate and skillful system of cultivation. Some of the planters, who have no new lands near them, are unwilling to abandon the costly buildings required on their estates, and consequently give very particular attention to improving their lands by manuring and the use of the plough.

Our black calesero drove around numberless small and large stones, up and down hill, and along the trenches made by the carts, and more than once approached close upon the verge of a precipice, but without diminishing the rapidity of his motion. Occasionally he would meet an acquaintance of either color, to whom he bowed with a courtly smile. Although my friend Don Santiago did not usually stop for any meals on the road, to gratify my desire of seeing every thing, the calesero drove gallantly up to the tavern of "La Perfecta," in the village of ——. Under the shelter of a wide shed, which ran round it, a number of horses were standing—some tied to the posts, others with their riders on them, who, without dismounting from their large straw saddles, were making purchases, or conversing with those standing about them. We were shown into a small room, a little more cleanly than the rest of the house, and in a short time were served with some very tough beef, strongly seasoned with garlic, some fried eggs, a bit of very salt ham, coffee with dirty sugar, and no milk.

The tavern-keeper, who seemed delighted that he was able to supply us with such inviting fare, asked us at times how we liked the service, adding that it was lucky for us that we had come on Wednesday, because Sundays and Wednesdays were the days for killing. "But your beef is rather tough," said Don Santiago. "And how could it be otherwise?" he answered. "In the first place, old oxen are the cheapest article to be found. They are the heaviest also, which is another advantage, as the duty is just the same on large as on small cattle. When the butcher happens to kill a two-years'-old calf, he is sure to lose by it, as the duty disproportionably increases the cost." Don Santiago also remarked to me, that as the treasury agents sold the privilege of killing to the highest bidder, without any particular regard to the wishes of the public, the only point they considered was the increase of the revenue, the provision for the benefit of the community being observed as mere matter of form; and that a petition was never made or expected to be made on the part of individuals, who found it always more to their interest to to endure abuses than to complain of them.

We were thus far beginning to discuss matters of importance, when, the inn-keeper having retired, Manuel, our black driver, in the uncouth accoutrement I have described, somewhat bespattered with mud, holding his whip in his left hand, and his hat in his right, entered our room, swinging like a sailor, in order to avoid the embarrassment in walking caused by the large ears of his boots. "Child," said he, addressing his master, who was certainly much older than himself, "I want to speak privately with the child;" and he looked toward me. Don Santiago told him that I was a foreigner, and he might speak without reserve. I was so anxious to pick up any interesting matter regarding the country, that I gladly availed myself of the opportunity, and remained in the room.

"The child knows," added Manuel, "that ever since

I came to this country, ever since I was a mere baby, I have been with your bounty, and in the child's family. Your bounty is my father and my mother. I have nothing in the world besides. When I have my sorrows, to whom shall I tell them but the child? And if the child reject me, what shall I do? Oh, my God!"

"But, Manuel," interrupted Don Santiago, "what is the matter? what ails you? have you been whipped? have you been in want of any thing? are you ill? do you wish to have another master?"

"Another master!" continued Manuel; "it is well for the child to suspect one of that wish after being so many years in the house! Alas! what would the good old gentleman say, were he to rise from the hole, if he saw and heard the strange things that have happened in these days! The negro name, how it has gone down! And after passing all our life in the service of such good masters as the child, no matter what we do (because there are some bad slaves, who have acted improperly), we are all doomed to lose the confidence we enjoyed. If I say, me, Manuel, the old calesero of the family of Cisueros, that I love my master, or his children; if the child is sick, and I inquire, as I always have done, why, I am only making believe."

Don Santiago kindly reproved Manuel, wishing him to be more precise in his expostulation.

"Very well, my master," said Manuel; "I know this is not a suitable place; but at home I could not speak, and my heart was so low, I could not wait."

"But, Manuel," said Don Santiago, "have I ever accused you?" "No," answered Manuel, "you have not. But I will tell you all, right away. You know how much I have tried to please the 'nina.'* My

* By "nina," the feminine of child, Manuel meant Don Santiago's wife. A distinguished Spanish writer observed to me, that the term "child" was a delicate flattery (since it implied youth), invented by the negroes to avoid the more humiliating expression, "*Sumerced,*" which siguifies "Your bounty."

business always has been to have the volante clean and ready. But if your nina wishes me to go of errands, to help the cook on some holidays, let any one say if Manuel refused; let any one say if he put a bad face to it, as would have done the caleseros of the Montalvos, the Charones, or the Herreras, or any of those great families, who are no better than the family of the child. No such thing: always at hand, always to be found, always cheerful; and now the nina says I am surly; I want to shake off her authority! 'Well,' says I to myself, 'the nina is not pleased with me, but if I go tell my master, in these hard times for the black color, he will, perhaps, think bad of me. Ah, Manuel! have patience!' says I; and then I go and purchase a wax candle with the same money the child gave me last week, and which I always spend in lottery tickets at the grocer's store at the corner,* and right before the image of the Virgin of Mount Carmelo, which I nailed in the room of the harness of the volante, I lighted it all day and night until it wasted away. I am a little ashamed to tell these things, because I know you gentlemen laugh at them. But pardon me; for the poor slave, when his heart is made so very small, has no help but to go to prayer. Then I thought things were going to right again; when yesterday morning, because the wheel of the volante went once over a stone, which certainly seldom happens, when I am mounted on the horse, the nina said I did it on purpose; that I was as great a conspirator as any; and because I staid late at the street-door last night, playing on the 'tiple,'† as I have always done, your nina said your bounty ought to get me a place in the opera-house, and have one enemy less near her person. Alas, child, I cannot help it; I can no more bear it; the child knows my heart."

As the scene was becoming too pathetic for the place, Don Santiago urged Manuel to be consoled, adding,

* The negro spends nearly all the money he can get in this way.
† A favorite negro instrument.

that he would remind the lady of his good services, and do away any unfavorable impression she might have respecting him. Manual appeared relieved, and walked to his horses, carefully balancing his body as he went along. We followed, jumped into the volante, and hurried from the tavern.

On arriving at the estate, we stopped at the dwelling-house, which, as the don was not expected, was far from being properly prepared to receive us. He apologized, and explained that he preferred all these inconveniences to giving previous notice of his coming. He calculated too much, perhaps, on the idea of taking his *operarios*, or workmen, by surprise; and observed to me that he once found all the white persons employed on his plantation gone to a ball, and the negroes left by themselves; and that an estate was not unfrequently made the rendezvous of gamblers. We walked over to the square of buildings, which are generally placed in the centre of the plantation, and found them in the invariable respective order observed here: the mill and the boiling-house in the west part, the baggage-house still farther west, and the purging-house and drying-drawer in the north, so that the latter may receive the rays of the sun from morning till night.

During our short absence the house had been comfortably arranged. We found two or three black damsels, just dressed in new and shining calico frocks, with silk shoes, worn slip-shod, red shawls, and hair arranged in very fine tresses, and very tight on the head. The table was set, our rooms neatly disposed, and our beds ready to receive us, should we feel disposed to take before dinner what the Spanish call the prebendary's or canonical nap. I preferred a small room where I found some old books covered with dust, which appeared not to have been disturbed for years. Don Santiago, divining my intention, ordered one of the black girls to dust them off; and, sitting down, awaited what I should say of the assortment, which I was determined to examine. I read aloud the title of the first pamphlet I laid my hand on: "Expediente de las Cortes Extraordinaria, Sobre Trafico, y esclavitud de Negros;" 1811.

"Quite other days than the present," said my friend; "read that single phrase;" and he turned over the pages until he found it; "read it, and be astonished at the change. That was the way our public bodies addressed the government when they had dignity, and were not spurned as they now are." The phrase which seemed to have fixed Don Santiago's attention was the following: "And we would conclude by saying on these subjects, what our fidelity and honor require, that Spaniards should be Spaniards every where, especially in those countries which, moist with their blood, or the sweat of their brow, acknowledge them conquerors and founders; and that if we were loyal under sufferings, we could not be less so, enjoying the splendors and advantages which now encircle the Spanish name."

"How changed! how changed!" continued Don Santiago; "nobody can speak so now; and, if he did, he would be obliged to lament, as the calesero did this morning, that no one believed or dared acknowledge he believed him. The *moneda-corriente*, the password of all the government people, is to assert and maintain, whether they really think so or not, that we, the creoles, are all insurgents. We have been placed in Manuel's case, you see."

Don Santiago's burst of indignation, like all such emotions with the Cubans, soon subsided; and adjusting his rather loose vest over his ample stomach, he went out to meet the sugar master, whom he had been for some time expecting. The latter was a pale, thin man, about five feet six inches in height. This being the season when those of his occupation have no employment, he appeared in full dress: a wide-brimmed straw-hat; blue striped breeches, fastened to his waist; a white embroidered shirt hanging loosely over them; a very large straight sword, made at the factory of Guanabaioa, with a silver handle, ornamented with precious stones; his shirt-collar and sleeves confined with gold buckles; an embroidered cambric handkerchief tied loosely round his neck; pumps cut quite low; and heavy silver spurs. Were it not for the finery above described, you might fancy, from his mode of wearing his shirt, that he was not altogether dressed. I have often thought what a figure a man thus attired would make on the sidewalks in Broadway! But you may be assured, that were he placed there, he would be perfectly at ease; for you can have no idea of the bold, independent manner peculiar to the "guageros," or country people of Cuba.

"How has it fared with the Senor Don Santiago?" said he, as he presented his hand to his employer, in the most cordial and easy manner.

"Very well, Perez," said the former; "as well as it can fare with the planters now-a-days, with such terrible occurrences, and such small crops and low prices."

"Ah! the Senor Don Santiago has no reason to complain. He fares better than many; and as for the quality of the sugar, he must be aware that there is none better in the market."

"You are mistaken there," replied the planter; "for many better sugars than mine have gone from the port of Havana."

"You say so," continued Perez, sitting himself down as Don Santiago had done, "and so it may be too; but considering the quality of the cane, and the materials, and the fuel, I am sure that the man is not yet born who could improve my sugar."

"Remember," answered the don, "remember my near neighbor, with the same quality of land, and, I am certain, with no better help than I give you, what a superior article he makes."

"So have I, ever since the Senor Don Santiago turned away the impudent ox-driver, who used to throw sour juice from the ditches into the juice-gutter, in order to spoil my sugar. But as for any man's improving my work, that cannot be. The Senor Don Santiago must know that I was born in the boiling-houses, was brought up in them, and my hair has grown gray in them. The senor should likewise bear in mind that I do not wear a hat* in the boiling-house. No, sir, no hat. Why should I? That will do for those who are new in the trade. I can smell the 'guarapo' at one league's distance. The senor may perhaps remember the old Count of ——. He it was who made me follow the trade; and never did that estate produce a better article than while I was there; and so the count used to say, and make me presents, and call me when he had company; and we went along very well. He used always to take me along with him to the cock-fightings, and say he did not care for two or twenty boilers-full lost, for the pleasure of having me at his side on these expeditions. At that time he had an Indian cock, the most sprightly and sure bird I ever saw; and the count would have nobody touch him but myself. But I perceive the senor has a visitor, and I can come another day."

"No matter for that," said Don Santiago, who noticed how delighted I was; "tell us how you came to leave the old Count of ——."

"Leave him! why I should have left him a thousand times, if he had been my own father. I had just worked the old cane-fields, and coming to a new one, which was overgrown and mostly decayed, the sugar, of course, did not look like the rest in the boiling-houses; although, had the clay been laid on it, I am sure it would have given the very best result. I remember it was the countess' birthday, and just after dinner there comes a large party of gentlemen and ladies into the boiling-house, all gay and lively, while I was cursing

* The hat is used to attract the vapors over the kettles, in order to smell and judge how the sugar is.

the cane. They all looked at the sugar, and made faces at it; and by and by, who should come to me but the countess herself, and before every body, even the overseer's wife, who came peeping in, to rejoice in my trouble, tells me, 'Why, Perez, I see you know how to manufacture *dirt* as well as sugar!'"

"Was that all the cause of your leaving the count?" inquired Don Santiago.

"No, sir; it did not end there. The senor may remember how devout the old countess used to be. She had always gowns for the Virgin and Saint Francis to make; and she was proud of it, too, the sweet lady! Well, I turned to her at once, and said: 'My lady the countess would do quite as well to attend to the dressing of saints, which she understands, than to the making of sugar, which she does not.' If you had seen what an uproar was raised then! All I can tell the senor is, that I heard the countess tell her husband, 'Pancho, do not let this man sleep here this night!' But I had the pleasure, many years after, to be recalled to the old count. Twenty sugar masters had been tending his boiling-house. All lost; not one grain of sugar fit to be looked at. At last the count sent for me. 'Well, Perez, you see how I am,' said he. 'But the count has been permitting himself to be ruined,' I answered, 'because he wishes to do so. Now from here is nearly one league, yet I can without hesitation say that they are burning the juice with too much lime.' Two hours after the best sugar ever made was drawing from the kettles. They had been using twelve cocoanuts of lime; I at once reduced it to three. My nose could not fail me!"

It is on account of this use of the olfactory nerves, Don Santiago informed me, that his utmost care with the sugar masters during "crop season" is required to prevent their taking cold.

Before dismissing the sugar master, I must tell you an anecdote, which I heard from Don Santiago.

The latter had given him a short elementary treatise on the manufacture of sugar; and having asked him several times whether he had read it or not, Perez, after saying that he had a tiple; that he understood the trade: and repeating all the praises of himself with which I have favored you, finally broke out with: "The Senor Don Santiago must excuse me; but what could a man like me, brought up in boiling-houses, learn from any of those foreigners, or their foreign contrivances? I am in nature's way, which is always the best, and am no child to begin my A B C now!"

Among the various means of spending my time, I have occasionally read some of Don Santiago's books and pamphlets, endeavoring to obtain from them some information upon the political situation of this island in latter years. If you would have exact ideas take the subject as patiently as I have; for there exists in the United States, a lamentable ignorance of the political system of government in Cuba, and very erroneous opinions of its nature.

From the following extract some idea can be gained of the musical taste of the Cubans, and the hyperbole and fiction which are necessary characteristics of the Cuban press:

"I was presented not long ago at the tertulia of St. Cecilia, one of the three very respectable philharmonic societies, which are the constant resort of the fashionable world of Havana. By means of a small stipend the members of these communities are enabled to have concerts and two hours of dancing every week, which in a great measure take the place of the agreeable parties we enjoy so much at home. Of late, complete operas have often been performed, altogether by amateurs. The Lucia di Lammermoor, the Pirata, and the Barbiere de Seville have repeatedly called forth the applause of crowded audiences. Indeed, we must admit that there is throughout this country a very general and delicate taste for music, which is not to be found in our colder region. I do not however consider the higher latitude the sole cause of this difference. Where the genius of man is crushed, and forced from its natural channel, like the waters of the fountain it will rise to the level of its outlet in another. Take from American society the exciting interests of political ambition; restrain their bold mercantile, manufacturing, and agricultural enterprise by unwise legislation; shackle and repress their free spirit, and they would instinctively seek other spheres of exertion, and consequently become greater proficients in the fine arts. Give free institutions to Italy, and her dazzling musical superiority would gradually sink to an equality with the rest of the world.

"In most countries you would naturally conclude that by taking up a newspaper a correct knowledge of all the interesting events of the day might be obtained: not so here; and the reason is to be found in the strict censorship exercised over the publication of the most trifling article, the grant depending upon the mere will of the censor. This state of the public press originates a conventional emphatic style of writing, which every body reads without surprise in all the periodicals of the city, and every body translates into the veritable meaning, as a matter of course. To a foreigner, however, unaccustomed to this everlasting hyperbole, extending its poetry and fiction to the most common acts of every-day life, it is difficult to get into the habit of translating. It is, withal, very important that the newspapers of the United States should be put on their guard; for it often excites a smile with those who are here, to see the apparent or real candor which they exhibit in repeating the fairy dreams of the Cuban press. But I am occasionally amused with the efforts of some able writers, who give interest to the periodicals by an airy, delicate style, which, though characterized by great enthusiasm and warmth of feeling,

6*

vented in exaggerated expressions, is still pleasing to the reader. The editor of the "*Diario de Avisos*," Don Ramon de Palma, is a remarkable specimen of this kind; a distinguished literary character, and both as a poet and a prose writer, excelling in that lively and graceful, I had almost said ethereal, manner, for which the French are distinguished. His introductions to the periodical reports of the fashions, of the public amusements, and various little incidents which entertain the fashionable world, affect one almost like the perusal of an oriental tale; and yet how melancholy to behold such a waste of genius, such a perversion of mind, and of intellectual effort, arising solely from the tyranny of a government whose intent appears to be to encourage every thing that can render the inhabitants forgetful of their own interests."

Here is an extract illustrating the peculiar method of administering justice in Havana:

"I have some how or other become quite attached to a little neighbor of mine, a colored woman, who every morning is to be seen at the vegetable market, sitting near the corner of the *Calle de la Cuva*, in the *Plaza Vieja;* surrounded by sweet potatoes and plantains, and little piles of beans, turnips, tomatoes, egg-pears, dried corn, and so forth, set upon several coarse straw mats; animated and cheerful, and turning round in her large, easy leather chair, to talk to her numerous acquaintances, or to persuade her customers into a bargain, and occasionally answering some flattering, and but too significant, though public, insinuation of her enamored gallants, as naturally and coolly as if it in no way concerned her. I have often wondered, while observing her at her usual station, so active, so busy and pleasant, and so perfectly agreeable to every one, how the apparent art of a coarse, but withal grateful, politeness had been acquired by this woman. There she would sit for hours and hours, in her very loose calico dress, with a yellow-and-black shawl, a clean

Madras handkerchief on her head, green silk shoes, no stockings, a fat, fresh, happy face, beautiful white teeth, rings of all kinds on her fingers, ear-rings, bracelets, and a coral necklace, brilliant on the black surface of her smooth skin. Why I should feel any more interest in 'Maria del Rosario' than in any of the other dealers in the market, I know not; but certain it is, that I was agreeably attracted by her manner, and thought I read in her looks evident demonstrations of a feeling soul within.

"Having got into conversation with her one morning, when I was tempted to buy some of her really beautiful Avocado pears, I soon after had a fit opportunity to be convinced of the truth of my surmise. At ten o'clock, having paid the commissary a tax for the privilege of selling in the market, she would retire to her dwelling, which was a small wooden house, away off in the *Barrio de San Lazaro*, facing the boisterous beatings of the ocean at the Punta, and looking as desolate and dreary as the countenance of the inmate was invariably cheerful and calm. There she would commence a new task, that of washing and ironing, which kept her in constant labor until late in the evening. As her industry appeared to me so unavailing and endless, I was induced to question her particularly about her private affairs. Thus I became acquainted with the following facts: Poor Rosario had come from the country of the Mandingoes, in her early youth; had been sold to a wealthy family, where she had enjoyed many hours of leisure, which she so employed as to obtain the means of purchasing her freedom. But since the patronage of her former master was no longer hers, the petty exactions of the commissaries and sub-commissaries of the police ate up nearly all her earnings. On a great festival she had not complied with the order of having a lighted lantern at her street-door, and was obliged to pay a fine for the infraction. One of the female servants living with her had let her license run five or six days beyond its time without renewing it, which brought upon poor Rosario the charge of keeping unlicensed persons of color at her house. There was a number of similar unfortunate unavoidable little committals, which caused her incessant trouble and expense. But her most serious source of misery arose from her determination to obtain from a captain of a regiment, stationed at Havana, her long-standing bill for washing. All her endeavors, through the under-menials of justice, with whom she was in constant contact, having proved fruitless, she appeared one morning at the audience of the captain-general, to establish her claim against her debtor. From the moment she stated at the lower bureau her object, she was evidently an unwelcome visitor, and was looked upon as a most daring woman. She lost the whole of one morning to get the order to appear; she could hardly find any one to execute it; and was harassed and kept waiting for a number of days, until her perseverance overcame all obstacles, and she had the satisfaction of appearing at the tribune with the representative of her debtor, a shrewd, diminutive, sly, dapper, old man, abundant in words, scant of ideas, and as little concerned in the clearing of the case as she was desirous of making it distinct. Her heart nearly failed her when she saw that instead of the imposing presence of the captain-general, she was only heard by a beardless officer, verbally commissioned by his excellency. The latter, nevertheless, took special care to sign all the judicial acts, as if he had been present at them, so as to receive the fees. It was alleged, on the part of the debtor, that though the instructions received from his party were not perfectly satisfactory, there had at least been what the law styled *plus petitior*, the bill having been overcharged; that it was subject to a liquidation, and that the case should be written down and followed through the regular order of proceedings. There was no one to answer for her, that the amount being a small one, it should be decided at once, and Rosario had the sad alternative of abandoning her claim, or throwing herself in the ocean of a Cuba law-suit, with the additional cause of dread of her antagonist, who was a European officer in active service.

"On the evening of her appearance at court, I called on my poor friend, whose fate became interesting to me; and soon after my inquiries had been answered, the same little man who acted for the captain at the court, came in.

"'Well,' said he, at once, with the air of most profound indifference to her sorrows, 'I have come to see you merely for your own sake, for I would not have you get into trouble. You are yet in time: it will be my business to press the suit hereafter, and you will be obliged in three days' time to name your own *procurador*, or law-agent, and supply him with about as much money for expenses as the debt amounts to. I propose to you to reduce the eighty-two dollars you claim, to thirty-four, which will be paid by me in a reasonable time; and you pay the charges of the suit as far as they go, now, and thank me too; for you do not know what it is to get yourself into trouble with the army.'

"During this conversation, Rosario occasionally looked at me, as if to seek advice; and whether she read in my countenance decided marks of indignation, or not, she mustered courage, and in spite of the threats of the agent, and of the under-commissary of police, who came to stand by him, and to censure the steps she had taken, she insisted upon going on with her suit.

"From this time, it was no longer in Rosario's power to appease, with comparatively trifling gifts, the insatiable avarice and ill-nature of the commissaries. Just as the law-agent had threatened, the suit was followed on in writing, with more activity on the part of the defendant, who represented himself as very indignant; and the wretched and disconsolate washerwoman was obliged to borrow money in order to carry it on. She had of course named an agent for herself, such as she could find, who would take charge of so troublesome and unpromising an affair; and though now and then soothed with the hopes of obtaining one favorable resolution, there was nothing very positive in the result, excepting that time, money, and patience were lost. At last, I was so moved by her distress that I resolved to do something for her; and, having secured a respectable friend among the lawyers, I prevailed upon him to see into her case. Immediately after this, my friend had the woman's agent called to him, so as to obtain and peruse the proceedings, so far as they had been advanced; and I saw such a change in the manner of the commissaries, and the little contemptible set of agents employed in the business, that I began to feel as if I had done a great deal for the woman. To satisfy myself on the subject—for Rosario was already overpowering in her thanks, and in the fullness of her heart, begged me to allow her to do my washing for nothing—I hastened one morning to my learned friend of the law. Behind a rather high table, literally covered with processes, or 'autos,' my friend was negligently seated, in a huge, Spanish easy-chair. He was surrounded by a few business men, who seemed waiting for their turn to speak with him; and altogether taken up with the brief instructions of notary clerks and agents. At times he would place his signature at the bottom of some petition or writing; and invariably sustained the unmoved countenance of an old warrior, no matter what ponderous or dreadful tale or information was communicated to him. On seeing me come in, he for one moment looked as if he were going to rise from the drudgery which surrounded him, and as if he could smile over it with me; but the next instant he sank back into his usual tone, bowed slightly to me, and turned unconsciously around on the anxious circle which pressed about him.

"'I have seen the process of your protegé,' said he, at last, when an opportunity offered to attend on me, 'and am afraid that nothing can be done for her. In the first place, the act of *comparescence* is enacted in such language as best suited the party of the captain. She appears herself more desirous of having her account approved of, than of collecting the sum. Then, in the numberless petitions of her own agent, this seems to have been the principal point of his requests. On the other hand, the protests of the captain, from the very first act, as to his readiness to exhibit the sum, provided it be ascertained, are calculated to make the expenses bear on the poor woman. This is probably an explicit or instinctive combination of all the law-agents, assessors, and lawyers in the case, who generally endeavor to stamp some weak point on the party who is more ready or able to pay, so as not to lose their fees by giving all right to the innocent.' My friend added, however, that he would call upon the captain-general himself, and have some conversation with him, and would then see me again. The uncommon circumstance of a respectable lawyer appearing privately to demand attention to a case like this, produced some useful effect. The general ordered instant payment of the sum; but what he could not interfere with, as he said, was *the expenses*, which were far beyond the amount sued for; so that, upon the whole, it was understood and settled that poor Rosario should neither claim her bill nor pay any charges, and endeavor thereafter to be as amiable and generous to the little set of menials of justice as she had been previously.

"This little history is every day repeated in a thousand different shapes; and surely no one who sees occasionally in the city of Havana the appearance of comfort and civilization, the pompous records of reforms, and the annual speeches of the judicial courts, glowing with equitable principles of justice and humanity, could imagine that the society which seems thus prosperous and lofty is devoured by a cancer so destructive to their fortunes, ease, and repose. Speaking on this subject, the *Revista de Espana* once expressed itself thus: "Were you to withdraw the brilliant mask which hides the state of the country, a lacerated and deformed skeleton would present itself to our sight. * * * Other evils, other abuses, may chiefly fall on interests and classes better able to support them; but those coming from the administration of justice, prey upon every class and condition in life, impairing and absolutely ruining the most indigent and helpless."

CHAPTER V.

Visit to the Country Residence of a wealthy Marquis.—Singular Occasion of it.—The Marquis and his Creditors.—The Spanish Judge and the Advocate.—The Marchioness and her Guests.—Her Children.—Mode of bringing up a Family.—Easy way of dealing with stubborn Creditors.—The unfortunate Potrerero.—Early Dawn in Cuba.—The Morning and Evening.—Tacon's Opera House.—Insolence of the Soldiers.—Anecdotes.—Beauty of the young Cubanese.—The married Women.—Their Habits and Customs.—Shopping.—Exercise in the Volante.—Children.—The lower Classes.—The Guagiro.—His Courtship.—Obsolete Customs.—The hours of the Oracion.—Conclusion.

THE epistolary style is continued in the present chapter in order to present more vividly the social habits and customs of the native Cubans. In this way many things can be introduced and described of which no proper conception can in any other manner be afforded. The following, then, may be considered as taken from an unpublished letter:

You desire me to describe the social condition of the Cubans, and as the request is coupled with an intimation that this must be done forthwith, I have concluded, under the urgent necessity of the case, to throw aside forms, preambles, and introductory remarks, and report quite abruptly the result of an invitation I had lately to the country residence of a wealthy marquis. At one of the stations of the railroad we found several empty volantes, with their mounted drivers and gaudy liveries in attendance for our party. The marquis was a man of easy and amiable manners, though not particularly clever in conversation. He seemed to attend on his friends as if by starts, and unconsciously relapsed into an habitual revery. His dress, of clean, colored linen, constituted the regular traveling habit of a Cuban gentleman. In singular contrast with this, but one quite peculiar to the country, he wore an immense diamond-pin at his breast. This little insignia might, in the present day, when railroads are depriving tourists of their descriptions of solitary and dangerous scenes and localities, be a substitute for the ornamented uniform, which, with the honors of an army officer, not long ago was regularly purchased by men of rank, to secure to them the right of traveling unmolested by petty officers of justice, or *fine-gatherers*, as they may well be named. But to return to my company. The marchioness, a fine-looking woman, of about fifty, wore a dress of the thinnest cambric; her still small and pretty feet were encased in delicate satin slippers; while a bonnet of transparent texture, more appropriately trimmed for an opera-box than suited to the heavy red dust of the Cuban roads, completed her traveling attire. She seemed all activity; to the several gentlemen who formed our party she had continually something to say; she gave her orders to the drivers, determined where we were to have breakfast, ordered the several stoppages, and even seemed to whisper now and then to her docile husband what was best for him to say or to do. I observed that her attentions were especially divided between two rather remarkable members of our party, with whom she had, alternately, long conversations, which were at times very private. One of these persons was a native of Castile, in Old Spain, a man of about forty, though from his rather bulky figure, one would have judged him to be considerably older. He appeared to be fully impressed with his own dignity—when he spoke, he seemed to listen to his own remarks, which he could do to perfection, as no one presumed to interrupt him, while all heard him with deep attention. His complexion was dark, his eyes jet black, and in his speech, the clear

Castilian pronunciation, in which even the commonest of that province appear to delight, was evident to the most careless ear. With all the deference paid to this important guest, whose attire, with the exception of a rather shabby discolored ribbon in the button-hole, was similar to that of the other guests, he did not always retain the manner of one quite at ease; on the contrary, it seemed as if it were more natural for him to court those by whom he was surrounded, than to receive their homage. I soon ascertained that he was one of the judges recently sent from Spain, elevated to the office, though ignorant of the country, and its habits and usages, from his fortunate relation to members of the cabinet or Cortes. The other gentleman engrossing the attention of the lady marchioness, was a young lawyer, full of activity, and with the money-making spirit of a true Catalonian; his particular influence with courts of justice, was owing to his Spanish birth, and was the origin of his great practice and profits in the profession.

"Una flor," said he, picking a flower and presenting it to the marchioness, "a flower that will appear as beautiful on you, as your bountiful gifts will in my purse." I was struck with, and have since remembered, this remark, which in its very insipidity and coarse allusion, gave an idea of the aping, at what is gallant and graceful in the Spanish gentleman, on the part of the upstarts of the present military administration in Spain; and at the risk of being charged with digressing, I cannot resist the inquiry, whether the Spanish gentleman of days gone by, is a character now altogether historical? The intermixture in the best society, for the last half century, of men risen through party influence, especially from the Carlist ranks—the utter annihilation of that faith in his church which gave a serious cast to the natural dignity of the native Spaniard—the mercenary motives which from the throne have penetrated down to the humblest cottages—every thing has conspired to efface the simple but haughty and noble-minded Spanish gentleman, both from the Peninsular and from Cuban society. Let me, however, be just; the class does exist, and Spain may yet boast of the distinguished "caballeros," whose manners may have become even too polished to reflect the plain Castilian courtesy, but whose truthfulness and uprightness of character would excite the envy of more advanced nations. I could point out as a specimen, Don Miguel Rodriguez Ferrer, whose recent visit to Cuba, apparently to report the physical condition and historical reminiscences of the island, produced the most able and impressive political sketches, which, privately communicated to the court as they were, would have brought about, under an enlightened administration, immediate reforms and concessions. But so great is the habit of acting the part of conquerors, which has become almost intuitive in the old Spaniards, that even Rodriguez Ferrer manifested a tinge of haughty arrogance while in America, of which, as a native of Spain, he could hardly divest himself.

To a foreigner, the object of the party assembled at the estate "Santa Gertrudis," which I had accidentally joined, would have appeared incongruous and extraordinary. The Marquis of Santa Gertrudis, through the reckless extravagance of his wife, had become entangled in his affairs; and were it the practice for men of wealth to pay off their debts at once, he would very likely have become a bankrupt. This, however, is not the custom in Cuba; but such matters are managed on this wise.* The creditors are assembled; yearly installments are agreed upon; the extravagant living of the noble family is considered a necessary expenditure, and the majority, *usually made up of family or fictitious creditors*, force the rebellious claimants to lay down their arms, and enter into private compromises. The effect of this course is to set the family at ease; the lady returns to her habits of luxury; the sons to their dissipation; the daughters to their careless waste

* See Appendix.

of finery; while they spend their time in love-sick fancies; the poor relations and parasite friends to their customary dependence on the old trunk, raised from the ground for a few more years; and the head of the family to fresh undertakings of new estates. And all this is carried out with as much indifference as if, in place of an extorted compromise from clamorous creditors, payment in full of every debt had been promptly made.

The lady who, on the occasion, had the management of this important domestic matter, was the daughter of the Count of M——. She belonged to what may be called the staunch nobility. Nature, and the teachings of her noble-minded parents, had made her a modest and virtuous woman. But the habits of her new home, and the circle surrounding her, were calculated to impair her superior qualities. The universal custom of the country, rather than indolence, influenced her, from the very first years of her married life, to give into the hands of her slaves the nursing and early training of her children. The recollections of her father's home now and then directed her attention to books and foreign literature. But she found none to sympathize in such tastes; the ball-room, the "sociedades," the operas, her visits, the tedious and loquacious shoppings, the "paseo," the correspondence which she found it necessary to maintain with the country-estate clerks, and, what is more than all calculated to destroy the freshness of modesty and beauty, the gambling-table, to which she gradually became habituated, not only deprived her of time for more intellectual and domestic enjoyments, but destroyed by degrees her original taste for them. "Mamma," said her son, a boy of fourteen, dressed like a small gentleman, and with all the nonchalance and airs of a gallant, "I don't know how you or papa are arranging your business with the creditors, but you must recollect that my own private property, now in your hands, must be so left that I may have all the necessary resources for living, and for my customary pleasures; and as to my carriage, I cannot give it up on any consideration, for there is not one of my cousins who is without this convenience." He went on at this rate, until the poor mother, conscious that she was reaping the fruits of her own errors and neglect, sighed in despondency. I must add, with pain, that this specimen of filial coldness and depravity is by no means the exception; the too fond and over-indulgent mothers, who are themselves the direct cause of such examples, are far more to be pitied than condemned. What teaching or light have they enjoyed to guide them in their incipient path when starting in life? The magistrate is corrupt, and his misconduct is the subject of every-day anecdotes and scandal; the minister of the gospel teaches neither by example nor from the pulpit; the husband has no idea of performing what would elsewhere be considered the most ordinary duties; the society is frivolous; books are looked upon with aversion; the press is an instrument of oppression; and the mainspring of civilization and civil liberty, faith in Christ, is unknown.

In what able manner the marchioness succeeded in exciting the energy of her lawyer, by the offer of ample reward, what secret understanding went on between him and the unintellectual Castilian judge, how each creditor was coaxed or frightened into acquiescence, I cannot say. I will only add, that some of them obtained favorable arrangements through the cunning arguments of the judge, which were the more ludicrous from contrast with his reasonings with other creditors, whom it was his policy to discourage in their claims. It was painful to see how poor neighbors had to yield to these influences out of utter incapacity to counteract such disgraceful combinations. Among the company of creditors, I was much amused with the appearance of a potrerero (cattle grazier), who was particularly urgent on the occasion. The fact is, the daughters of the potrerero, whenever they appear in public. dress most extravagantly, quite after the style of the wealthiest ladies of the island. To satisfy this thirst after finery of the female portion of his household, the potrerero has invariably to contract debts for the paying of which the earnings of the year are hardly sufficient. What wonder, then, that the poor cattle grazier urged his claim with a desperate but unavailing earnestness. He, with the other persevering creditors, were overruled, and the marquis was thereupon left to his new projects, his wife to her accustomed routine of folly and of fashion, the sons to their pleasures, and the daughters to the enjoyment of new dresses, new finery, and new fancies. Have I not drawn a revolting picture? Alas! it is absolutely a true one.

* * * * * * *

I had intended before this to allude to the climate and atmosphere of this enchanting island. It is quite impossible, however, to give to one who has never enjoyed it, an idea of the delicious fragrance of the early dawn. The exquisite freshness of the morning, the soft, cool breeze of evening, when the very soul is refreshed and purified, and the pulse of life beats fuller and clearer, produces a sensation to be enjoyed only, but never to be described to those living in the forbidding north. An intense gratitude to the Giver of all these beauties fills the heart of the stranger, and the human voice rings through the early morning air with such a clear freshness, that one would fancy the inhabitants would instinctively raise their first notes in thanksgiving or hymns of praise; but alas! how does the heart of the good man thrill with anguish, as he sees the rich beauties of this lovely island perverted to the wicked uses of more wicked men. The first beams of its glorious sun light upon the wearied souls of worn-out and exhausted slaves, and serve but to render more visible the degrading bondage of their masters; while too often the clear light of the heavenly moon reveals sights of infamy and vice which make the soul shudder. One feels at times almost afraid to be happy in a country upon which the judgment of God seems to have fallen in wrath. The absence of all refinement, religion, education—in fact, of decency—among the lower classes, is a contemplation painful enough to mar all enjoyment of society in Cuba. The invariably idiotic faces of the women and children make the heart ache; for an humbly pious or modest *young* face, I have never seen among the poor. What is not vice or bold recklessness, is generally stupidity or sickly indifference. I do not think this is prejudice or exaggeration; I am sure it is not; for I love Cuba, I pity the poor oppressed Cubans, and I look with loathing upon that infamous government which has systematically destroyed all moral and social good among them. When I see the half-naked women—the all-naked children—the desperately bad (when not too lazy) men—I look away from these to their mother-country, and feel my heart stirred, in spite of me, with a desire of revenge. As these and similar thoughts were disturbing my spirit this morning, the elegant-looking and lordly young Bishop of Havana, in his gorgeous robes and costly jewels, swept past me from the altar, amidst a train of ignorant and servile priests. Not one gleam of piety or grace could be discerned in his vain, worldly countenance—not one single mark or sign to denote him a follower of the meek and lowly Jesus. I feel a wonder that there are none around whose hearts do not burst forth into audible expressions of disgust; I marvel that Spain and her infamous government have one voice left to defend them in Cuba.

A stranger in this island will be vividly impressed with the contrast between the insolent hauteur of the Spanish official, and the cringing deference of the prostrate Cuban. The commonest Spanish soldier assumes the impertinent swagger of his superior, as a creole passes the point of his bayonet, while just as surely his cowardly eye falls before the independent glance of an

American citizen. I remember to have been struck with an illustration of this, upon going one night into the beautiful opera-house of Tacon, in Havana, where guards of soldiers and dragoons are regularly stationed, as it appeared to me, for no better purpose than to annoy ladies, by the freedom of their gaze and their half-whispered insults. A young man, while hastily making way for half a dozen beautifully dressed girls with their fat mammas, placed himself too near this imposing array of military, and within forbidden limits. The gentlemanly quiet of his manner deceived the officer on guard into the belief that he was "only a creole," and he arrogantly, with lowered bayonet, ordered him aside. "Come, come, my famous soldier," was the reply, "if I have done wrong by standing here, inform me of it with respect; I am a gentleman and an Englishman, not one of your poor Cubans." I turned to observe the effect of this reproof, which to my surprise was evidenced by an humble salute, and a courteous wave of the gold-laced hand in the direction to be taken by the young Englishman!

Now that we are here, let us enter the opera-house, where we may, indeed, be surprised to see no external evidence of all this degrading tyranny. Elegantly dressed and polished men crowd the boxes and seats; while the beautiful repose of countenance and figure, characteristic of the ladies, are expressive of dignity and content, to say the least. Their noble outline of feature appears to great advantage in the retired light of an opera-box, while their full busts and rounded arms, contrast finely with the richly plaited, dark hair and simple white dress, rarely ornamented by more than a fall of soft lace or a natural flower; and one is tempted to overlook the absence of intelligence and brightness in those magnificent eyes, in consideration of their almost bewildering depth and softness. The vivacity of the Spanish lady is lost in the creole; but in its stead, we find a charming gentleness very pleasing, and an amiability of manner absolutely captivating to the stranger. One dare not, however, raise the eye above the third tier of boxes, for there again are only met the depraved countenances and loose manners of the lower classes, unrestrained by either good taste or shame.

The outward decorum of the better and upper classes may be, to a great extent, only in appearance, as is often asserted by prejudiced foreigners, for it is hard to understand how the fresh cheek of a young girl can retain its ordinary color, as I have often witnessed in the public paseo of Havana, under the bold and free —I may not hesitate to say licentious—gaze of the young men assembled to render this tribute to their too generously exposed charms. Indeed, there seems little reluctance to be thus admired, for no change in the expression, no falling of the long and lovely black eyelash, ever indicates a shrinking from it. With all this, in no part of the world has it been my fortune to see more devoted wives and mothers than in Cuba. There are few, indeed, who could teach their sons to become great men; but their deep, abiding love, untiring care and devotion, many a northern mother who never allows a new publication to escape her, and who laments in elegant English the ignorance of the Cuban ladies, may, with advantage to her own nursery, emulate. Literally speaking, however, there are no children in Cuba: men and women, they descend from their nurses' arms. Little girls of three years old are dressed in long dresses made in the extreme of fashion; artificial flowers and jewels are quite common; and the little debutantes sit gracefully opening and shutting their tiny fans with perfect incipient coquetry. Very funny little men, too, are manufactured at five or six years, after the complete toilette of a Parisian exquisite, not omitting diamond-pins and a wonderful variety of cravats and canes.

We hear a great deal of Cuba as the land of gallantry and love. The former it may be, but for the latter, the sentiment, or holiness, which should hallow the union of hearts, is scarcely understood; the wives too frequently degenerate into mere household drudges, scolding their servants and petting their children all day, and sitting at night, when the former are quiet and the latter asleep, in their luxurious butaque or easy chair to play with their fans, the use of which is often the only grace left to them. A creole girl before marriage is a beautiful object, graceful, gentle, and loving; but a creole woman after forty is very generally quite the reverse. The ravages of time are never concealed; gray hairs are not considered worth adorning, and old age is made disgusting. Instead of the "nice old ladies" and elegant matrons of our American homes, we too often find in Cuba only fat scolds with voices loud enough to frighten a regiment of men into submission, and faces so brown, so wrinkled, and so ugly, and with so evident an absence of all feminine softness, that we listen in wonder when we are told that they have been the beauties of their day. Delicacy of habit, and even of feeling, are in my opinion smothered in their infancy by the constant association with negroes; the loud, coarse laugh and low jests, they imbibe with their first milk from the same source; the habit of command and arrogance, also acquired in their childhood, appears in after life to destroy all tenderness of manner, and increase that harshness of voice so universally remarked upon by foreigners and ascribed entirely to the effect of climate.

The daily life of a Cuban lady is monotonous in the extreme. It is utterly devoid of intelligent exercise of mind or body, and as a natural consequence both deteriorate sadly. A host of nervous diseases attest the truth of this. Early rising is a virtue common to all ranks; but the manner in which they contrive to kill time without reading, household occupations, or, in fact, any employment except, perhaps, a little embroidery, is indeed a mystery. Shopping, which is generally confined to the morning, is, to be sure, a great resource; hours are consumed in passing from one shop to another, bargaining for goods, and chatting with the very polite, but extremely familiar shopkeepers, quite elegant-looking men, who do not hesitate to address ladies by their Christian name, and to pay them most elaborate compliments upon their beauty and grace. Still, I can scarce find fault with this, there is so much amiability of manner, such an entire absence of intention to offend, so much cheerful alacrity in complying with every whim of a lady, and, above all, such an exhaustless, untiring patience in running back and forth from the volante to the counter, that one finds it quite natural to smile at the flattery, and return, at parting, the salutation "a los pies de usted, senora," an "adios" with gracious good humor. Many a foreign lady has been deluded by this exquisite politeness into the belief that she has made a very great bargain; and one which "none but so charming an *Americana* as herself could have made;" in a fan, at fifty dollars, which a *Habanera* would have passed an hour in reducing to half the price.

Eating fruit, and the routine of the bath while away many a morning and after-dinner. Happily, for the Cuban girls, the sun is ever shining, the volante, with its easy motion, ever ready; the negro maid, living only to plait and pomatum their beautiful hair, and the good mamma patiently waiting to escort them to the public drives, or "paseos." Operas, and visits of interminable length, pass off the evening, and by ten all are again at home, the massive house-door turns on its hinges, the lazy porter goes to sleep, and the young maiden to dream of the few whispered words she may perchance have caught from some one of her admirers. I reject all the scandalous accounts given by most foreigners here, of the immorality existing among the better classes. I have seen no little of good society in Havana and the surrounding cities, and within my personal observation have witnessed the highest degree of womanly devotion and virtue; the reverse I have very rarely seen pass without severe censure. The surveillance exercised over women possessing the least pretensions to youth or good looks, is the argument generally made use of against them. In Spain, where much more freedom exists, the wives and daughters are less pure. I would venture the assertion of an impartial and quick observer, that entire fidelity and high domestic virtue exist among the women of Cuba, especially when one considers that the many irksome restraints imposed upon them, with the lack of mental resources, are calculated to produce indifference, or a mischievous frivolity of character, even where the neglect of the husband does not induce a reckless despair. Among the lower classes, as I have before mentioned, this is all very different, and the very meaning of the word virtue is lost. This disgrace, with countless others, Cuba now flings back with reproaches upon the mother-country, whose representative, General O'Donnell, dared even to suppress the incipient organization of Sunday schools for the poor, lest, through the little children, a faint glimmer of light might awaken their parents from the dark night of their ignorance and superstition. In towns and villages where, as in most civilized countries, one would expect to find some softening, at least, of the vices of the city, we see the people, young and old, sunk still lower in stupid ignorance and in an immorality of life too revolting for me to dwell upon. A little romance perhaps remains among the country lovers. The Guagiro, with his wild, dark eye, wonderfully expressive gesture, and usually imperturbable self-possession, becomes ridiculously silent and shy in his courting. In a richly-worked shirt of fine linen, worn upon the outside as a sack; a long, and often elegantly embroidered cambric sash-fastening to his side, the silver-handled sword, or "machete," silver spurs, and low slippers, he will sit for hours opposite his lady-love, only venturing now and then a word of reproof, to be interpreted in affectionate playfulness, and to which she retorts in the same style; yet, now and then, at a glance, and when unobserved, they do venture to exchange some very tender word. But gestures, shrugging of the shoulders, little dashing airs of coquetry in the lady, and bashful approaches on the part of the gallant, fill up the measure of the wooing of the Cuban peasant.

There are many customs in the island nearly obsolete, which have had their origin in a most simple and true spirit of religion. One particularly struck me in a fine old Cuban family at Havana, the mother of whom would grace her position in any country. I paid her a visit at the hour of the "oracion," announced at sunset by the convent bells throughout the city. In past years, as in Spain, at that moment every voice and occupation was suspended, and every knee bent in silent prayer; but now the only observance of it I have any where seen, was (in the family I have mentioned) the quiet dropping in, one after another, of the children of the donna, to ask her blessing, and affectionately kiss her hand. The action in itself, though not intended to produce the least effect, was most touching, as she, placing her hand gracefully and feelingly upon each young head, replied, "Dios te haga bueno hijo"—God make you good, my child. Among the slaves in another family I have known the same custom observed, and I found it peculiarly touching to see a large, coarse African slightly bending his knee to his master and mistress to ask of them the evening blessing. This too would be asked for and received with a sincere and marked affection on both sides. The above, however, are instances which I am sorry to say now stand nearly alone. By degrees, religious observances and true piety have given way to a careless indifference or an open disbelief; and unless a change is speedily effected in the general administration of the island, it will sink still lower in the scale of humanity. Heaven forbid that this should be. Is it not time that philanthropists every where should awake to the fearful condition of Cuba, and use every effort to free her from her present degrading bondage?

CHAPTER VI.

State of Religion in Cuba.—Contrast with the same in former times.—The "Angelus."—Flirtations carried on in the Churches.—Infidelity universally prevalent.—Absence of all Religious Feeling in Families of every class.—No piety among the Priests.—Their disgusting Debaucheries and Excesses.—Horrible instances of this in the priest Don Felix del Pino.—Roman Catholicism.—Why many of the Cubans desire Annexation with the United States.—An appeal to the Christian philanthropist.

AMONG the many reasons for sad reflection afforded by the present situation of the beautiful Queen of the Antilles, there is none so appalling as the low and wretched condition of religion. The seeds of infidelity which were so widely diffused through the world at the close of the last century, have been greatly checked within late years; and the Christian observer now rejoices daily more and more at the general extension of the Gospel influence. But in unhappy Cuba those fatal seeds seem to have found a more propitious nurture under the influence of depressing and deteriorating government; and nowhere therefore is presented a more dark and distressing picture of unbelief, corruption, and immorality.

Twenty-five years ago, if one happened to be an inmate of any respectable Cuban family, one would be sure to meet with religious practices and feelings which, even to a foreigner of a different creed, appeared cheering and grateful. At the hour of twilight, a church bell rung through the city would create every where a sudden and simultaneous excitement. It was the "*Angelus*," and at its sound all persons, of all classes, would at once rise to say their evening prayers; children and servants would, at its conclusion, ask a blessing from their parents or masters; while every carriage and passenger would pause in the street, every workman would suspend his toil, and a general manifestation of religious reverence would be exhibited. In those days frequent sermons, from pious and eloquent preachers, would awaken the congregations that filled the churches to the solemn truths connected with their spiritual welfare; slaves and free blacks were instructed in the precepts of the Saviour, and the service of the temple was attended with devotion and decency.

At the present day, in all the churches of Cuba, a brief mass, scandalously hurried through, and witnessed by a very small portion of the inhabitants, is all that attests the Sabbath of the Lord. And even this poor and meagre performance of the solemn services of the church whose creed bears sway in the island, by whom and how is it attended? By few others than those who resort to it as a public place of meeting, gayety, and flirtation. The ladies ply the telegraphic fan with the same airs of coquetry and playfulness as they may have done the evening before at the theatre, or as they will probably do the same evening at the opera. The young gentlemen attend at the doors for the interchange of glances with their fair friends, and perhaps for a glimpse of the pretty ankles ascending the steps of the *volantes*, in waiting. All seem intent on showing, by their smiles and their undisguised disrespect, that they are neither believers, nor ashamed of their unbelief. In the church itself, are no expounding—no reading, even of the Gospel—no visits of the pastors—no consolations carried to the dying—none of the charitable communities that abound in other countries, both Catholic and Protestant.

Among the shopkeepers and artisans, is manifested the same utter disregard, not to say scorn, of the Christian Sabbath and the Christian faith; for with wide-open doors and windows, and on the public street, they pursue, without even the affectation of a difference, the customary employments of the week in labor or traffic.

But to explore further the moral results of the state of things thus imperfectly described, go to the aged head of a family, and behold him incapable of exercising any influence over his own offspring, who have never been taught the divine mission of Christ; to the neglected wife, who weeps over the cruel and mortifying treatment experienced from a depraved partner, and see her endeavoring to forget her griefs at public amusements, at cards, or elsewhere, ignorant of, because never taught, the only balm that can restore peace to the most embittered soul; to the injured husband, and there witness a similar hollow wretchedness of the heart, searching vainly for the relief he knows not how to search for aright; or, what is more probable, behold him plunged in the most deadly course of debauchery and vice.

Leaving the cities, go to the country, and see the poor African, condemned to a toil not less incessant than severe—doomed to remain forever sunk in the imbruted ignorance in which he was torn from his native and distant land—adoring a serpent—and encouraged to suicide, by the superstition which he believes, of the immediate return of his body to Africa after death. Few of them are baptized; scarcely any married; but they live together for the most part in the most disgusting habits of promiscuous intercourse; while none are ever instructed in the consoling and humanizing truths of the Gospel. Look farther around to the white laborer who commands the negro as overseer or *mayoral*, or who tills a piece of land, or who moves along the road with his cart or draught horses; look, too, at the countryman's family—and every where will be found the same indifference, and in general worse than indifference, the same sneering contempt of all that their ancestors revered as holy.

The gentry also—the masters of estates—the officers of government—nay, the very priests themselves—exhibit the same painful picture of an all-pervading, all-demoralizing infidelity. The country curates may, in general, and as a class, be set down as an example of all that is corrupt in immorality, all that is disgusting in low and brutal vice. Of the number there is one—Don Felix del Pino—too notorious, too illiterate, and too shameless to care for even this publication of his name, whose career presents so shocking and frightful an example of vice that I will mention a few of its characteristic traits, as a proof of what is possible in the island of Cuba at the present day. This man, who is the curate of an interior town, is in the habit of exacting $200 for an insignificant pretended attempt at the great ceremonies of a funeral. On one occasion, at a meeting of his low associates, he announced that he was preparing for a pleasure trip to the city of Havana, and in reply to their inquiries as to the pecuniary means on which he relied for that object, he simply answered, that a certain respectable old woman, whom he named, was on the eve of death, and that her funeral expenses would supply him the means. Having afterward ascertained that she was unexpectedly improving, he vowed that she *should* die, and hastened to her bedside, where, prostituting the rights of his sacred ministry, he labored to dissuade her from any hopes of recovery, and harassed her mind with such agonizing and terrible pictures, in such a tone, and with such evidently evil design, that the friends of the poor despairing sufferer felt compelled to interfere, and rescue her from his guilty hands. On another occasion he informed a couple who wished to marry, but whose family relation of consanguinity required a dispensation from Rome, that he could obtain the grant for that purpose at Havana. He therefore went to that city, and shortly afterward returned with the full license, as he pretended, to perform the marriage; to which, however, he insisted on naming the attesting witnesses, or the *godfather* and *godmother* of the ceremony. He accordingly married the parties, and received six hundred dollars as his reward. When the couple, at a later day, discovered that no such authority could be procured at Havana, and that they had been made the victims of a foul deception, they called on him and were met by a cool denial of his having had any thing to do in the matter; in support of which he exhibited his books, where he had carefully omitted to set down the case. He was, however, arrested for a time in consequence, but no more serious penalty ever ensued. His last act was one which, indeed, can hardly be credited, though its truth is beyond question. In a letter coarsely written, in the most obscene and revolting language, to his brother in Havana, he expatiates on the violation of a young white female, for whom he had paid to her own father, and says that on the occasion of his first possession of her, he had ordered the bells of his church to be rung! The signature of the letter he acknowledged to be his; and the young girl, only thirteen years of age, was found at his house, and the truth of the case so fully proved by her testimony, and other corroborating evidences, as to cause the imprisonment of the father, and the suspension of the priest from the office so foully scandalized. Of course, it must not be understood that there are many priests in Cuba who have reached such a depth of corruption as is exhibited by this revolting and hideous instance; but the general degradation of the clergy and the church, and the deep demoralization of the country where such a monster is not at once visited with signal punishment, must be sad indeed. This wretch may, on the contrary, be seen even now, though suspended from his parish cure, attending in his clerical robes on the public ceremonies of the Church at Havana!

The responsibility of this dreadful state of things,

in reference to the religious and moral condition of the island of Cuba, should not be considered as resting upon the Romish Church or creed. It would be illiberal indeed to carry to so unjust a length those prejudices of Protestantism which are doubtless founded in reason, and which cannot but be stimulated to a great degree at the exhibition of Roman Catholicism in Cuba. Yet in the United States no one can deny that it is a very different institution, both in its spirit and its practice, from that which is presented to the eye of the most superficial observer in Cuba. The Church proper is not the responsible cause, but the corrupt political government which has invaded its domain, paralyzed all its good energies, corrupted its entire organization, and poisoned its very fountains of spiritual purity. The central military despotism, in the hands of the Spanish officials, clustered in and about the palace of the captain-general, may be said to have absorbed to itself the Church, with every other good institution possessed by the island in its better days. Its influence has been destroyed, its revenues and property, together with all the patronage of ecclesiatical appointments, appropriated by the government. The nominations to all religious offices are made, directly or indirectly, *by* the creatures of the government, and given, directly or indirectly, *to* the creatures of the government. The very members of the chapter of the cathedral at Havana are now named at Madrid, in disregard of the canonical proposals from the board according to law. Day after day and year after year have been suffered to pass without an appointment to fill the long vacant bishopric of Havana, and thirty years have elapsed since the sacrament of confirmation, as it is termed by the Roman Catholics, has been administered in the several districts of the diocese, which should be regularly visited once a year.

In short, the principal reason given by the serious and reflecting Cubans for desiring annexation to the

United States, is derived from the present condition of religious and moral degradation of the island. It only requires, say they, the fresh air of liberty and light of free truth to be let in upon it, to secure that reform and regeneration which should be the object of the hope and desire of every Christian observer. With annexation to the United States, will come the free Bible, the free Pulpit, and the free Press; the healthful and stimulating influence of Protestant competition in the labors of the spiritual harvest; the infusion of a new spirit, a renovated vitality, into the moral being of the population of Cuba, now corrupt with disease and palsied well nigh beyond recovery. Surely the Roman Catholic clergy and community of the United States cannot but unite in the desire, which must be to Protestants an anxious one, to witness the termination of this miserable and scandalous condition of a neighboring community—a community with which this country is already connected by so many ties of interest and intercourse, and which, all know and feel, must at no very distant day become an integral portion of it. Ought not, then, the Roman Catholic clergy of the United States, alive to the dignity attached to their ministry in America, to speak out in the name of those of their brethren who, by the corrupt and corrupting interference of civil power, have become careless of the holy cause which they do not even profess to sustain? Ought not the Pope, whose course of reform brings back the Catholic Church to the earlier period of her career, when she was the natural ally of the poor and the oppressed, to be made to know that there is a portion of his wide-spread flock, purporting to obey and follow his Christian standard, who are yet sunk deep in the abyss of infidelity and vice? When in that beautiful island, so bountifully favored by God, the family circle shall once more be comforted by the cheering peace of Christianity—when the master shall learn to cherish a Christian care for the slave who is now treated by him as a brute beast of burden and labor—and when the latter shall be rescued by Christian instruction from the superstitions and practices of his present state of heathen destitution, and taught the precious lesson of Christian hope for the future, and Christian comfort in the sad present, then what grateful and fervent hymns of praise shall arise from hearts now ignorant of their own immortal nature and destiny, mingled with prayers in which will not be forgotten the names of all such as shall now bestow on them one look of sympathy, and extend a helping hand to bring them out of their present bondage.

CHAPTER VII.

Public Education.—Attempts to falsify Statements.—Official Items from the Census of 1841.—Schools pillaged by the Treasury.—Saco's Parallel between the Spanish and British Colonies.—Degradation and Ignorance in the Country Regions.—Frightful Pictures of Vice.

THE organs of the Spanish administration may boast of progress in the island of Cuba, and endeavor to hide the deficiencies of public education by tedious and sophistical reasoning. Of late this has been attempted with an earnestness which bore evidence on its face of a conscious desire to produce an untrue impression. But why not silence, in the face of the world, the complaints of the Cubans with statistical numbers, and the report of facts which come naturally within their reach? It is true that the census has not been taken, or at least published, since 1841; but whose fault is it? It is also true that the committees lately appointed by the government, are ignorant and lukewarm —whose fault? It is also a fact that the officials authorized for the purpose, are not furnished with adequate supplies to carry out the object of diffusing knowledge among the poor; but again, whose fault?

The condition of education in the island is here exhibited by appealing to the official items. It must at the same time be borne in mind that an intimate knowledge of the country and people, would bring to light many facts of daily occurrence, which, with the open immorality of the multitude, and the ignorance stamped upon their countenances, must strengthen the conviction that however erroneous these official items may be, a correction of them would present a still more revolting picture.

The census of 1841 gives the following results as regards the free and slave population:

White inhabitants	418,291	
Free mulattoes	88,054	
Free black	64,784	
Total free		571,129
Mulatto slaves	10,974	
Black slaves	425,521*	
Total slaves		436,495
Transient population		38,000
		1,045,624

The number of schools, according to the most recent and certainly the most favorable accounts, amounted to

Of white male children	129
" " female "	79
Of colored male "	6
" " female "	8
In all	222

Those receiving instruction in them were

White boys	6025
" girls	2417
Colored boys	460
" girls	180

From this data, it results that through the whole island 222 schools existed, and that 9082 free children, of all classes, were instructed in them. Of this num-

* There is little doubt that this number should be augmented by one third to make it correct.

ber, it is all-important to observe that 5325 paid their schools, and that 3757 was the pitiful number under gratuitous tuition. Of the latter, 540 were supported by the branches of the once comparatively flourishing "Sociedad Patriotica," whose resources were derived from personal subscription of the members or voluntary taxation of the citizens; 2111 by local subscriptions or taxes; and 1106 gratuitously taught by the professors, through the suggestions of the society, or other functionaries, whose request might almost be considered as actual command.

The census also shows the number of free children between the ages of five and fifteen, to be 99,599; of whom, as before stated, 9082 are only educated, and that chiefly by private means and efforts. Scarcely ten per cent. of those requiring instruction receive it, four per cent. of whom by public contributions, and not any by appropriations from the general treasury. On the contrary, so far from receiving aid from the treasury, the schools have been pillaged by it; for when the custom-houses have taken charge of collecting the local taxes established for public instruction, ten per cent. commission has been deducted for the service, and large sums imposed on commerce and trade for this object, have been, and are to this day, withheld and unaccounted for by the treasury. When the enormous amount of Cuban taxation, as explained in another part of this volume, is considered, who can restrain his indignation that with at least twenty-two millions of dollars of imposts—an equivalent to $38 77cts. to each free soul—the first duty of a civilized government should be so dishonorably neglected.

By referring to the above items, and those found in Mr. Saco's "Parallel between the Spanish and British Colonies," the following discouraging comparison is drawn:

		Number of children educated in proportion to the whole free population.		
In the Bahama Islands	1831	1	to every	16
" St. Vincent's	1830	1	"	19
" Jamaica	1827	1	"	18
" Antigua	1830	1	"	5
" St. Christopher's*	——	1	"	11
" Lower Canada	1832	1	"	12
" Nova Scotia	1832	1	"	10
" Prince Edward's	1832	1	"	14
" Terra Nova	1834	1	"	8
" Mauritius	——	1	"	11
" Presidency of Madras	1834	1	"	5
And the island of Cuba	——	1	"	63

By withdrawing from the Patriotic Society, established under the most favorable auspices, first, its very name, that the word *patriotic* might be erased from the colonial vocabulary; then, the care of watching over, and directing public education; and, lastly, the resources voted by the citizens from the origin of the corps—the most sacred cause, one always commanding the noble excitement and enthusiasm of philanthropy, has been placed in the sordid and debased hands of the officials of a venal and corrupt administration. Were this the sole grievance inflicted on Cuba, by Spanish despotism, no greater motive could inspire the bold cry of her indignant sons against tyranny so oppressive.

Let not the traveler, from whatever land he may have approached that island, even though he be a native of the beautiful Spanish peninsula, discredit the sad truths which are here recorded. But should the enormity of the evil induce a momentary doubt of its existence, let him visit the comfortless home of the village poor, and there witness the most convincing proof of what is here affirmed. He will find the villager, like all his humble associates, continually called to do public duty, for which not even thanks are ex-

* There is a slight inaccuracy regarding this island.

pected; while there is no individual service he demands of society for which he is not made to pay dearly. His children, in the mean time, wander around amidst vice and filth; both parent and child exhibiting a benighted ignorance which is absolutely unparalleled. Not a feeling calculated to ennoble his nature, finds a place in the heart; vice, in no instance, is regarded with aversion, for its deformity is not even perceived. Alas, for the community affording pictures of human degradation so revolting. And what shall be said of a government on which the awful responsibility rests of causing, of promoting, and of perpetuating so much moral hideousness and desolation!

CHAPTER VIII.

Cuban Grievances.—Personal Liberty.—Personal Security.—The Right of Property.—Instances of exercise of despotic Power.—Senor Saco.—Number deported and banished by Tacon.—The same System continued.—Taxation in Cuba.—Details.—Summary of Grievances.

THROUGHOUT the preceding chapters continued allusion has been made to the wrongs and grievances which the Cubans are forced to endure, and the despotic sway with which the island is governed. It is proposed, in the present chapter, to enter more in detail upon these wrongs and grievances, that the world may judge between the island and her rulers. This is a subject that can no longer be shirked by Spain. Either Cuba has a right to redress, or she has not; and that question cannot properly be settled by the voice of mankind, without a fair investigation of the causes of complaint.

In the Declaration of Independence of the United States of America, the right of life, liberty, and the pursuit of happiness, is claimed for all men. A less rhetorical, but a more definite, proposition is laid down by the great English commentator, in his division of rights, into the right of personal liberty—the right of personal security—and the right of property. The Cubans are deprived of all these.

The liberty of the person is constantly violated, and often with no other warrant than the arbitrary order of the meanest official, and from which no redress can be obtained, except by means of heavy bribes.

During and since the time of Tacon, the seizure and immediate deportation of persons of respectability and distinction. were, and have been, of common occurrence, and this without a hearing of the party accused, and without granting any opportunity for defence.

Individuals, for the slightest possible causes of offence—often, indeed, without any cause whatever—are seized and banished from the island, or, what is still worse, are incarcerated in loathsome prisons.

One of the most flagrant acts of despotism was the deportation, by Tacon, of Senor Saco, a man universally known and esteemed in the island for his high character and unblemished reputation, for his benevolence and philanthropy, and for his attachments to Cuban interests. All these, however, were of no avail against the tyrannical exercise of arbitrary power.

Within a period of little more than eighteen months, about 200 persons were deported, and about 700 banished for life, from the island by Tacon. These acts of despotism are continued, with more or less frequency, to the present time.

Innumerable instances might be named to sustain an assertion which no one will venture to contradict.

So far from affording personal security to the Cuban, the government has taken every method to endanger it, under the pretence that it is necessary to keep the native inhabitants in a state of constant apprehension in order to insure their continued allegiance. To this end, every kind of judicial enormity prevails, and every description of imposition is practiced upon the helpless creole. If he commits a wrong he is punished without an opportunity of being heard in his own defence, or, what is the same thing, he is tried before a prejudiced tribunal. If he has suffered an injury, he finds the means of redress so tedious that endurance is preferable to the formidable task of obtaining justice. There is but one means of avoiding persecution—but one way of escape when persecuted—but one method to obtain justice when seeking ordinary redress. It is by bribery. Gold will open prison doors, procure dispensation for falsely imputed crimes, obtain a tardy decree of long-sought justice. Thus personal security is only to be enjoyed at the expense of the right of property, which brings the third division of rights to be specially considered.

The plan of robbery and plunder—it can be called by no milder name—has been reduced to so complete a system, and that system has been brought to such a state of perfection, that it will be more satisfactory to undertake the subject in its details.

Without enlarging upon the difficulty of obtaining legal remedies, and the insecurity attending the possession of property when claims are made against it by those in favor with the government, it is proposed to examine the method of taxation now adopted in Cuba, and also its extent and operation.

Whatever may be the cause of the mystery in which the gross amount of taxation is involved, it is a fact that the publications which are made by the local administration neither comprehend the whole range of taxes, nor do they generally affix to each head any thing more than the balance subject to the control of the general treasury. We commence the list by the official statement of 1844, which is mainly composed of *balances* of different taxes, the chief names of which are the following:

Alcabala (or six per cent. on sales of real estate, of slaves, on auction sales, on sales in shops).

Bulls of the Pope.

Brokers' tax.

Cattle tax.

Shopkeepers' tax.

Tax on mortgages.

Tax on donations.

Tax on cockfighting.

Tax on grants of crosses, or uses of uniform, etc.

Tax on promissory notes, or bills of exchange.

Tax on the municipal taxes, yearly tribute of the counts, marquises, and other titles.

Tax on all deaths of non-insolvent persons.

Tax on investments in favor of the clergy, sale of the public offices, sealed paper, penalties in favor of the royal household.

Tax on the property of the Jesuits, sales of public lands.

Tax on establishment of auctioneers.

Tax (four per cent.) on law expenses.

Water canal tax, royal order of Charles III., etc.

To this must of course be added the custom-house duties on imports and exports, and tonnage on vessels.

The proceeds of the revenue for the year 1844, comprehending the custom-houses, maritime and inland, of the Provinces of Havana, St. Jago, and Puerto Principe, and net proceeds of lottery tax, and *balance* of tax on religious orders, are, according to the before-named official statement....................	$10,693,626 01
To the above must be added the amount expended on smuggled goods which have been paid to those concerned in the act without any material relief to the consumer. In the official statement above referred to, $7,364,005 is the amount given for maritime duties; and deducting one fifth for tonnage charges, we have left $5,891,204 for duties on imports and exports. As a moderate calculation, add one fifth of this sum for what is paid on smuggled goods......	1 178,240 00
The lottery tax, though called voluntary, is no less a burden, and the greatest incentive to idleness and dishonesty amongst the poorer classes, and especially among the slaves. The ancient custom of purchasing freedom is becoming almost obsolete among the latter—their hopes being exclusively fixed on the freaks of fortune, which, as it may well be supposed, do not always favor the most worthy, and therefore the most capable of enjoying the rights of freemen. 35,000 tickets at $4, in sixteen drawings, and 20,000 tickets at $16, in one	
	$11,871,866 01

		$11,871,866 01
drawing, make the whole sum drained from the public in one year	$2,560,000	
There being a scandalous connivance to prevent the public from obtaining tickets from the offices, 6¼ per cent. additional must be added	160,000	
	2,720,000	
Less the amount included in the official statement	761,000	
		1,959,000 00
The post-office expenses, which left, in 1843, a balance to the treasury of $5734 01½, amounted to $997,341, according to Sagra, in 1830. Since then the population, which in 1827 was 730,562, according to this writer, who was officially employed, and is a native European, has increased to 1,045,000. The country surrounding Cardenas, Jucaro, Sagua la Grande, and San Juan de los Remedios, and Nuevitas, has also greatly increased, and correspondence as well; new branches have been established to convey the mails, so that it will be quite safe to calculate upon half a million increase, calling it now		1,500,000 00
Census on land, according to the same Sagra...................................		4,000,000 00
The 4 per cent. on law expenses in the statement commencing this calculation, gives the sum of $62,240; but as 10 per cent. is deducted previously as a commission in favor of the revenue, the amount received in the treasury is really $69,155, which by 25 is......................	$1,728,875	
Deducting the sum included in the statement	62,240	
		1,666,635 00
The municipal taxes received by the corporations from those who purchase the right of collecting them, amounted, according to the memoirs of the Economical Society and the		
		$20,997,501 01

$20,997,501 01

Faro Industrial of the 5th June 1847, with reference to the year 1843—

For the Province of Havana, ...	$552,577 75	
" " St. Jago...	101,063 00	
" " P. Principe	76,997 25	
	730,638 00	
To this, in order to cover expenses of collection, and profit to the speculator, add 25 per cent.	182,659 00	
	$913,297 00	
Apart from these municipal taxes received by the corporation, there may be others received by the very contractors who supply the object of its creation. There is one called the "limpieza," or cleaning of the city, which the same Faro Industrial values at	53,400 00	
This gives for municipal taxes, at least		966,697 00

The next tax, is that in favor of the alguazils-mayor, as far as it weighs on cattle and animals.

This charge was originally allowed by the crown in compensation of certain pecuniary services. In the course of time those services have become insignificant, and more than paid by the country. For large cattle, $1,25 each must be paid to him, and $4,75 to the crown; and more or less, in the same proportion, for smaller animals. The true items not having ever been published, the amount of $652,408 is adopted, which the above quoted Faro Industrial fixes as the government tax in the island on cattle, and for the proportion as follows: As the duty, $4,75, is to the $1,25 alguazil-mayor charge, so is $652,408 to the whole amount of charges of alguazils-mayor in the island 171,475 00

The licenses given by the captain-general,

$22,135,673 01

$22,135,673 01

governors of towns, and captains of county districts, is another subject of heavy taxation. The negro slaves, or their masters for them, are frequently subject to it; but to simplify the estimate, take the amount of the free population, which, in the census of 1841, ranges thus:

White,....................	418,291
Free Colored,................	88,054
Free Negroes, ...	64,784
	571,129

Supposing one fifth of this number to be heads of families forced to have a license, the number will be 114,225

50 cents for the certificate of the commissary of the ward, and 31¼ for the signature of the magistrate, viz., 81¼.................... 92,807 81

But as the above does not comprehend the whole of the licenses given for separate excursions, suppose that only one fifth of the number before accounted for shall make one single trip in the year, say 22,845 individuals, at only 31¼ cents 7,139 06

Another charge of this nature is that on passports, for which take the amount of 38,000 individuals, given in the census of 1841 as garrison and transient population, and deducting 18,000 for troops, there will be left 20,000; of which, from the number of crews, and other causes, suppose that only 6000 passports are given. The charge made is $1,50 for the captain-general, or other subaltern governor, $1 for the warden's report and sealed paper, and $2,75 for the certificate of the judge of property of absent heirs; in all $5,25; amounting to, for the 6000 mentioned...................... $31,500

But out of this number, 2000, it is fair to suppose, will apply for the passport to the "agencia," an office kept by military officers who have remark-

$22,235,619 88

		$22,235,619 88
	$31,500	
able advantages in procuring ready-made passports for $8,50 apiece, which, less than $5,25, leaves $3,25.	6,500	
		38,000 00

The crown derives another source of revenue from the sale of offices, vendibles, and renunciables, that are subject to being sold or renounced in favor of another person. In the statement of inland customs and revenue for the year 1843, the sales of the kind were stated to amount to $92,737; but whatever the sum of the present year may be, it is supposed to be included in the official statement or first item commencing this estimate. Among the many offices of this kind, are the alguazils-mayor, whose various fees are counted in the law expenses and in the slaughter of cattle, both herein estimated. Another of them is the fiel executor, also a member of the corporation, whose duty is to examine the weights and measures of all retail and wholesale dealers, visiting the different stores. It is assumed that the one holding this office in the city of Havana, which gives a handsome income for a family, renders $8000 net, which is equal to $12,000 on the country, to pay clerks and other expenses; and judging that the corporation taxes of Havana, $384,000, will bear to $730,000, and the taxes of similar nature of the whole island, the same proportion, it follows that all the fiel executors will amount to 22,812 00

The government has also sold archives for notaries, where deeds are entered and recorded. There may be presumed to be about fifty in the whole island, and to be sold from 3000 to 50,000 dollars apiece. Although the latter price is nearer the general one than the former, the majority may be much beneath it; adopting the price of $15,000 as the true rate for the whole, it gives $750,000. They are very productive, and must be so, on ac-

$22,296,431 88

$22,296,431 88

count of the peculiar conditions of all offices, vendibles, and renunciables, which, whenever they pass from one possessor to another, or even to the lawful heir, leave a portion of their price in favor of the crown. They are also subject to confiscation, when a monthly injunction of a renouncing deed is neglected; and there are even days each month in which should the death of the proprietor take place, the crown takes back its grant. This also applies to the alguazils-mayor, fiel executor, etc. Great profits must be the recompense of such disadvantageous conditions. It is not therefore an exaggeration to suppose these archives to produce forty per cent., of which sum we consider ten per cent. the just price of the service; and the remaining thirty per cent. is the penalty which the community pays in extra charges for the resources anticipated to government at these monstrous sales.—$750,000 at thirty per cent.................. 225,000 00

Fines which are constantly imposed by subaltern officers of justice in Cuba will continually strike the eye of a foreigner, on looking over the Havana newspapers. The infractions of the by-laws are the pretexts; but the menials of government are guided often by a thirst for money, which excludes a just and impartial exercise, since they are interested by having a portion assigned for their benefit. It is fair to compute the amount of fines at $25,000 publicly avowed, and $25,000 privately exacted and not accounted for. That the above calculation may not appear altogether arbitrary, it may be added, that the fines of the royal household, which are the most insignificant in the island, amounted, according to the statement of 1843, to $10,881 .... 50,000 00

Fees in the captain-general's tribunal are likewise another tax not included in any other calculation. The present captain-general has designated two days in the week to hear actions

$22,571,431 88

$22,571,431 88

verbally established and decided in his presence, or in that of officers whom he appoints in his lieu. Persons having difficult claims, who do not find in the usual course of proceeding, the easy attainment of their object, apply there, and orders of immediate payment issue often in utter disregard of law, or the state in which the case may be in another court. No pleadings, but the order of payment, under threat of imprisonment, constitute the course of this strange, all-powerful judge. Calculating on 100 days of audience, in which he or his delegates hear ten suits each, and estimating his fee at $8,50 for each, though the sum may not publicly be acknowledged, it will give 8,500 00

The fish and meat markets, monopolized by General Tacon, according to his own report, published in 1838, have had the effect of elevating the price of these commodities at least thirty per cent. The yearly consumption of large cattle, being 86,000, gives, at

this estimate	$1,500,000
Suppose smaller animals and service one sixth of this value	250,000
	1,750,000
The fish consumed can be at least estimated at one eighth of the meat, viz.	218,750
	$1,968,750

And thirty per cent. on this sum will render .. 590,625 00

N. B. The seller of cattle obtains only $2,50 for each arrobe of 25 lbs. of meat, while the consumer pays really, whatever may be published to the contrary, $5,50. Here, then, is a measure for the weight of the monopoly. There is another official data which is subjoined. It is a statement published by General Tacon, as an appendix to his report of his own acts, containing estimates of the buildings by

$23,170,556 88

$23,170,556 88

him reconstructed, the revenue they produced previously, that which they produce now, and that which they would produce to the corporation after the time should be elapsed for which they were bound to the contractors.

	Valuation.	Old Revenue.	Present Revenue.	Future Revenue.
Fish market	$34,031 06½	$864	$864	$7,000
Christina meat mkt.,	115,521 00½	8,712	11,100	38,100
do. do.	67,876 03			
Slaughter at Tacon Sq.	47,780 06			7,800
" the Jail,	480,640 04		18,600	18,600
At Governm't Palace,	102,434 04	2,400		13,900
	$848,282 24	$11,976	$30,564	$85,400

In the present case, this exorbitant rise in the rent is only the expression of the forced monopoly, unheard-of petty renting of apartments of sale, and strict severity in preventing the sales elsewhere, in the city and its suburbs.

In the general statement are not counted $4,25 per death, and 75 cts. per christening, and generally what are called Renta Ovencional, which Mr. Sagra calculated, for 1830, at 250,000 00

Private extra fees demanded for marriages, under various pretences 15,000 00

The charge for renewing what is called the apprenticeship of emancipated slaves, an authority *de facto* exercised by the captain-general, is $102 apiece. Since General Valdez, whose honorable conduct reflects honor on his nation, granted about 3000 patents of freedom during about one year, it may be supposed that at least one thousand become due every year . 102,000 00

The custom of extraordinary and expensive services on the death of a relative, imposing a ruinous tax on the survivors, is another source to the priesthood, which may be appreciated from reading the by-laws of General Valdez, regulating the prices of the use of the scaffolding, carpets, etc. A mortality of five per cent. on the 418,000 white inhabitants, will

$23,537.556 88

	$23,537,556 88
give 20,900 deaths, of which one fourth we may suppose capable of doing something to save apparent neglect of their deceased friends; and this number, 5225, if only calculated at the minimum rate of $10 each, is...........	52,250 00
Tolls on the bridge of Marianao	56,000 00
Private gifts for nominations of captains of districts, city ward commissaries, watchmen, etc.	10,000 00
Permits for gambling, etc. (private)	50,000 00

Tithes. In the general statement which is taken as guide, summing up the amounts of the revenue in 1844, two main divisions are found—the maritime and the inland taxes. There is no specification of the latter corresponding to that year; but in the year preceding, the only sum belonging to tithes as a deposit, was $19.831 03.

From the memoirs of the Economical Society, are subjoined the following statements, which were also published in the Faro above quoted:

Four years from 1833 to 1836—

Jurisdiction of Havana.

1833	$227,780 00½
1834	247,036 04½
1835	262,653 01
1836	246,102 04¼
	$973,571 10¼

Jurisdiction of St. Jago.

1833 . . .	$50,260 04
1834	50,260 04
1835	37,822 05¾
1836	37,822 05¾
	$176,164 19½

Four years from 1837 to 1840—

$23,705,806 88

$23,705,806 88

Jurisdiction of Havana.

1837	$220,438 07¼
1838	217,928 06½
1839	190,164 00¾
1840	186,555 06
	$815,085 20½

Jurisdiction of St. Jago.

1837	$37,822 05¾
1838	37,822 05¾
1839	49,547 00
1840	49,547 00
	$174,738 11½

Province of Havana, first four years, ...	$973,571 10¼
Province of St. Jago, first four years, ...	176,164 19½
	$1,149,735 29¾
Province of Havana, second four years, ...	$815,085 20½
Province of St. Jago, second four years, ...	174,738 11½
	989,823 32
Total . . .	$2,139,558 61¾
This by 8 years, gives .	$267,444 82½

The above result, having been obtained under the law which only required the tax on sugar from estates founded previously to 1804, is no criterion to what the tithe on sugar estates will be from the year 1847. To endeavor to fix on some items by which its present product can be calculated, it is necessary to know what is the relative importance of sugar estates compared to other agricultural pursuits subject to tithe. For this pur-

$23,705,806 88

$23,705,806 88

pose, take from Ramon Sagra's "Breve Idea," published in 1836, the following estimates:

	Capital employed.
For raising cattle, . . .	$26,767,977
Pastures, ...	21,691,610
Sugar estates	83,780,877
Coffee "	85,825,000
Farms "	111,861,984
Tobacco vegas (valleys), . .	6,532,420
	$336,459,868

Sugar consequently represents one fourth Therefore out of the $267,358 tax of a common year, $66,839 should be deducted, as corresponding to sugar, and the remainder will be the tithe on all the other articles 200,519 00

Now, as regards the tax on this article, which according to the new law has commenced to be exacted, and is 2½ per cent. on the gross products of all estates not having had fifteen crops (the latter being exempted during that period, provided they have not been erected on woodlands), take the crop of 1834, which, being thirteen years ago, may be supposed to constitute the quantity now subject to pay, though it will certainly be greater from the increase of each individual estate. In that year the chief imports were

8,408,231 arrobas of sugar.
1,817,315 " coffee.
104,213 hogsheads of molasses.

In the year 1841—

13,082,288 arrobas of sugar.
1,998,846 " coffee.
119,138 hogsheads of molasses.

And in 1843, the official balance gives 889,103 boxes—equal to 14,225,648 arrobas, adding to which the enormous quantity of Moscavado sugar in the districts of Sagua, it is safe to call it, with the subsequent increase, twenty millions of arrobas. The coffee of the said year was 1,631,782 arrobas, and 191,093 hogs-

$23,906,325 88

$23,906,325 88

heads of molasses. The sugar crop is now, therefore, equivalent to 1,252,000 boxes of sixteen arrobas; and that of 1834, say 8,500,000 arrobas to 531,250 boxes. The increase which has taken place from 1834 to 1847, in fourteen years, is 720,750, or 51,482 boxes a year; of which the two and a half per cent. will be 1287 boxes; which, at fifteen dollars apiece, will give a yearly advance of $19,305 to the sugar tithe. Two and a half per cent. on the crop of 1834, will be 13,281 boxes at $15..... 199,215 00

The above will be yearly increased with $22,305 more, until the whole sugar crop will be subject, which, not counting the progressive extension of culture, will give on the present production of 1,250,000 boxes, $468,750.

N. B. Against any suggestions calculated to impair the exactitude of the above inferences, it is to be noted that the proportion of sugar paying taxes was much less under the old law, and therefore the fourth deducted, as if all sugar were subject to it, in order to obtain the tithe on other articles, was much beyond its real importance. As a general rule, great caution has been exercised in admitting data not official.

Spoliations of Taxgatherers. The exemption from this tax being founded in the number of crops made by an estate, and on the fact of its being erected on woodlands, the formula to establish these facts, and the right of exemption, was decreed by the Board of Authorities to be a summary course, without law expenses, or any tedious proceedings of the kind. Under a spirit of corruption, this safeguard has been broken through, and whole apartments have been hired in Havana to store the enormous and numerous packages of processes unjustly, and under various pretences, issued to threaten the planters, and force them in spite of their rights, to a private compromise. There is no doubt it is much under the real sum, snatched

$24,105,540 88

	$24,105,540 88
in this manner from the country, to estimate it at twenty per cent. of the whole sugar tax, say	40,000 00
Passengers landing to and from steamboats, where the latter come near the shore, are forced, in Havana, to pay twenty-five cents for each person, and something additional for freight or excessive baggage. Calculating that the number either going or coming from the buetta abijo, or Matanzas, by steamboats is 64 in a day, at 25 cts. .... $16 00 One fifth for baggage................ 5 20 $21 20	
Corresponding to a year	7,738 00
In the present administration there is a monopoly of manure, which, by compelling it to be thrown on one spot, and preventing its being carried even to farms, secures a profit which, weighing on the city, is computed at	5,000 00
The custom which forces the poor often to be suddenly deprived of their horses in the midst of their excursions, in order to convey military baggage, which being paid for by the treasury of the island might as well be contracted for beforehand, added to the gratuitous conveyance of troops by railroads, is a tax equal to	5,000 00
Port charges of vessels paid to captains of the ports, health officers, etc., on 2586 vessels, at an average of forty dollars	103,440 00
Tax on coastwise seamen	10,000 00
Subscriptions. Notwithstanding the taxes established for building and support of churches, those of Monserratte, Cardenas, Matanzas, the cemetery of Bejucal, and of every country place, the old theatre, and whatever public work or dispensation is undertaken by any one chief of town, is always carried through by means of subscriptions obtained by the coercitive influence of those in office; the barracks for Roque, Matanzas, Coliseo, and Cardenas, the support of veteran guards for the country, bridges, repairs of roads, public subscriptions	
	$24,276,718 88

	$24,276,718 88
and entertainments, are thus capriciously taxed. The very military hospitals are built by such means. In fact, there are no objects, however sacred, exempt from liability to subscription, not excepting even those entitled to an extensive support from the public treasury. The amount derived from this constant source of taxation cannot be less than..................	25,000 00
Error of 10,000 less in calculation of lottery, in sixteen drawings, as per note.*...........	160,000 00
The tax on the mineral ore exported of 20 per cent. on its value, say $2,013,543, will give..................................	402,708 60
	$24,864,427 48

The detail of Cuban taxes is here concluded. When it is considered how small a portion, comparatively, of the sum collected is applied to the legitimate object of taxation; when it is considered that for variety and extent, for amount and oppressiveness, they exceed any taxation imposed by any government in any country upon the earth; when the enormity of the whole subject is regarded in all its features, no one can repress a feeling of abhorrence at such acts of tyranny, and of wonder that they have been so long endured in silence.

So much for taxation in Cuba. For grievances generally, the following may be considered a correct and faithful abstract.

On the death of Ferdinand VII., Cuba was included in the constitutional reform published in the Estatuto Real.

In 1837, the democratic constitution of 1812 was proclaimed, and when General Lorenzo repeated its promulgation in St. Jago, General Tacon sent an armed expedition to put down the system authorized by law, which act was rewarded by the court.

* The number of tickets advertised lately being 37,500 instead of 35,000, makes $10,000 for each drawing, which, for the sixteen drawings for the year, makes a difference of $160,000.

The Cuban deputies, legally elected, were refused admittance in the same year at the Spanish Cortes, and a resolution was then passed establishing that Cuba should be governed by special laws.

The organs of government in Spain and in Cuba have since declared, that the civil laws, as they are executed, and the paramount authority of the agents of government, are all that is required in the island; while arbitrary rule and rapacity are the known results.

Besides representatives in Congress, Spain has deprived Cuba of all means of redress. The press, under the most infamous and servile censorship, is a weapon only wielded against their rights. A petition, signed by more than two, is condemned as a seditious act. The corporations have no longer a representative character, besides being under the immediate control of the captain-general, who appoints their members, and dictates at will their resolutions. The Board of Improvement has become a mere arm of the government, to sanction despotic acts, to support additional taxes, and to introduce mixed races into the population.

All good and enlightened patriots are forced into obscurity, or persecuted, or expatriated.

Martial law, since 1825. The captains-general have increased their encroachments until they now exercise the legislative, judicial, and executive power.

No trade can be followed, no shop opened, no goods sold in the street, without a license.

The creoles are excluded from the army, the judiciary, the treasury, and customs, and from all influential or lucrative positions; private speculations and monopolies are favored and established with a view of taking from the former their means of wealth.

Services are extorted from the poor in the country, to serve in the precarious police sustained therein; fines are imposed, and forced aid for the repairing of the roads, all according to the will of the officer in command, or the pliancy of the individual.

More than twenty millions of regular taxes are collected by the order of the Spanish government, the captain-general, the lieutenant-governors, and of the country district judges.

These taxes are employed in supporting an army of twenty thousand men to intimidate and oppress the peaceful inhabitants of Cuba; and likewise the entire navy of Spain, unnecessarily stationed in the ports of the island for the same purpose; in the paying of a vast number of officers residing either on the island or in Spain; and in remittances to the court.

In spite of the enormous tithe collected, it is only by subscriptions that the inhabitants can secure to themselves temples for their worship, or cemeteries for their dead; and for a baptism or a burial, or to obtain any of the consolations of religion, the care of which is indirectly under the all-absorbing power of military rule, it requires a large additional sum to be paid.

The military government has taken from the other political and administrative branches the control of education, in order to restrict, to limit, and to embarrass it.

The tributary system has drained many sources of wealth. The flour monopoly has put down the cultivation of coffee; and the grazing of cattle has become a sad speculation from the tax on its consumption.

The heedlessly supported slave trade—which carries with it additional danger to the existing slave property, from an increased number of the savage Africans, and the entanglement of diplomatic relations with England—though rejected by the enlightened portion of the community, is kept up because of the clandestine profits it brings to the captain-general.

The farmers have to pay 2½ per cent. on sugar, and 10 per cent. on their other harvests, when gathered; the same is paid by all engaged in raising live stock, for all their cattle, exclusive of the charges arising from an exportation.

There is a tax of $1,25 cents upon every fanega of salt (about a hundred weight), which causes the price of that article to be raised to an immoderate sum.

The Cuban pays 6 to 6½ per cent. of the value of any slave, or any property in town or country, that he may sell; besides all other charges of notaries, of registration, of stamped paper, etc., etc.

There is stamped paper, for a special purpose, the use of which is enforced by the government, and sold by it at the price of eight dollars every sheet; and it is necessary on solemn oath to prove one's poverty, in order to be admitted to the use of cheaper paper, a sheet of which costs six cents.

No one can have in his house any company or amusement of any sort, if he does not solicit, obtain, and pay for a license ($2,50), or he must submit to be mulcted for an infraction of the regulations.

Every inhabitant is compelled to ask for a license, and pay for the same, when he wants to go from the place of his residence.

No citizen, however peaceful and respectable he may be, is allowed to walk through the city after ten o'clock in the evening, unless he carry with him a lantern, and successively obtains leave of all the watchmen on his way, the infraction of which law is punished with immediate arrest, and a fine of eight dollars.

He is not permitted to lodge any person in his house for a single night, either native or foreigner, be the same his friend or a member of his family, without giving information of the same, also under the penalty of a like punishment.

He cannot remove his residence from one house into another, without giving notice previously to the authorities of his intention, under the penalty of a heavy fine.

An order has been made which in effect prohibits parents from sending their children to the United States for purposes of education; and such parents are driven to the expedient of proving ill health, or feigning it, in their children, in order to obtain passports for them.

In the whole island a most brutal spirit of despotism is strikingly prevalent in all officials of the government, from the captain-general down to the most abject of his hirelings, without even excepting the municipal and other local authorities.

A diabolical scheme, concocted in the chambers of Alcoy, exists for perpetuating the importation of African slaves into Cuba, the primordial cause of her present hazardous position.

In that scheme enter not merely some members of the royal family of Spain, but all its dependents, favorites, and satellites, including the captains-general of Cuba, and their subordinates.

The "gratification" of half an ounce in gold, which was formerly received by the captains-general for every *sack of charcoal* (the nickname given by those engaged in this infamous traffic to the African slaves brought over), has risen to the large sum of *three doubloons* in gold.

The colonial government and its confederates, not being able to elude the vigilance of the cruisers of the nations engaged in the suppression of this traffic, in order to continue the same, have had to appeal to a forced interpretation of existing treaties, pretending to show that such slaves are imported into Cuba from Brazil.

These machinations are carried on by some members of the royal family in concert with the colonial government; and the cabinet not only has full knowledge of the same, but authorizes and protects them, or, at least, winks at the practices.

Within these last months various cargoes of African slaves, amounting in number to more than 3000, were imported into the island of Cuba, and there sold almost publicly; and in *gratifications* set apart for the captain-general, Senor Alcoy has already received the sum of 12,000 doubloons in gold—about 200,000 dollars.

The sons of Cuba are persecuted, imprisoned, buried in dungeons, banished, sentenced to fortresses, and condemned to death for calumnies, for imaginary crimes of disloyalty, on no better foundation than flimsy suspicion, or false denunciations by infamous spies.

CHAPTER IX.

What is to become of Cuba.—Spain and her American settlements.—Cuba cannot be held by Spain.—Progress of Events.—Right of Cuba to Revolutionize.—Must ultimately belong to England or to the United States.—Reasons why it will fall to the latter.—Conclusion.

Having presented briefly the past history and present situation of the Cubans, the inquiry naturally arises, what is to become of Cuba?

Spain was the first to plant her colonies in the new world. Taking the lead in European civilization, she became possessed of the entire extent of the American continent which lies between the forty-third degree of south, and the thirty-seventh degree of north latitude, a region possessing every variety of climate, capable of yielding every variety of vegetable product, abounding in mineral treasure, remarkable for the richness of its virgin soil, and promising inexhaustible wealth to the European adventurer.

Compared with this magnificent range of country—exceeding the whole Russian empire in extent—England occupied a meagre and barren shore, the possession of the greater part of which had to be disputed with the French and Dutch.

Three hundred years have elapsed, and how stands the account? Spain has not a single foot upon the mainland of the American continent. Cuba and Porto Rico alone, of all her western possessions, have been preserved to her by the force of circumstances. In view of past history, with reference to the peculiar state of things in the island, as they now exist, considering the advance of the age in liberal sentiments, and in free institutions, regarding the inevitable progress of events, it cannot be held an unwise affirmation that Cuba must soon be lost to Spain. Much has been said, of late, about "manifest destiny," and the term has got to be a sort of watchword in the mouths of patriotic orators and political speech-makers. It is, however, a poor excuse for the unlawful seizure of the territory of a friendly power, or for the unwarrantable interference with their rights, to raise, in avoidance of the charge of robbery or oppression, the plea of "manifest destiny;" for the same plea is as good in the mouth of the highwayman as in that of a power who shall take to the high road of nations, and, armed to the teeth, prey upon the weaker. But for all that, there is a sense in which "manifest destiny" becomes no longer a byword; for when the reflective observer of events endeavors to form an opinion as to the future, and from past examination, and from all that he can see in the present, a result presents itself which is not to be mistaken, and which tells, with unerring certainty, what is to be; he is content to say that it is the manifest destiny of a nation to do, to become, or to achieve this or that.

It has not been owing to the good management of Spain, or to the loyalty of Cuba, that up to now the former has retained her colony. Rather has it been the good fortune of the one, and the misfortune of the other. It has always been understood that the United States would never consent that any European power other than Spain should hold that island. Important as the possession of Cuba was, Spain was supposed to be too powerless and inert to render her presence dangerous to the United States. But the island has, notwithstanding, been watched by this government with jealous interest. This country interfered in 1826 when the invasion of Cuba and Porto Rico was resolved upon by the combined forces of Mexico and Colombia, not because it was desirous of opposing the extension of liberal principles, but because it was apprehensive that independence would not result from the proposed invasion, and that Cuba might in consequence fall into the hands of some other European power—which on no account could be permitted. As a proof of this, the following extract is made from the message of John Quincy Adams, who was then President.

"The condition of the islands of Cuba and Porto Rico is of deeper import, and more immediate bearing upon the present interests and future prospects of our Union. The correspondence herewith transmitted will show how earnestly it has engaged the attention of this government. The invasion of both those islands by the united forces of Mexico and Colombia, is avowedly among the objects matured by the belligerent states at Panama. The convulsions to which, from the *peculiar compositions of their population*, they would be liable in the event of such an invasion, and the danger therefrom resulting of their falling, ultimately, *into the hands of some European power* other than Spain, will not admit of our looking at the consequences, to which the Congress of Panama may lead, with indifference. It is unnecessary to enlarge upon this topic, or to say more than all, our efforts, in reference to this interest, will be *to preserve the existing state of things*."

It is a sound proposition to put to the civilized world, that no nation shall, at this period, oppress by any arbitrary or tyrannical despotism, a dependent country or colony. Although the means of redress may not always be at hand, no one now disputes the right of the oppressed to seek for and to use them.

If a true statement has been given of the situation of Cuban affairs, Cuba has a right to attempt her freedom. Taking what has been said for truth, a case is made out which shall justify Cuba, by the unanimous voice of mankind, for the act of revolution. In the struggle she will be entitled to the sympathy of all Christendom. How far nations should adhere to the doctrine of neutrality remains, as yet, unsettled. A deviation from it is a dangerous departure; for although there is not one rule of morality for a nation, and another for an individual; and although, as individuals, the whole world should sympathize with, if not assist in the effort of an oppressed people struggling with despotism, still, in such an instance, a nation cannot be held to the same rule. The reason is plain enough. If one man beholds another inflicting blows and wounds upon a weaker and unresisting fellow-creature, he does not hesitate to interfere in his behalf, without stopping to inquire whether or not he may be committing a technical assault. But a nation cannot interfere in the same way. The individual who comes forward to protect his fellow is amenable to the law of the land in which he lives, and he must answer to it if he has done a wrong. But a nation is amenable to no constituted earthly authority. How far is this forbearance to be carried? Is there any limit to it? It is certain that the government of the United States did not hesitate to sympathize with the Greeks in their struggle for liberty, and were only prevented by a constitutional objection from granting them substantial national aid. To preserve a settled state of things, the United States, as has been shown, promptly interfered to prevent the invasion of Cuba by Mexico and Colombia. How far the same government ought now to interfere, again to preserve things from change, or how far it ought to forward the change, it is not necessary to discuss here.

Spain is too weak much longer to hold her Cuban possessions. It needs but to strike the blow, and independence is achieved to the island. In this instance the first step is emphatically half the journey, and that step will not long be delayed.

Cuba has the power, as well as the will and wisdom to be free. She cannot be kept forever in bonds, endowed as she is with a population of 1,200,000; with a revenue of $20,000,000; with the intercourse and light attending $60,000,000 of outward and inward trade; with a territory equal to that of the larger states;

with a soil teeming with the choicest productions; with forests of the most precious woods; with magnificent and commanding harbors; with an unmatched position as the warder of the Mexican Gulf, and the guardian of the communication with the Pacific; Cuba, the queen of the American islands, will not consent always to remain a manacled slave, and when the chains are to break, the United States can no more say, "Cuba is naught to us," than Cuba can detach herself from her anchorage in the portals of the American sea, or her sentinelship over against the entrance of the thousand-armed Mississippi.

Then arises the question, what is to become of Cuba?

She will remain independent; she will come under the protection of England; or, she will form one of the confederated United States.

So far as the interests of Cuba are concerned, a connection with England of the advantageous character which that country would inevitably grant to the island, or annexation to the United States, would be more for its welfare and prosperity, than for her to maintain the position of solitary independence. It is rational, then, to suppose she would adopt one of the two remaining positions.

That Cuba shall ever fall under the power or influence of England, is a thing simply out of the question. The United States cannot permit any European power to erect a Gibraltar which shall command both north and south, and which can at any moment cut in two the trade between the Gulf and Atlantic states, and break up at pleasure the sea communication between New Orleans and New York. In a military point of view, Cuba locks up in a closed ring, the whole sweep of the Mexican Gulf. Its seven hundred miles of coast is one mighty fortress; each one of its hundred hill-crowned bays is a haven of shelter to an entire navy, and an outpost to sentinel every movement of offence and to bar out every act of hostile import.

Standing like a warder in the entrance of the Gulf of Mexico, yet stretching far to the east, so as to overlook and intercept any unfriendly demonstration upon either of the great thoroughfares to South America or the Pacific, it is in a position to overawe the adjacent islands, and watch and defend all the outside approaches to the Isthmus routes to the Pacific, while it guards the portals of the vast inland sea, the reservoir of the Mississippi and Mexican trade, the rendezvous of California transit, and, what has not yet been duly heeded, the outlet of an immense though new-born mineral wealth, which is yet to control the metal markets of Christendom.

In short, it makes the complete bulwark of the Mexican Gulf, and only leaves to it two gates; one between Cape Antonio, the western extremity of the island, and Cape Catoche, which advances from the coast of Yucatan to meet it, and forms a strait less than 100 miles wide; and the other between Hicacos, the most northern point of Cuba, and Cape Sable, the southern extremity of Florida, but a little more than 100 miles apart, and between which passes the "Old Channel" of the Bahamas.

Half a dozen steamers would bridge with their cannon the narrow straits between Yucatan and the west point of Cuba, and between Florida and Matanzas on the north, and seal hermetically to every aggressive stranger the entire coast circle of the American Mediterranean. This simple geographical fact constitutes Cuba the key of the Gulf, and it would be felt if it passed into the grasp of a strong and jealous rival. England, firmly resting on Cuba, and with Jamaica and the Bahamas to flank her steam operations, would have full retreat and succor for her fleets, and would be able at need to concentrate the force of an empire against the coasting trade. With such a firm and convenient cover as that island, with its self-defended coast and secure harbors, she could face, Janus-like, in every direction. With Canada and the Bermudas—raised for that purpose into a strong naval station—opposite our centre on the Atlantic, and half way between those strong extremes, she would present a dangerous front to the whole northern coast, while she executed the bold threat of her minister, to "shut up the Gulf of Mexico, cut in twain the commerce between it and the Atlantic states, and close the mouth of the Mississippi and its hundred tributaries to the trade and assistance of the shipping and manufacturing states." But strike Cuba—the central and noblest jewel—from this diadem of power, and her broken circlet of American strongholds is no longer formidable.

England—controlling Cuba on the north as she claims to control the Mosquito shore on the south, and mistress of Balize on the west as she is of Jamaica on the east—would be the arbitress of the Caribbean Sea, even now almost her own, and well guarded by her long array of Leeward and Windward Islands from other intrusion.

The same steam fleets that watch, and the same island key that locks and unlocks the Gulf of Mexico, with the long chain of rivers and states depending on it, also watches the inlets of the Caribbean and locks or unlocks the gates of the Pacific. Cuba, the queen of the Antilles, unrolls her long line of coast exactly in the path to the Pacific, whether by the Gulf or Isthmus; and whoever holds her, commands the great highway to Mexico and South America, to Oregon, California, and the Pacific.

In view of all this, can the United States permit England to control Cuba? As well might England give up to the United States the command of the entrance to the English Channel and the Irish Sea. In short, it is a question about which there can be no argument. It is settled by the mere statement of the case.

But, in conclusion, what inducements has Cuba,

when independent, to become one of the states of the American confederacy; and what advantages will the United States reap in admitting Cuba into that confederacy? Enough has been said of the geographical situation of Cuba, when speaking of the tremendous power the possession of the island would give to England. Cuba seems placed, by the finger of a kindly Providence, between the Atlantic and the Mexican seas, at the crossing point of all the great lines of an immense coasting trade, to serve as the centre of exchange for a domestic commerce as extensive as the territory of the Union, and as free as its institutions. It is only after a careful study of the incredible extent and variety of the products of thirty states, with all their grades of climate, and in the whole circumference of their natural and manufactured wealth, and then only with the map of North America distinctly before the eye, that the importance of Cuba as a point of reception and distribution can be fairly understood.

From the moment Cuba becomes an integral portion of the United States, all the exactions and oppressions which now weigh so heavily upon it, will be at an end. The island would enter at once into the enjoyment of civil and religious liberty; and with her ports open to the commerce of the world—her inhabitants educated and religiously impressed—her soil cultivated to its full capability—her products sent to an unrestricted market—and under the influence of the moral and political force which are the vital elements of the American Constitution—she would become the most prosperous of the states.

On the other hand, the advantages to be obtained by the United States by the annexation of Cuba, are incalculable.

If annexation was fully and freely established, Cuba would be as valuable to this confederacy as New York itself. As an outpost, vital to American trade and defence, and as a centre of transit and exchange, Cuba would grow in importance to the whole family of the confederation, in even measure with the growth of the states on the Pacific, and the rising tide of the oriental business which the flag of the Union is about to lead from Asia across the Isthmus. She lies exactly in the track of the golden current, and none of the states are, like her, in a position to watch and defend every inlet and outlet.

In the circle of production, essential to a home supply, always sure, and independent of foreign interference, Cuba can fill nobly the remaining gap, with her coffee, cocoa, and tropical fruits. In this, too, she would serve all her sister states, for she would sell to every one, and buy of every one, which is not true of the special product of any other state. She would also add as much as the Union really needs of sugar lands, and would make that, henceforth, a strong and distinct feature in the national balance of interests.

A new sectional interest always implies another mediator in the councils of the confederation—a proved truth in favor of the permanent equilibrium of the Republic, which the opponents of annexation refuse to take fairly into account. The manufacturing east, the wheat and cattle-raising west, the commercial middle states, the cotton-growing southwest, the rice and sugar-planting south, and, last and latest, the new-born and gigantic mineral power starting up on the great northern lakes, and seaming the continent, down to the far Pacific, with its sudden influence—have each and every one their independent sectional weight and representation, as well as a diffused reciprocal dependence on each other, and on the Union as a whole. In the perpetually recurring—but under these balance checks never fatal—state opposition, every distinct interest is a distinct guarantee for the general equity of adjustment. It has been seen in the slavery discussions how far sectional bitterness can go, when the whole Union is reduced to two parties, with no disinterested and intermediate powers between them to urge peace, and teach conciliation. Yet even in this stress it will be found, at last, that the counsels which open the way, and the votes that compel moderation and compromise, will come from almost a third interest. The states that lay along the line of division, and that are themselves, in transition from slave-holding to emancipation, will come to the rescue and forbid extreme measures. Cuba may suffer from the dispute between the free and slave cultivated states; but apart from this, she wants to come into the Union without offence to any, and to the absolute profit of every partner in the confederation. In bringing to the commonwealth a class of luxuries which every state largely demands and consumes, and which are not produced by any, she also brings to the Union fresh elements of mediation, harmony, and stable equipoise.

The money value of this circulation of natural products would be more conspicuously evident if Cuba could trade with the United States on family terms, unembarrassed by the heavy and wasteful hindrance of the Spanish tariffs. Official documents show that out of the twenty, or twenty-two millions of dollars of annual exportation into Cuba, fifteen millions are in provisions, fabrics, lumber, and materials which one or the other of the United States could better supply than any other country, but through the multitude of taxes and restrictions imposed by European policy, not more than a third of it comes from the fields and factories of this country. The industrial classes here lose by this system the stimulus of ten millions a year—sufficient to employ and support forty thousand laborers—while the Cubans only obtain, under these exorbitant imposts, about one half as much for their money as they would get in a free, fair market.

Provisions for example, such as flour, salted meats, butter, and all the etceteras of American abundance, are imported into Cuba to the amount of nine millions of dollars annually, and all are loaded with duties that average 34 per cent., and what with delays, high appraisals, tonnage duties, local exactions, and retail taxes, cost more than double the just market price by the time they reach the table of the consumer. American flour from American ships pays a duty of $10,50 a barrel to "protect" the *inferior* article from Spain, and in consequence, none but the rich in Cuba can afford to eat good wheat bread; while in open family reciprocity, American agriculturists would yearly be called upon to supply a million barrels of flour to its 1,200,000 inhabitants.

New England is not less concerned in unbinding this trade, for besides the nine millions which should be paid to the farmers of this country, and the two millions in metals, implements, and machinery, which of right should float to her from down the Ohio and Mississippi, Cuba annually requires cotton and woolen fabrics, and ready-made furniture and apparel, to the invoice value of three millions more, all of which New England looms and mechanics should create. Fifteen millions are therefore imported into Cuba which the citizens in the mining, manufacturing, and agricultural states should supply, and which the ships of the commercial section should convey; and this mass of needful food, raiment, furniture, and implements for house and land, when broken up in detail, and overwhelmed at each step with fresh impositions, do not cost the Cubans less than thirty millions of dollars.

By reason of this system of preventions, the shipping interest can only employ 476,000 tons in a year in this trade, for which it pays $1,50 a ton duty to Spain —while it would find advantageous service at once for a million of tons, if the ports of the island were free to this country.

This brief outline of the domestic and pecuniary inducements to annexation is based on official data, and it is kept within the mark for the convenience of using round numbers. From this it may be deduced whether the United States would gain or lose by the accession of Cuba.

On the other hand, with a multiplied population, with all her fountains of wealth open, with all her elements of prosperity developed, who can fix the limits to the benefits which will arise to Cuba, to America, and to the United States?

In conclusion, it must not be understood that the annexation of Cuba to the United States is advocated, without regard to the rights of Spain, merely because it would be advantageous on both sides. As between Spain and Cuba, the former has forfeited every right to her supremacy over the latter. This, however, does not justify an unlawful interference on the part of the United States. But this country must look to it, when the island shall become free from Spanish dominion—an event to take place speedily—that, in the words of the late distinguished ex-President, John Quincy Adams, "Cuba does not fall into the hands of any other European power."

It is the natural right—it is the solemn duty of the United States to watch over the interests of Cuba. The present captain-general has threatened to emancipate and arm the African slaves in case of the least movement on the part of the Cubans. Who can regard with any thing but horror this most outrageous, most fiendish avowal? Would the United States permit this? Dare the United States permit this? Who can look back to the enormities and awful excesses of St. Domingo, and hesitate for an answer? What, then, is to be done? Cuba will undertake her freedom, and that speedily; the captain-general will be proud to make good his threat, and what then? It is with a shudder that this picture is contemplated; but the struggle is close at hand, and cannot be delayed.

There is one method by which all the difficulties and

perplexities attending the Cuban question can be avoided; by which Cuba shall be free, and Spain content; by which Cuba shall join the United States, and England have no cause to complain; by which an entire revolution shall be effected in the island, and no blood be spilled.

One method there is by which all this may be accomplished, viz., the purchase of Cuba from Spain by the United States. Applying carefully what has been said in the preceding pages; as to the advantages resulting to the island and to the Union by the incorporating of the former into the latter, and the inadequacy of Spain to hold her colony longer in subjection; to the question whether it is not best for Spain to sell, and the United States to purchase Cuba, no one can hesitate for a decision.

On the cabinet at Washington, with the President at their head—on Congress assembled there—a heavy responsibility rests. It is in their power by a firm but prudent, a just but conciliating course, to save a people from the conflict of a revolution, which is certainly close at hand—a revolution bloody and desperate from the nature of the elements which shall compose it—and place them on an equal footing with the states of the confederacy, while, at the same time, they protect Spain by paying for a colony which would otherwise be absolutely lost to her.

That negotiations may be successfully carried through which shall have this consummation for their object, should be the devout prayer of the philanthropist.

Map; showing the relative situation of Cuba, and other West India Islands, and different parts of the United States.

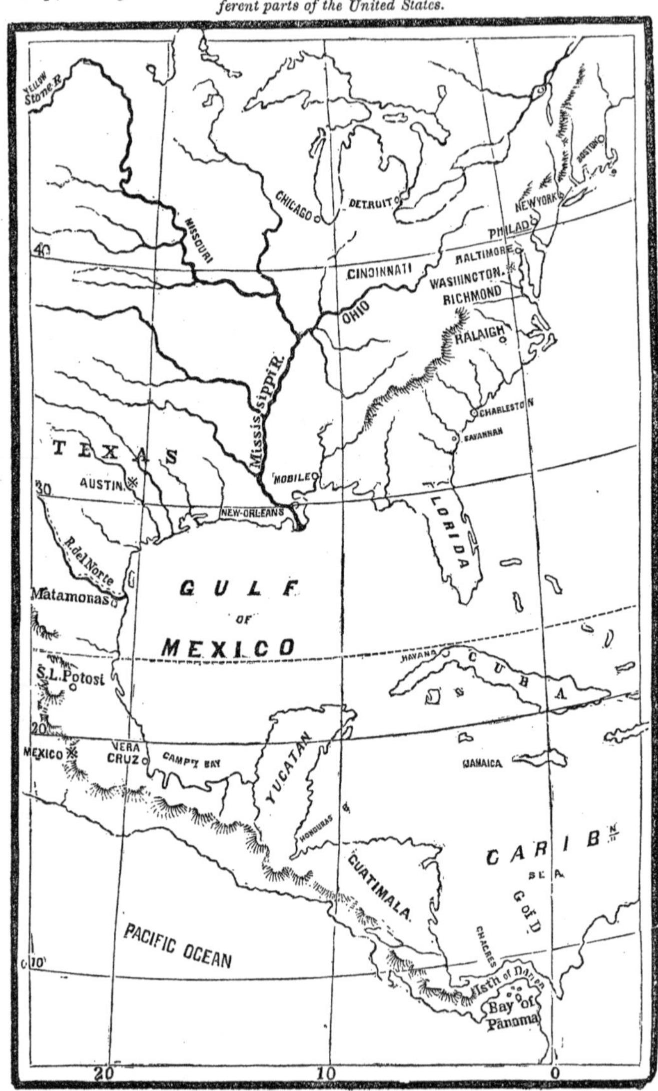

APPENDIX.

No. I.

Cuba, the largest of the greater Antilles extends from Cape Mayzi on the east to Cape St. Antonio on the west, in a curved line of 790 miles. It is 117 miles wide, in the broadest part, from Cape Maternillos Point on the north to the western point of Mota Cove on the south, twenty-one miles east of Cape Cruz. The narrowest part of the island is twenty-two miles, from the mouth of *Bahia del Mariel* on the north to the Cove of Mayana on the south. From Havana to Batabano it is twenty-eight miles. Near the centre of the island, the breadth north and south is about seventy-five miles.

The periphery of the island, following a line the less tortuous, and cutting the bays, ports, and coves at their mouth, is 1719 miles, of which 816 are on the north, and 903 on the south. Its area is about 55,000 square miles; and taking into the estimate the adjacent islands or keys which belong to it, it is 64,000 square miles.

The form of the island is exceedingly irregular, approaching that of a long, narrow crescent, the convex portion of which looks toward the arctic pole. Her situation in regard to said pole is nearly from east by south, to west by northwest. It is the most westerly of the West India Islands, and her western part is placed advantageously in the mouth of the Mexican Gulf, leaving two spacious entrances. the one to the northwest 124 miles wide, between Point Hicacos, the most northerly of the island, and Point Tancha or Cape Sable, the most southerly of East Florida. The other entrance into the Gulf to the southwest is ninety-seven and a half miles in its narrowest part, between Cape St. Antonio of Cuba, and Cape Catoche, the most salient extremity of the peninsula of Yucatan. From Cape Mola or St. Nicholas in the island of St. Domingo, the eastern extremity of Cuba, or Mayzi Point, is separated by a channel forty-two miles wide.

From Mayzi to great Enagua, the nearest of the Lucayas or Bahama Islands, the distance to the northeast is forty-five miles. From Point Lucrecia, in Cuba, to the most easterly point of the great Bank of Bahama in the old Bahama channel, called Santo Domingo's Key, thirty-four miles. From *Punta del Ingles*, on the south of Cuba, to the nearest point of the northern coast of Jamaica the distance is seventy-five miles.

Cuba contains the following ports on the north,* viz.: Guadiana, *Bahia Honda*, Cabana, Mariel, *Havana*, *Matanzas*, Cardenas, Sagua la Grande, San Juan de los Remedios, Guanaja,† *Nuevitas*, Nuevas Grandes, Manati, Puerto del Padre, Puerto del Mangle, Jibara, Jururu, Bariai, Vita, *Naranjo*, Sama Banes, *Nipe*, *Leviza*, Cabonico, *Tanamo*, Cebollas, Zaguaneque, Zaragua, Taco, Cuyaguaneque Navas, Maravi, Baracoa,‡ and Mata: thirty-seven in all.

On the south, Batiqueri, *Puerto Escondido*, *Guantanamo*, *Santiago de Cuba*, Mota, Manzanillo, Santa Cruz, Vertientes, *Masio*, Casilda, *Jagua*, Ensenada de Cortez, and Ensenada de Cochinos: thirteen in all.

* Those marked with *italics* are spacious bays, affording anchorage to ships of the line.

† This was the first place on the island visited by Columbus, October 28th, 1492.

‡ This was the first town built on the island by the Spaniards, under Diego Velasquez, in the year 1511, and till 1522 was reckoned the capital.

There are besides some other anchorages, good for small vessels. It must be observed with astonishment, that a great many of these fine harbors are deserted, without a single fisherman's hut.

The climate of the island cannot be more pleasant, as well in spring as in winter. In the latter prevails what we call *la seca*, dry weather. The rainy season begins in May, and continues until November.

The annexed tables of the rates of Fahrenheit's thermometer, will afford an illustration of the almost uniform temperature of the climate of Cuba.

MEAN TEMPERATURE.

			deg.	min.
Mean temperature of the year at Havana and northern part, near the sea,			77	00
"	"	at Havana the warmest month,	82	00
"	"	" the coldest month,	70	00
"	"	in the interior for the year, where the land rises from 600 to 1050 feet above the level of the sea,	74	00
"	"	in the coldest month,	62	30
"	"	for the year at Santiago de Cuba,	80	30
"	"	for the warmest month,	84	00
"	"	for the coldest month,	64	00

EXTREME TEMPERATURE.

	deg.	min.
At Havana it is cold when at	70	00
The coldest day at Havana has been	60	30
The warmest day " "	92	00
In the interior, the thermometer many times has sunk to	53	00
And even to	50	00
In the grottos and caves near St. Antonio and Beitia, and on the Chorrera Creek,	71	30
In a well at the depth of 300 feet,	77	00

The vegetable soil of the island may be said to rest almost universally on one great mass of calcareous rock, of a porous and unequal character. (*Seborucos* or *Mucara.*) Near the middle of the northern coast, a slaty formation is to be seen, on which the calcareous rock seems to rest.

As to the fertility of the land in Cuba, little can be said which may be new, it being so well known that it is almost proverbial. An area of 65,000 square miles, equivalent to nearly 34,560,000 acres, the greater part of which are of the first quality for cultivation, and a great portion of them still remain uncultivated, are circumstances which offer to every emigrant fond of labor, a vast field to exert his efforts in, and the prospect of a very brilliant reward.

With respect to the salubriousness of the country, it is usually remarkable, and particularly so in the interior of the island. It is certain that in the largest towns situated near the coasts, during the intense heats of the summer season, it is usual for the yellow fever to make its appearance; but besides this being not, as it formerly was, a mortal disease, thanks to the actual improvements in medicine, its attacks are almost surely avoided by observing a good hygienic regimen.

The population of Cuba does not correspond to its area, nor to the infinite advantages offered by its climate and its riches, nor to the time since which it was constituted a colony.

The statement on the following page was made out in accordance with the official accounts and census of the government of Cuba.

From that statement it appears that the white population of the island has only increased in five years, in 7476 individuals, while that of the colored people has decreased, in the same space of time, in 116,348 individuals, of which 3612 belong to the free class.

POPULATION OF CUBA IN 1846

DEPARTMENTS.	WHITES.			FREE PERSONS OF COLOR.			SLAVES.			GRAND TOTAL.
	Males.	Females.	Total.	Males.	Females	Total.	Males.	Females.	Total.	
Western -	133,968	110,141	244,109	28,964	32,730	61,694	140,131	87,682	227,813	533,616
Central -	62.262	52,692	114.954	17,041	17.074	34,115	32,425	14,560	46.985	196.054
Eastern -	34,753	31,951	66,704	26,646	26,771	53,417	28,475	20,506	48,981	169,082
Total -	230,983	194,784	425,767	72,651	76,575	149,226	201,031	122,748	323,779	898,752

POPULATION OF CUBA ACCORDING TO THE RETURN IN 1841.*

DEPARTMENTS.	Whites: Males.	Whites: Females.	Whites: Total.	Free persons of color: Males.	Free persons of color: Females	Free persons of color: Total.	Slaves: Males.	Slaves: Females.	Slaves: Total.	Grand Total.
Western -	135,079	108,944	244,023	32,726	33.737	66,463	207,954	113,320	321,274	631,760
Central -	60,035	53,838	113,873	15,525	16,154	31,579	34 939	15.217	50,156	195,608
Eastern -	32,030	28,365	60,395	27,152	27.344	54,796	38,357	26,708	65,065	180,256
Total -	227,144	191,147	418,291	75,703	77,135	152,838	281,250	155,245	436,495	1,007,624

* Vide "Resumen del Censo de Poblacion de la Isla de Cuba.—Habana, 1842."

Population of some of the principal cities and towns on the island, according to the census made in 1841 *and in* 1846.

	1841.	1846.	Increase.	Decrease.
Havana - - -	137,498	106,968		30,530
Puerto Principe -	24,034	19,168		4,866
Santiago de Cuba -	24,753	24,005		748
Guines - - -	2,515	2,612		912
Matanzas - -	18,991	16,986		2,005
Cardenas - -	1,828	3,103	1,275	
Cienfuegos - -	2,437	4,324	1,887	
Trinidad - -	12,718	13,222	464	
Villa Clara - -	6,132	5,837		295
Santi Spiritus - -	9,484	7,424		2,060
St. Juan de los Remedios	4,313	4,106		207
Nuevitas - -	1,352	1,222		132
Manzanillo - -	3,299	3,780	481	
Bayamo - -	7,480	4,778		2,207
Holguin - -	4,199	3,065		1,132
Baracoa - -	2,605	1,853		732

The natural riches of the island are immense, many resources of which still lie unexplored. Sugar, tobacco, and coffee are the three principal branches which have hitherto absorbed, and will continue to command, the united efforts of industry and capital, as long as the increase of population shall require no other veins, which though less important are still rich and productive.

In her vegetable kingdom she need envy none. The catalogue of her indigenous alimentary plants is large, to say nothing of exotics. In grains, excluding coffee, she has rice, corn, and wheat; also, every variety of vegetable; in roots, the name, the yuca, the boniato, the malanga, the sagu, the ararut, etc. (all indigenous), besides potatoes, onions, and garlic; and others of the horticultural class.

The different varieties of fruit-trees are very numerous, as in all tropical climates. Plantains, orange-trees, pines, and lemons, in great variety, cocoa-nuts, all these are well known and esteemed in the United

States; but could the following reach this market, they would be no less appreciated, the anon, the zapote, the mamey, the guanabana, the guyaba, and other varieties, not including wildings. The pasturages are extensive, abundant, and perennial.

Cuba is well provided with the best qualities of building timber; among which are the acana, the jucaro, the oak, cedar, etc. In valuable woods the island no less abounds; fustic and brazil-wood for dying, is a principal source of wealth, in the eastern division. With regard to other varieties of the vegetable kingdom, the following paragraph from a recent number of a periodical of the island, will throw some light:

"Many persons believe that various natural productions imported into the island of Cuba (and for which we pay so exorbitantly), could not be raised here to advantage. It is an error, since we now have before us a piece of a cinnamon-tree which has the same smell, color, and taste as the imported, and yet is the product of a plantation in the jurisdiction of Santiago de Cuba. On the same soil may be seen nearly all the fruits of Europe and Asia, including cloves, oregano, and pepper."

The medicinal plants also are in great abundance, and are very efficacious.

The riches of the mineral kingdom have hitherto not been sufficiently explored, to make known their extent. Copper mines are now being worked to great advantage, in the Eastern Department; they are also found in all parts of the island, as had been proved by researches in the neighborhoods of Matanzas, Villa Clara, Cienfuegos, etc. Only a few months ago, a rich mine of lead with silver was discovered which promises to be very profitable. In the Western Department there are rivers (such as the Arcos or Cuevas de San Antonio), which deposit on their banks that same sand of native gold, in search of which thousands are now flocking to the distant shores of California.

Coal is also found in the neighborhood of Havana and in other parts of the island; and with the produce of Guanabacoa, steamships have always been supplied.

On all the coasts of Cuba, principally on the northern, are found immense deposits of salt, which would open a profitable fountain to labor and industry, were it not for the exorbitant duties imposed by the government, levying a tax of $2,50 per fanega (200 lbs.)

There is also an abundance of sulphur, loadstone, granite, clay, flint, crystal, and marble. This latter is one of the principal branches of wealth, in the Isle of Pines, where the quarries of O'Donnel have been worked to great advantage.

The animal kingdom is not less prolific. Exquisite fish abound on all the coasts, rivers, and streams; an endless variety of wild fowl people the groves and lakes; the luxurious vegetation of the soil affords ample nourishment to immense flocks and herds, which multiply abundantly in the meadows and inclosures.

No. II.

The following statement comprehends the details relative to those articles of commerce which by their value as branches of the public wealth in the United States, and by their large consumption in the island of Cuba, are of the highest mercantile importance, and are of great interest to all the industrial classes, agricultural and manufacturing as well as commercial. The details are given of the duties with which each of these articles are burdened by the tariff of the government of Cuba, the mode of valuation so exaggerated as to double and triple the amount of the duties, etc., etc.

Summary of the importation of certain articles that have a large consumption in Cuba, produced by the United States; to which is added a classification of the prices on which they are valued by the tariff of Cuba, and the duties charged on them:

Article	Valuation		per cent.
Joist or scantling, per 1000 feet,	$20		27½
Tar, per bbl.	3		do.
Ploughs, each	6		do.
Rice, per qq.	6		33⅓
Morocco, per doz.	7	50	do.
Codfish, qq. lbs.	3	50	27½
Plaids, Scotch, not exceeding 38 inch., per yd.	0	25	33
Trunks, leather, each	8		33
" covered with hide	4		33⅓
Flannels, coarse, 6-4 yd., per yd.	0	31	do.
" " to 58 in width, per yd.	0	50	do.
Hogsheads, each	2		27½
Hogshead shooks	1		do.
Half boots, pair	3	50	33⅓
Boots, "	5		do.
Brass, manufactured, qq.	37	50	33
Mackerel, per bbl.	4	50	27½
Geldings, each	150		33⅓

Item	Value	per cent.
Copper boilers, qq.	$37 50	27½
Settees, wood, each	10	33½
Negro cloths, per yd.	3	do.
Preserved meats, per lb.	0 50	do.
Salt beef, per bbl.	9	do.
Pork, "	14	do.
Willow wagons, each	12	do.
Carts, "	100	do.
Straw wagons, "	4	do.
Hogs, live, "	10	do.
Baskets, "	1	27½
Copper nails, per qq.	25	do.
Copper, manufactured, per qq.	37 50	33½
Russia sheeting, ordinary, per yd.	0 06¼	do.
Cabs, gigs, etc.	400	do.
Bureaus, each	25	do.
Small bureaus,	12 50	do.
Cotton rope or cord, per piece	0 06¼	do.
Staves, per 1000	25	do.
Floor matting, per yd.	0 25	
Oakum, per qq.	4	33½
Fringe, cotton, per piece	1	do.
" silk, per yd.	0 25	do.
Flannels, "	0 21	do.
Blankets, each	1 25	do.
Corn meal, per bbl.	5	do.
Flour, " duty, $10 50		
Sugar moulds, per doz.	6	do.
Soap, per bbl.	2	do.
Cordage, per qq.	12	do.
Pianofortes, each	300	27½
Bricks, per 1000	6	33½
Valise, leather, each	6	do.
" for horsemen, each	2	do.
Cotton shawls, per doz.	4 50	do.
Silk " ordinary, each	2	27½
Stockings, cotton, per doz.	3 50	33½
" wool, "	4	do.
Merino, not exceeding one yard wide	0 37	do.
Tables, card, one leaf	10	do.
" " two leaves,	12	do.
Candlewick, per arr.	6 25	do.
Cotton handkerchiefs, per doz.	1 75	do.
Potatoes, per bbl.	2 50	27½

			per cent.
Ruled paper, not exceeding 26 inches	-	$6	33½
" white, " " "	-	5	do.
" " " 30 "	-	8	do.
" letter	-	2 50	do.
Shot, per qq. - - - - -	-	5	27½
Powder, " - - - - -	-	18	do.
Oars, per 100 ft. - - - - -	-	6 25	do.
Bags, per doz. - - - - -	-	2 25	do.
Silk sewing thread, per lb. - -	-	3	do.
Napkins, per doz. - - - - -	-	0 75	33½
Mahogany chairs, per doz. - -	-	50	do.
Maple " " - -	-	31	do.
Ordinary " " - -	-	15 50	do.
Saddles - - - - - -	-	17	do.
Hats, each - - - - - -	-	3	do.
Boards, pine, per 1000 - - -	-	20	27½
" maple, " - - -	-	25	do.
Shingles, " - - -	-	3 75	do.
Sperm candles, per qq. - - -	-	32	do.
Tallow " " - - -	-	12	do.
Shoes, men's or boys', per doz. -	-	15	33½

Summary of the articles of importation charged with duties, the way in which they are taxed, and those which are free.

The duty of 33½ per cent. is imposed on	824 articles.
" 27½ " "	1908 "
" 2 to 7½ " "	13 "
Free from duties - - - - - -	25 "

☞ The articles not valued, nor precisely taxed by the tariff, are appreciated discretionally, and charged with duties according to the prices assigned to them.

This document alone, if examined with attention, will be sufficient to demonstrate plainly the innumerable and grave injuries which the producing classes of the United States, and the consumers of Cuba, suffer by the colonial system of Spain, which can find no better means for filling the royal coffers than multiplying the impost with which it fetters, if it does not annihilate, the commerce of its rich colony.

No. III.

Reply to a pamphlet, entitled, " Thoughts on the Annexation of Cuba to the United States, by Don Antonio Saco," addressed to him by one of his friends.

Preceded by applause from a quarter whence the productions of Saco had never before obtained it, we have seen a pamphlet entitled " Thoughts," etc., the work of the distinguished Bayamere, who is the honor and pride of his country. It would be needless to dissemble the pain experienced by the truly Cuban party, on seeing voluntarily and spontaneously separated from their ranks a man of so high value, and still more painful must it some day be to Saco, to find that the prophetic part of his paper is marked by the same fallacy which more than once has accompanied his political annunciations. Happily for the eventual fate of Cuba, it is not dependent on the opinions of any one man, howsoever high his authority may stand, and least so of those of one who, notwithstanding his genius and acquirements, is controlled by blind fanaticism. Linked, as the fate of Cuba is, with that of the fortunate people who surround her, relying on the progress of republican institutions, and on the philanthropic cosmopolitism of the neighboring commonwealths, and on the American beneficent policy contrasted with that of Europe, which is tyrannical in its exercise in this hemisphere, she will fulfill her destiny notwithstanding the only obstacle, exercising a moral influence, as yet presented in its path, which is the pamphlet of Mr. Saco.

Before continuing in this ungrateful task, I wish to

acknowledge the embarrassment I experience on account of the inequality of a contest with one enjoying a European name as a writer; the strength of my convictions, and the urgency and gravity of the subject, must be my excuse.

Of a certainty, the friends of the unfortunate Saco will not be the ones to accuse him of receding in his views through apostasy, or of staining his honorable career by being sold to any party. The explanation of his conduct is much more natural and in harmony with himself, and it will appear altogether so if we first examine what constitutes ultra radicalism in Europe and democracy in America.

During the past twenty years the political passions of the European countries being calmed, and they all enjoying uninterrupted peace, the extreme ultra liberal banner, of a nature speculative rather than active or profound, adopted for its own in Europe the cause of the emancipation of the negroes; and to this school, whose errors had always their origin in its fanaticism, Mr. Saco belongs. Its followers assumed, as a fact, the want of good faith on the part of the slaveholders, who demanded time and preparatory measures for a change in the condition of the slaves; and in order to surmount their opposition, they always resisted the idea of colonial independence, because they understood that to secure prompt emancipation nothing could be more expedient than an authority distant, European, free from the influence of the colonists, and subject to that of the British government, and abolitionary disturbers of the Eastern Continent. Experience has shown the precision of this calculation; violent emancipations have already taken place, or are expected in the several colonies governed from Europe, and in them property, the value of which depends on slavery, is constantly suffering from uncertainty and depreciation. In the United States, on the contrary, the moral progress of the enslaved race, and of the legislation which regulates the same,* is slow but certain, and the property of this nature does not exhibit in the market the absolute impossibility of being sold, or the unexpected depression of value which affects them with us at each political transition of the metropolis.

Let us now see what constitute the banners of progress in the North American Republic.

The democratic majority of the United States supports political, religious, and commercial freedom, and believes in the philanthropic mission of their country to extend the same throughout this hemisphere; and at the same time acknowledge that slavery is *constitutional* and beyond the reach of abolitionary cabal, but not beyond the moral influence of civilization which slowly prepares its peaceful termination. Such is, in my view, the expression of public opinion in the United States, of that opinion which, being the result of the contest of of parties, guides the acts of the government. The democracy of the South is distinguished by their wisdom, their daring, and the tenacity and address with which they exert their influence in the counsels of the nation, and defend their rights over their slave property.

I would have wished to have succeeded in drawing the above sketch so as to explain the position in which Mr. Saco appears at this moment, and why he dislikes annexation to a government which does not assign an absolute importance to his *negrophitism*. We will now go on to examine his pamphlet. His opposition to annexation is founded on his regret for *Cuban nationality*, which would become extinct, and on the dangers attending the change, although he acknowledges the material advantages which would result from the act.†

The *Hispano-Cuban* nationality should be adorned

* The greater part of the asperity of the Code Noir has disappeared.—*Debon's Magazine*, 1846.

† This concession is very important, and quite distinct from what we read in the official gazette of Havana, wherein it is stated that the fountains of wealth would be dried up by annexation.

with the characteristics of Spanish. It should love its origin. It should reproduce its habits, glory in its historical remembrances—in the institutions and deeds of their people and of their government. As long as Cuba be a colony, can the spirit of national unity be aroused without laws, or institutions, or public life, or political dignity? Can we glory in any thing similar to that which despoils and oppresses us? Can it be that the establishment of a Cuban nationality for the future, requires of us to preserve the dependence which is physically and morally ruining us?—that is to say, the present political system! Can we expect from an ignominious school of progressive degradation noble and generous effects? Will it be said that Spain will follow the impulse of the age—granting, in imitation of the other European powers, institutions to Cuba, and that by this means another sentiment of Cuban nationality will be nourished? I answer that this is morally impossible. Spain, or rather the cabinet of Madrid, will ever keep the only order of things advantageous for the ministers. To give institutions to Cuba is to put a limit to fiscal demands, to the inexhaustible mine of grants and monoplies; to the security of favorite claimants on the treasury; to the monopoly of flour, and of the Spanish flag. To give institutions is to invite emigration of the white population of other countries, to establish militia, and to put a stop to that uninterrupted outpouring of forced recruits, who impoverish Spain at home without insuring her dominion here. To give institutions is to open the eyes of the Europeans as well as of the Creoles, and to inform the industrious and honest class, no matter where they are from, that the fruit of their labor disappears under the irresponsible rule of the officials of government. To give institutions is to do away with the economical obstacles which impede the agricultural development of Cuba. It is thereby to give her the means to compete with all countries producing sugar, and to raise her to that position which is her due in this hemisphere. To give institutions is to secure slave property, and to improve the condition of the slaves which is the immediate consequence of that security. Lastly, to give institutions to Cuba is to substitute relations of reciprocal advantages for the tyranny of the strongest, thereby making the metropolitan court indifferent in holding the reins of the government.

Is there any one of these effects of institutions which is not opposed to the policy on which Spain grounds her dominion? When all the officials employed, or, if you please, the participators in the spoils of the island, unite in praising the liberality and the advantages of the present system, is there any sense in anticipating change or reform? What less could be expected from a government having some self-respect, not merely for the weal of the American subjects, but to preserve the unity of the administration of distant provinces, and to consolidate their dependence, than the establishment of a colonial ministry? This was the only request of the Cubans in their paper published in Madrid, under the title of the Observador (de Ultramar), edited, with courtesy and talent, by Senor de Armas. Was the object attained? If this demand, which was useful to the Spanish nation, was not granted because it was opposed to the personal advantages of the several members of the cabinet, what can be expected with reference to such as are solely to benefit the colonies, however equitable and just they may be?

Were it possible to give birth to a Hispano-Cuban nationality, the first step to be taken should be to blot out the past, above all, the most recent, acts of the Spanish administration—those from whence can be inferred what is to be expected in future. To forget the policy which subjects, the administration which destroys, the barbarous cruelty which despoils and insults, and then to bring to mind the glories of ancient Spain, and awaken the love to our ancestors innate in the heart of man, would be the true, the only course. Without the previous separation, there is no hope of political reform, and while oppression is weighing upon us, the patriotism of the Cubans will only dwell upon grievances and bitter recriminations. To preach another philosophy, is not to know the spring of the human heart, "*Because the eternal laws written by nature in the heart of man* (Mr. Saco's own words) *prohibit that we should love the tyrant that oppresses; no, not even if he be our own father.*" But take away from the Spanish creole the weight of his political degradation, and the obstacles curtailing the fruits of his industry, and he will be observed, as it has happened in South America, to turn his eyes to the land of his forefathers, and to press to his heart sacred ties which, on the basis of equality, cannot vilify him. Spanish America after her independence, and Louisiana after her annexation to the United States, gave testimony to this yearning of the Americans toward the European races from whence they derived their origin.

The last-named country has so many points of resemblance and contact with our island, and its history so fully contradicts the inferences of Mr. Saco, that it has seemed to me the most victorious refutation, to lay before him facts which are something more than groundless prophecies. Forty-five years are now elapsed since the First Consul sold Louisiana. Has her French nationality been forgotten? Have French habits, customs, and tastes been lost? Has even the trade with their ancient metropolis become diminished? We read in Marbois' history, written twenty years after the purchase, that the commerce between Louisiana and France had swelled to ten times what it had been with the colony. "Our commerce of import," said the minister of commerce, in his report to the French chambers in 1838, "however satisfactory in its development, ought to be more important yet, with a country where two thirds of the population have preserved French habits and tastes."

In our day, the domestic customs of Louisiana; the manners of her inhabitants; the public amusements on Sunday, which take place on that day in no other state in the Union; the French theatre and opera, all testify to the origin, and fondness for their ancient habits, of those citizens of the republic who are still French.

Their laws, which have gathered the good of those of Spain and France, accommodating it to the type of the new institutions, written in French, and the whole sessions of their assemblies and courts, with the speeches uttered alternately in either language, all of which is published in French, equally testify. Louisiana's very history has just been given to the public by Monsieur Gallard (1846), in the language of their fathers; on which subject the author says, "Je dirai donc que sachant que la plupart de nos Louisianaises ne lisent guere l'anglais, j'ai pensé qu'en écrivant la langue qui leur est familiere, elles seraient tentées par un sentiment de curiosité de jeter les yeux sur les pages de cette histoire, et peutetre de les lire jusqu'aux bout," etc., etc.

What else is this than the preserving of nationality, or at least of that part of the feeling which moves and satisfies the heart. Can it be said that the result will be different in Cuba? Is it the intention to alarm the Spanish race with the word absorption? Why will the Americans absorb a population of one million two hundred thousand inhabitants, when they did not do so with the seventy-six thousand inhabitants who peopled Louisiana in 1810? Can the circumstances of the time and of the soil be different? Let us see: scarcely had Louisiana become a part of the American confederacy, when she was freed from the colonial ties which embarrassed her progress, and the quantity and fertility of the lands which the new government placed within the reach of speculators and settlers, and the instantaneous appearance of her productions in the sugar market, make it evident that there existed great stimulants calculated to call American emigration, which are not to be supposed in Cuba in case of annexation; first, because Oregon, California, New Mexico, and other free states, offer greater inducements to white emigrants, without the competition of the slave, nor the obstacles of the climate; second, because we are not in possession of the immense tracts of land not appropriated, which were in abundance in Louisiana; third, because Spanish emigrants would naturally find better reception among those of their race than foreigners; fourth, because among the various signs which Cuba has of constituting in herself a nation, not to be found in the early history of that state, one is, the possession of vast capital of her own; and scarcely would the rise be foreshadowed which the new institutions would give to landed property, when the resident capitalists of the Spanish Main would be the first to compete with foreigners in speculations of this nature.* Mr. Saco supposes that the peninsular Spaniards would abandon the soil of Cuba immediately after annexation. What took place in Louisiana, with the French?

The latter were in want, in America, of an asylum with the type of their nation, where the industry of man should be unfettered by legislation. The magic of liberal institutions, therefore, produced its inevitable effect. So far from abandoning their new country, the French settlers of the colony shared the advantages of the new rule, and when the insurrection of St. Domingo took place, a large number of the fugitive colonists, in preference to other dependencies of their government, found shelter and wealth in that reflection of their distant country.

* "If I were to adjust the conditions," said Napoleon, while treating for the sale of Louisiana, "on the value which those immense territories will have for the United States, the indemnification would be without limits."

The Spaniards on both hemispheres are, perhaps, the people who more seriously suffer from having begun their political reform in a selfish and speculating age, which sneers at warm enthusiasm and patriotism. Corruption and discouragement seem to be the inseparable concomitant of the useless attempt at self-government of the large Spanish family, both in Europe and in America. When a nation, like the island of Cuba, governed by its own laws, sheltered from the scourge of intestine commotions under the mantle of the American confederacy, were to present itself to the Spanish people, with their customs and habits, peaceful, prosperous, and free, who can doubt that from all America, and even from Spain, the sons and descendants of the latter would flock to the island, and that in the concurrence of European races, which constitute the emigration from the United States, the Spanish *trunk* would preserve the supremacy which appertains to it. America is the asylum of the oppressed of all Europe, and the government of the Union, that which approaches most to perfection, by indefinitely diffusing enjoyments: her nationality is the practical realization of cosmopolitanism. The expansive views of her policy find no obstacle in the origin of her citizens. The Dutch peopled New York, the Swedes New Jersey and Delaware, the Germans Pennsylvania, the French flew to South Carolina after the revocation of the edict of Nantes, and in Louisiana and Florida the French and Spanish still preserve the usages of their ancestors. The American citizen, therefore, signifies the participator, the admirer, and defender of free institutions, and this democracy propagating its principles, which has commenced to diffuse its breath through Spanish America, is chiefly composed of Europeans. Under the shade of the splendid tree of liberty, planted in the last century, by the persecuted of the old world, all nationalities have flourished. Can it be that the Spanish race are the only one incapable of expansion, and regeneration, far from the vices, the exactions, and the privileges of despots?

Such is the extension that in these states has been given to the right of citizenship, and such the consequent political importance acquired by foreigners, that not many years ago a party came into existence called the Native Americans, who attempted to restrict the rights enjoyed by the former. This useless attempt, after having created great excitement, had to be given up, and the liberal policy became, if any thing, better established and secured, which had so much raised that people in the scale of nations.

But Mr. Saco expresses fears on account of religious belief, which we cannot comprehend, coming from him. Is Saco ignorant that the Catholic, Apostolic, and Roman religion has always existed in the United States, and is diffusing itself to a great extent? Is he ignorant that the Catholic institutions of education and beneficence shine throughout the American Union? Does he not know that the Catholic clergy presents in these states an example of unction, of wisdom, and of evangelic charity, which produces the most salutary effects on public morals; or, peradventure, in order to preserve the national type, would he wish to preserve the scandal and the ignorance which are the distinctive traits of the priests in Cuba, and even in Spain? Infidelity, absolute indifference to the truths of Christianity, and looseness of the passions constitute the morality of which we take pride in boasting. Can it be that liberty of worship should appear foreign and in bad taste to Mr. Saco? If that liberty has purified Catholicity, and raised it to the noble station which it occupies in the neighboring republic, well might these advantages compensate the want of that exclusiveness in a religion without faith, having no object but the pecuniary advantages of its ministers.

Does Mr. Saco imagine that foreign absorption would be the consequence of annexation? Let him reflect that this important act has in itself no attraction to the emigrant; outlets to be opened to the exertions and natural scope of the human mind, institutions, liberty in its various applications; these are the stimuli which would induce the coming of the citizens of the neighboring republic. Let Cuba become a free republic and in that character open her doors to the whole human race, and then such as would look for a home in her territory annexed to the United States, would equally ask for an asylum in her as an independent and free state. Can it then be objected that deprived of American support, she would offer less security, stability, and, therefore, less inducement to the contemplated absorption by the latter? In that case, our better judgment would surely guide us not to sacrifice the peace and tranquillity of a people to the worship of nationality, to an idea which the tendencies of the times are fast blotting out for the benefit of humanity. The absorption which so much harasses Mr. Saco, will take place, he asserts, by the peaceful workings of the majoritics, because the Americans will form a majority when we shall appear at the electoral urns. Let us examine what happened in the neighboring state, and every body may judge for himself on this fixed and sure theme.

Eight years after the acquisition of Louisiana, its constitution was framed by a convention composed of forty representatives, of whom twenty-two were of French origin, and in the meanwhile the Louisianians had been sustained and protected in the enjoyment of freedom and their religious worship and property, and the laws in existence under the preceding governments had continued in force, all in conformity to the treaty of the 30th of April, 1803.

That constitution established the legislative power in two houses, senate and assembly. Every white citizen twenty-one years of age, and with property worth $500, and two years' residence in the state, could be elected representative. Every citizen twenty-one years of age, paying taxes, had a right to vote after one year's residence. For senator, four years' residence in the state, twenty-seven years of age, and property worth $1000 were required. Under a similar constitution would the inducements raise foreign over native or Spanish influence? But the political importance of Cuba, and her present mercantile relations with the civilized world, would call for her instantaneous settlement and quiet, and the immediate formation of her constitution without even the short respite which intervened in that of Louisiana. However great the intermediate emigration, it is idle to fear any other influence than that of our race would prevail in the establishment of the new government and the administration of the state.

Mr. Saco says he would not fear the absorption if we had a million and a half of white population, instead of 500,000. Let him consider that out of the 76,000 inhabitants which Louisiana possessed, only 42,000 were white, and, withal, that in the elections for the state department of 1843, the preponderance of the names of the ancient French families was yet preserved, while the whole population had swelled to six times their original numbers.

Well may he therefore vote for annexation in the case which he alluded to, suffocating in his breast, as he says, his national regrets. And in order to allay the intensity of his feelings, I will endeavor to revive before him some of the innovations which have been imposed upon Cuba since his absence from his native country. General Tacon, who, as Mr. Saco knows, commenced a series of encroachments on the rights of the Cubans, did not launch himself in that course which places the despotism of the sovereign in the hands of an irresponsible subaltern without some species of modesty, or some respect for public opinion. Not counting on the support of the ancient corporations of the country, he convoked meetings of proprietors, where measures of safety were discussed, and where the establishment of new taxes was solicited, and only obtained on conditions which he did not accept.

To commence from this one act, how great is the number which have followed, tracing the gradual usurpation of authority and contempt of Cuban rights. Not long since, with the single advice of one of the lieutenant-governors, the chief magistrate created a tax on the plantations for the support of jail prisoners, and this monstrous power, so varied in its attributes, was not at all embarrassed at having monopolized about the same time a profit on slaves judicially embargoed, which, had it been made available to the community, would have obviated the new impost in the very district where it was enacted.

The junta of six individuals named by the cabinet to enact the special laws for Cuba, suspended their labors, which were never recommenced, because at whatever time they should act, they would be obliged to limit the authority of the chief. As time passes, and the class of officials become more accustomed to justify their encroachment, and the opportunities of being heard and attended in their requests are taken away from the colonists, does Mr. Saco see greater chances of the reforms coming from Spain?

The faculties of the corporations have been restricted, and the filling up of their vacancies gradually made more dependent on the will of the captain-general. This has been done by means of royal orders, of secret requisitions, and of despotic acts.

The Royal Court of Justice declared itself incompetent to take cognizance of the complaint made by the corporation of Matanzas of the depredations committed by the troops during a fire, and the members of that body were fined and suspended from office by the captain-general.

The new tithe recently imposed without the advice

of the corporation of the country, as was the case with former taxation; the malice which has allowed a suit to be commenced against every owner who had to prove his exemption from the same; and the dark and corrupt dealings of the tithe gatherers, who enrich themselves on the sweat of the poor, on the economy of the wealthy, frequently defrauding the public treasury as a price of their report, allowed to play a singular unjustifiable part in the regular proceedings of the law, these are some of the astonishing signs of progress.

The liberality of the tariffs, since the ancient Consulado or Junta de Fomento has no consultive vote in the matter, is fast disappearing.*

The monopoly in the localities for the sales of meat and fish, established by Tacon, of his own will, and which at once raised the price of those necessaries of life to eighty per cent. of their value, is still in existence notwithstanding occasional conversations on the subject of their removal.†

On the occasion of the perspective want and misery, announced in consequence of the hurricane of 1844, the local authorities ventured to reduce the import duties on American rice and corn, not meddling with wheat flour, in dread of the all-powerful interest of the commerce of Santander; and these reductions were only granted for six months. A minister of finances was found who, before the expiration of the appointed time, ordered the suspension of the concession, and good faith toward foreign commerce was broken, and

* In comparing tariffs of different epochs, we cannot judge by the rates alone; the regularity and security of the contraband trade in times past, made their valuation and per centage duty in fact very moderate, and their effects very similar to that of free trade.

† Mr. Olozaza, the leader of the progressive party in Spain, proved in his defence of the corporation of Havana, that in the transaction of these sales, Tacon was moved by interested or pecuniary motives of a mysterious nature, never cleared before the public by that general. I intentionally quote the source, on account of the favorable prejudice in favor of the latter among a certain class of the American public.

the sympathy toward the afflicted colonists was met with a sneer.

The tedious course of obtaining personal licenses, and their price, have raised the charges on the citizens; have added to the insolence of the subaltern officers of the police, while the revenue of the latter, and of the only legislator in the matter, has been greatly increased.

The lottery which consisted of 17,500 numbers, has been raised to 37,500, and the drawings have likewise been increased.

On General Valdez (who is generally acknowledged to be both liberal and enlightened in his views) being apprised that the Junta de Fomento were going to make a report on the depressed state of the island, he commanded the board, through the commissioners who had called to ask his approval of their purpose, that they should abstain from so doing!

That part of the revenue drawn from the products of the industry of the country to cover the salaries, fees, and perquisites of the military, political, and civil officers of government, has been slowly and forever taken away from the native Cubans, and passed to the Europeans, who, by this cunning measure, deprive the families of the land of one of the most important sources of wealth and of influence in any community. If Mr. Saco could, by himself, examine the effect of this policy, in which the several rulers have united unhesitatingly, and if he would then compare the social importance that the creoles had when he was on the island with that which they now possess—even those who from their hierarchy he supposes might lose by annexation, how well he would understand what constitutes a true absorption, founded on the injustice and despotism of the conqueror!

The prudence and skill of the rural by-laws are at an end, as well as their observance, since the consulado has no hand in the enacting of the same, nor do the planters look after their execution.

The reports of the above-mentioned board having been remarkable for their opposition to the African slave trade, the influence of the despotic chiefs, by artful efforts and threats easier to be understood than explained, succeeded in introducing among the members speculators in the trade, and the result has been the first report decidedly opposed to white emigration which, in the present times, has emanated from that body.

From the want of police, disquietude was introduced and increased among the colored race.

Conniving at crimes and insubordinate acts of slavery, the venality of the officials and judges has been slowly nourishing the germ of servile insurrection.

The atrocious method of investigating and repressing the slave conspiracy in 1844, the horrors and inefficacy of which is now acknowledged by all, demonstrated, beyond any possible doubt, how absurd it is to deprive the class of proprietors from participating in the administration and government of a slave country.

The witchcraft and superstitious practices of the worship of savages, developed in the course of that frightful prosecution, discovered the hideous fact that not even the scant religious instruction which our fathers gave to their slaves, do our own receive, at present, at our hands. In truth, hardly can it be said that baptism is practiced; marriage is daily becoming more scarce, and the heart of the wretched slave does not even receive the comfort of faith.

The enactments regarding the colored people, contained in the by-laws of General Valdez, dangerous inasmuch as not consistent with a system in which the proprietors are excluded from the administration and defence of the country; the by-laws which, for the same class, were published by the last governor of Porto Rico, breathing cruelty and blood; the subsequent laws of the same nature recently published by his successor, announcing freedom and emancipation, and, generally speaking, the relaxation of discipline in the management of the free and enslaved blacks, which has been remarked in Cuba as either preceded or followed by excessive severity or cruelty, are so many means of keeping us alarmed, with which the abolitionists would desire ever to haunt the slave-owners, and which would not exist were the interested parties able to provide by themselves for the quiet and safety of both.

Without religious teaching, or political education, or the excitement of political ambition—without the light obtained by the interchange and freedom of thought, sordid motives of gain or a reckless routine has guided the actions of the agents of production; and while the slave trade supplied, at a low rate, the hands demanded by industry, it was found to be an insupportable weight to accompany, in the assortment of slaves on a plantation, a corresponding number of women, or to give additional care to the latter during their pregnancy, and their offspring after their birth: it has been also as bad business to take care of the sick, to prevent sickness, and to facilitate to the slaves the comfort which the most miserable of them obtains for himself as soon as he becomes free. It is by such a course that the friends of the African trade have succeeded in discrediting all essays of free labor, however partial, which have been heretofore attempted. Thus it is also that we may explain by what means the agriculture of Cuba has been productive. Reducing the price of labor, encouraging the neglect of the most sacred duties of the master, the African slave trade has in reality been the source of wealth, and the remedy which the planters found to withstand the excessive burdens which press on our productions. If they lent a sympathizing ear to the impulses of their own heart, they failed to prosper; cruelty and fortune they saw on one side, pity and ruin on the other. Let the responsibility of the results fall, not on the traders or cultivators who imported or acquired the slaves, but on those who over-taxed enterprise and industry, and sanctioned that trade which demoralizes the people, and removes farther off the regeneration of the negro. Here, then, lies the secret of the prosperity and progress of the island of Cuba; here the ability of the administration. The island might have prospered much more without building its fortunes on piles of African victims, by preserving and augmenting the number of her slaves, by natural increase, by improving their morals, and enlarging the range of their comforts under a more liberal government, and with lighter taxation. These are the advantages to be expected from annexation.

The efficacy of laws which are formed and executed under the eye of public vigilance, and the advantage of a militia which, without the expense of an army, prevents disorders, gives to slave property in the United States a security unknown in Cuba, as easily seen in the contracts, and purchases of landed property in both countries, which is a true basis for judging, not dependent on the principles or prejudices of a writer.

From so well regulated an order of things follow, in a slave country, the care of the mothers, of their offspring, and of the sick; the greater amount of individual liberty and comforts enjoyed by the slaves, and the mutual relations of confidence and affection between the master and his bondman, which have thus far disappeared in Cuba. By the suppression of the African slave trade, during nearly half a century, the neighboring republic has obtained a rare exemption from superstitious, and ungovernable, and ferocious habits; and, because more intelligent, they are less disposed to launch in insurrectionary attempts, which could, in the end, be mere vents of vengeance, always subject to inevitable and certain punishment.

From what has been said it can be proved that it is impossible to regenerate and prepare the slave gradually for any change in his condition, without the support of the owners. Abolitionism, such as we have seen, making war on property, may force a ruinous change, availing itself of the lever of the despotism of a metropolis; but it is only given to the quiet, undisturbed authority of a sovereign state to produce gradual reform in slavery, without compromising the existence of society. If this course appear too tardy for the impatience of the negrophilism of Europe, experience ought to have convinced them ere this, of the obstacles which the contrary system brings to the wealth, peace, and morality of any community. As to Cuba, where the slave population is chiefly African, and where the white portion is not permitted to be armed and formed into militia for their defence, general safety is consequently insured through a thousand privations imposed on the slaves who, as it has already been remarked, are not favored with any religious or moral instruction. There is therefore no country worse prepared for even the most distant announcement of emancipation, even in the opinion of abolitionists.

Free trade, which is another of the elements required to facilitate greater comforts to the slave, and method and implements for labor, more advantageous and economical to enterprise, thereby rejecting toilsome practices, to which the slave is subjected—how can free trade, I say, be established, while all Spain, and Mr. Saco himself, are bent on encouraging Spanish industry and trade by means of the commerce of Cuba, viz., by protective duties, and by enhanced prices?

But the island of Cuba, annexed to the American Union, might adopt a course of decided progress, combining the extension of her agriculture and commerce, and the philanthropic reforms claimed by the age, with a sacred respect to property. We have seen, in these latter days, the official press of Havana, endeavoring to sketch a dark future for slavery in that confederacy, on the occasion of the excitement created by the questions of introducing the institution in the territories recently acquired. Doubtless, it is attempted to impress on the Cuban public that the principle of non-interference in the domestic affairs of the several states is either attacked or threatened in this contest. It is therefore proper that the truth should be known as to what is contended for. The South, or the slave-holding states, hold that each one of these at the time of forming their constitution had the right to admit or reject the principle of the special institution, and that the General Congress cannot anticipate, guide, or oppose this future act of a new sovereign state. To be sufficiently courageous, therefore, to raise a cry against the very general desire of limiting slavery, in spite of the tendencies of the times, is it not a proof of the vigor of the South, and of the fact that there is no country in the world where slave property is better sheltered from the assaults of abolitionism? That which has been quoted as proof of the dangerous position of slavery, is it not what more decidedly proves the contrary? Cruelty and mystery (such as employed by the Spanish administration) are the weak arms of the pusillanimous —openness and energy, fronting our enemies, are the characteristics of a defence inspired by intelligence and conscious power.

In order to appreciate better the advantages of annexation, I will continue to avail myself of the example of Louisiana. The primitive constitution of this state granted at once to the inhabitants of it the important right of habeas corpus, the judgment by jury in civil cases at the request of either of the parties, the privilege of giving bail in all prosecutions not involving capital punishment, and lastly, the judgment by jury in all criminal cases.

"Twenty years of good government," said the distinguished and first historian of Louisiana in 1829, "have effected what could not have been accomplished in centuries under the previous prohibitory system.

General and local interests have sprung up, and advanced rapidly. The population, stationary, under an absolute government, has been trebled after the cession. * * * * After the last century, the Louisianians have better understood the wealth of the soil they possess. * * * New Orleans, founded in 1707, after dragging a languid life during almost a century, by possessing a liberal system for twenty-five years, has already become one of the most flourishing cities of America. The great facilities in her intercourse with Europe have reduced the price of all merchandise which the colony receives from thence, and pays back in her crops of corn, cotton, and sugar.*

"The lands of the interior," continues Marbois, "which were sold at the lowest rates under the French and Spanish rule, acquired a considerable value immediately after the cession. Ancient titles, forgotten during an age, were searched for with anxiety; and then it was that in the archives of the French colony of Illinois, the descendants of Philip Renaud, found the documents of the large donation which the Mississippi Company had granted to their ancestor."

Such is the vital impulse given by institutions, that the sugar lands of Louisiana, though exposed to a destructive frost, though requiring periodical replanting, and alternate rest and manuring, still have a *real* value in the market superior to those of Cuba.

The Louisianians, convinced of the immense advantages which annexation had brought to them, in February, 1825, expressed, by a unanimous resolution of the house of representatives, "their veneration toward Mr. Monroe, and their gratitude for the part he had taken in the acts which united Louisiana to the American confederacy."

* This was written twenty years ago; what could be said now, when the Mississippi river brings to the Louisianians manufactures, grain, dry goods, and merchandise of all kinds, without a custom-house, or any other intermediate cost than a moderate freight?

In the essay on the constitution of the United States, which precedes the history of Louisiana, already so much quoted, the author alludes to the formation of new settlements in the deserts, where families, assembled of their own accord, take the incipient steps in the infancy of their sovereignty. "They name their magistrates by themselves," he says, "and from districts and afterward from territories they become states. Until they acquire sufficient strength, it is necessary that Congress should guide and instruct these new communities and guard them against their own errors; and as this authority is exercised solely for their good, it is very seldom that it meets with any obstacle. The new states which are formed exist by themselves, and for themselves.

This independence and sovereign authority of the state is what Mr. Saco gives no indication of appreciating. Rarely is it that a stranger who has not observed closely the theory and practice of the American system, gives full value to the federal principle on which it rests, and which, while it unites all the states for determined objects, few in their number, and carefully explained in their nature, leaves untouched the equal and independent sovereignty which belongs to each, as also the absolute power to govern itself in all matters of internal administration and government, without interference on the part of another state, or even of the federal government. As a member in every respect equal to the rest in sovereign authority and independence, Cuba, admitted into the confederacy, would at once take the rank which belongs to her in the political world, on account of her geographical and natural advantages. From an humble and oppressed colony, trampled upon by oriental despotism, she would rise to be, like her sister republics, a nation within a nation, and for the first time would Cuban nationality, essentially Spanish in character, have an existence; while she would unceasingly draw to herself, as we have already intimated, the best class of Spanish emigrants, both from the metropolis, and the great Spanish family elsewhere. Giving to this principle of state independence, strictly adhered to in the United States, its true importance, could not Mr. Saco find, in annexation, the sure course to inspire life, activity, and character of its own, to the Cuban society?

I believe I have demonstrated that love toward our ancestors can be preserved, and, in fact, better preserved, purer and more noble, where it does not call for the sacrifice of our well-being; and also with the precedent of Louisiana, that there is no ground to fear annihilation of Spanish influence, by the *Americans*, through annexation. From what has been said, it is also definitively established that, as a European dependence, Cuba can hope for neither *quiet* nor *progress*; and lastly, that both can be reached by entering in the neighboring confederacy.

If the sketch herein traced of the posture of things be true, if the dangers surrounding Cuba are to cease with annexation to the United States, does Mr. Saco suppose that the European residents on the island will wait till it be too late to save her? They have given proofs of comprehending the danger on several occasions, one of them very recent.* It is true that late events in Europe, comparatively of a peaceful tendency, have served the views of our rulers, who take advantage of the love of their country to keep the old Spaniards in uncertainty and anxious wavering. But pictures of security, oftentimes confidently drawn, to be as often suddenly effaced, have excited misgivings and doubts, which are deeply rooted in the minds of the former. The industrious majority of them, which is not made up of the few who are conspicuously seen

* In 1841, when the agreement was proposed by the British cabinet to free the slaves; later still, on the intended sale of the island by a progressive cabinet; and lastly, at the time of the emancipation of the slaves in the French colonies.

surrounding the authorities, is identified in their interest with the creoles. Both parties are aware of their relative position, without daring to breathe the truth; they foreshadow the bond which is to bind them together in the future. A day does not pass by without thoughts flashing through the minds of the sensible portion of either band, as to the necessity of being united, and placing themselves under shelter against all vicissitudes, by becoming annexed to the American confederacy. Perhaps love of free institutions has a deeper hold in the heart of the Spanish European; perhaps a prejudice, a bare, frail wall is now separating their common interest and inclinations.

But when the rulers of a land have no other reliance for support than what is founded on error, their position is a false one. When the only thing wanted for a whole people to take a determination is the propitious opportunity, this soon presents; and what is in the minds of all, soon finds vent from thought to words and from words to action. The European Spaniards residing in Cuba know, just as well as the writer of these lines, that the sway of a distant metropolis is incompatible with the free-trade principle and the well-being of the citizens; that it must soon meet its terminus; and that the advocates of despotism and monarchy are daily losing their number and enthusiasm. They know that when free trade is established, if their commercial privileges come to an end, the sailor monopoly and other restrictive laws will also cease, and the ship-owner will be the gainer, being enabled thereby to man his vessels with greater economy; and the crews themselves will be exempted from forced services to the crown.* They know that with this and similar advan-

* England has likewise been obliged to disregard the clamor of her ship-owners—elevating by such means her mercantile marine in proportion as she took away privileges. "Protection," said her prime minister, "is the scourge of agriculture." We know that protection was the scourge of the manufactures of Spitalfields; that it ruined

tages of liberty, and their previous connection with the population, the mercantile class now settled on the island will flourish more than under the protection and restrictions of the present legislation. These restrictions, and not the want of activity and natural skill, as Mr. Saco thinks, are the cause of the backwardness of Spanish industry and commerce. What is wanting to those laborious and prudent men who, from Navarre, from Catalonia, from Arragon, from Galicia, from Andalusia, and from the whole of Spain, have come to this island, for their own advantage and that of their adopted country? What is wanting in them in order to extend and raise their commerce on a level with those who, with less toil, prosper on the borders of the Mississippi? What else than the political influence within the reach of the obscurest individual in the neighboring republic? What but to feel the worth of

our sugar colonies, and has given to Ireland misery in lieu of prosperity. In a word, protection has been the destruction of objects to which it has been granted. Like a tree, it shelters from the tempest those whom it protects, but brings down on their heads the thunder of heaven. And why should our mercantile navy be the exception to this universal law? Competition is the soul of skill. Those who never bear it are lazy and wanting in energy. They can neither avail of the example nor gain by the knowledge of others. To liberate men from competition, is to nail them on the ignorance of their fathers; to subject them to it, is to place their capacity to the test—it is to breathe into them energy and life, and to inspire them with ability. This should be equally applied to captains and sailors, and to ship-owners and other individuals. During the last seven years—which terminated in 1823—while the English navigation laws were in full vigor, the increase of the shipping amounted to five per cent. Then commenced a period of greater freedom; and the year 1842 shows an enormous increase, with this peculiar circumstance, that the shipping employed in the colonial trade, still enjoying protection, only augmented 67 per cent., while that engaged in foreign trade, under the reciprocity act, rose to 164 per cent.

	1823.	1842.	Increase.
Tonnage employed in commerce with British possessions - -	746,822	1,250,937	67 p. ct.
Tonnage employed in commerce with foreign neutral countries	802,686	2,124,333	164 "

[Economist, Nov. 27, 1847.

man and the respect due to every individual not actually convicted of some crime, even by the supreme head of the state. That democracy, independent and jealous of its own dignity, which the Biscayans practically possess, which the Arragonese hold consigned in their ancient laws, and which the Catalonians and Valencians carry stamped in their faces ; that democracy, the key to all the blessings of a nation, the path of which is quiet in America, because unobstructed by monarchical and retrograde ambitions—that is the ark of salvation for Cuba, and the bond of union for its inhabitants. Whenever it shall spring up and be understood there, the eloquent orators who shall better sustain its rights and immunities, will awaken the noble enthusiasm and the applause which is now only bestowed on a Steffanoni and a Marini. How far more elevated will the place occupied by the Cubans then be among civilized countries !

Had Mr. Saco, when discussing the dispositions of the peninsular Spaniards, taken into account the annexation symptoms manifested by them on the different occasions to which I have alluded, his opinion might command greater credit ; as it has reached us now, it too forcibly tells how long he has been away, and even now how distant from his country.

The manifest conformity, however, existing between the material interest and secret opinions of the several parties in Cuba, temporarily smothered though it may be, based as it is on the undeviating and victorious progress of democracy in America, convinces me that to obtain annexation it will not be necessary to resort to arms.

Peaceful in their habits, the Europeans, like the creoles, will not launch into a fratricidal war, injurious to their prosperity, solely to serve the class of officials or the prejudices of commercial monopoly. An order of things only supported through injustice and an armed force, is naturally on the eve of overthrow.

Good sense and the intercourse with our neighbors are doing wonders in the work of gaining partisans to pacific annexation, notwithstanding the ridiculous restrictions put to the press, and to individual liberty and action. There is no excess of credulity, therefore, in imagining that the Europeans, belonging to the industrious classes, will, on the first favorable opportunity, advocate what is their interest in common with all. The desire after freedom, impossible to satisfy white military despotism, exists; and a hope to give security to slave property, and to dispel, with one blow, the dangers attending on the actual, forced dependence, have influenced the minds of the peninsular Spaniards, and if the portion who speculate in offices, and office-holders, were not among them, they would have consummated the act of annexation themselves ere now.

As to the feeling among creoles, Mr. Saco is sadly informed; perhaps it is in the territory where he imagines annexationist views to be less advanced, that they are more extended. We cannot say now-a-days, that there is a political conspiracy in Cuba; what is to be met with is one common and universal idea. Some are ready to shed their blood for the banner which is to elevate them to the rank of men; some appreciate its advantages, and fear and hope to obtain the same results by convictions and treaties. Some, ill at ease with the law that might put a stop to the abuses on which they live, would oppose its course; but public sentiment advances daily, and all divine by an instinct, true messenger of the age,* and feel that the colossus of America is coming toward us, diffusing wealth and happiness in its path. It has been even asserted by a Spaniard, that the important act of annexation would have already taken place had it not been for the want of energy on the part of the creoles.

* Mr. Saco had called himself the messenger of the age.

But Mr. Saco would prefer that Cuba were first independent. Would he not dread to launch her in all the attempts at self-government which have been the constant reef of destruction to the Spanish family? Does not the picture of Spanish America, torn asunder by intestine dissensions, inspire him with sorrowful forebodings? Or would he deny the protecting shield which the government of the Union would lend to an incipient republic?

Informing Mr. Saco that even free-soil journals have shown themselves not averse to the acquisition of Cuba, and reminding him of occasional proofs given in the senate of a favorable disposition toward the same object, I sufficiently establish, I think, how strangely erroneous his information is regarding the opinions of the political parties in the United States. The northern states in defence of their manufactures and provisions, the eastern states of their shipping and lumber trade, the west of their grain and growing manufactures, and the south from the communion of slave interest, have but one voice—they all feel the want of Cuba. Polk, attempting negotiations at once, Cass, the candidate of the south, and Taylor, the President elect, are equally the servants of the popular will; and with regard to the latter's views, Mr. Saco must have heard, ere now, what was expressed in the senate on the subject, something like two months ago (written in December, 1847). It is but too well known that the annexation of Cuba is held as a national object, which cannot be made to serve as the banner of any one party. The masses who wish for it there, and who tolerate with displeasure the individual oppression suffered at the very threshold of the soil of freedom, do not, perhaps, busy themselves with the means of acquiring Cuba; but the states where slavery exists, aware of the political importance it has for them, do not slumber, and their prudence, their wise measures, and their enthusiasm in the cause, are sure guaranties that the annexation will take place at an early date. The pearl of the West Indies, with her thirteen or fifteen representatives in Congress, would be a powerful auxiliary to the South, and her value as an immense outlet for American manufactures, and a source of vast tropical productions in exchange, and also as a military post, would surely make the attainment of Cuba a bond of peace and union for all the states. With regard to ourselves, who can doubt that it will be a course calculated to develop the fountains of wealth, and at once dispel the clouds hovering on our future.

Now, then, the physical and moral wants of mankind *must* be granted, particularly in America, where democracy prevails, and obstacles arising from rights of conquest or possession, are settled by compacts at the risk of penalties or outbreaks more harmful to the parties opposing. If citizens can be oppressed under a tyrannical administration, when brutal force supports it, democracy may likewise use its might and strength to take off the irons from the victims of despotism. The power of the American confederacy lies in the number of resolute freemen who cover the surface of their territory—in the fact that their industry does not bear heavy taxation to pay debts contracted by preceding generations, nor to support menials, office-holders, or princes, useless to the land; or armies, only necessary to perpetuate wrong. More even than all this, does their power spring, especially in foreign countries, from the certainty that the cause of the Americans is the cause of individual liberty. Who, even though only partially enlightened, does not love this cause? What soldier, forcibly drawn from his country and home, would oppose an enemy in whose victory he sees his own and mankind's freedom? What parent, on leaving this world, would not prefer that his children, and the inheritance he bequeaths to them, remain under the guardianship of the laws of the Union?

If Texas had the advantage that her population consisted chiefly of American citizens, it had to beat against marked opposition, instead of the unanimous voice with which Cuba will be hailed by all the states and parties. The former had not the outlets and markets which the latter can offer, and when her cry of annexation sounded, France and Spain, still under dynastic influences, dared yet, the one to awe with her fleets, the other to concert pitiful combinations or expeditions for the restoration of monarchy in America; while England intrigued, and did every thing but launch into war, to prevent the annexation. What will France undertake, henceforth governed, as she is, by the law of popular majority, against American republicanism?

Without entering into a detailed examination of the aid which Cuban annexation may receive from the United States, it suffices my purpose to set down—

1. That there is not, in Cuba, the faith and determined will in favor of the *statu quo*, which Mr. Saco attributes to a part of the population.

2. That we would not consider any moral aid as such, coming from our republican neighbors, were it not based on the determination of the masses to make it real and effective.

3. That precisely when American democracy has given more proofs of energy, Mr. Saco's attempt to excite mistrust in the promises even of the President, were there any such, seems singular and unaccountable.

4. That so far from demanding twenty-five or thirty thousand men* of the government of the United States, were it a question of begging in such quarters, I would ask for fertile lands in abundance, situated no matter where, in order to give profitable occupation to the individuals of the Spanish army, who, instead of offer-

* Mr. Saco's ingenious system of annexation.

ing support to the government, as Mr. Saco supposes, are actually suffering the penalty of military service which the queen's party imposes on the prisoners in the civil war; and as the discontent is shown among them by simultaneous desertions and executions beyond what had ever before been noticed, Mr. Saco's remark that Spain *has a respectable army*, faithful under any circumstances, may very possibly be taken as ironical.

Whenever Mr. Saco shall appreciate, in its proper worth, the omnipotence, in this hemisphere, of the Great People, he will understand why it is that I rely upon them to watch and prevent attempts calculated to revolutionize the slaves. English interference in opposition to the United States, is a dream. A nation living on credit, whose masses are deprived of labor at the slightest threat of war, and whose capital and commercial business are so interwoven and confounded with those of the American people, cannot run the risk of even a temporary suspension of friendly relations with them. The denouements of the questions of the northeastern boundary—of Oregon—of Texas—and of the Mexican war, in all of which the republic gave the law, are the practical demonstration of this peculiar situation. England, even before the show of power and military skill exhibited in the Mexican war, had reconciled herself to the unlimited aggrandizement of the United States. On the other hand, the considerable consumption of English manufactures in Cuba, can but increase under the more liberal regulations of the federal government. Peace and markets for her manufactures are matters of life and death for England; the minister, tory or whig, who forgets these truths, would bitterly weep his error; because the mind of man is not able to compass the disasters which a war, especially with her ancient colony, would bring upon herself and the commerce of the civilized world. How can we then read, without wonder, the picture drawn by Mr. Saco, of England, intriguing to indispose and injure, involving in servile and sanguinary insurrection the nation whose peaceful relations are her first element of existence. The American people are too strong, their policy too open, their mission too noble for England to cause them, indirectly, the least harm, without suffering the consequences of her treason. And such is the respect which manufacturing and commercial wants have created for the United States, among the English, that Cuba will obtain the surest guaranty of the pacific views of Great Britain, whensoever the American cabinet shall openly enter into negotiations for her annexation as a new state. While this is not done, the crater which, owing to that kingdom or its American colonies, Mr. Saco noticed under our feet fifteen years ago, and which has suddenly disappeared to his sight, remains more dangerous than ever, for we have the misfortune not to ground hopes or faith in the cabinet of Madrid, or their agents, who, to judge from the men who have come in power to the island for many past years, will always be at the disposal of cabal and bribery. From the thoughtless or perfidious conduct of the Spanish ministers, who have tolerated the African slave trade, notwithstanding the danger it brings on Cuba, Saco infers that their successors in office, whatever party they may belong to, will have the wisdom to resist all advice or inducement, political or personal, calculated to emancipate the slaves in the Spanish West Indies. Surely, the administration has given proofs of being very systematical and consistent, for us to trust to the natural separation which ought to exist between the suppression of the slave trade and the emancipation of the slaves, as to a barrier, not to be leaped over by corruption, fanaticism, or incapacity. Did we see any signs that the local government, in Cuba, understood the true position of the country, and the changes that have been operated in what surrounds them, it would be some excuse for the confiding assertions which are in Mr. Saco's lips, both novel and contrary to his usually irresistible logic.

I will repeat once and again that so far from considering with this gentleman, that the demand of Cuba by the cabinet of Washington will induce the court of St. James to set at work sinister measures, I believe it to be the most efficient means of disarming the latter, who will always submit every other consideration to England's first essential wants of peace and markets.

Yes, without any hesitation we must assert, that to save slavery from a bloody crisis, and give to the institution the security which it should possess, as property, and which is not only compatible, but indispensable to its available reform, there is no other road than annexation.

"Spain dreams not," says our absent countryman, "of emancipating the slaves." Let us lay quietly to rest on this assurance. But on what is it based? Has she not withheld this assurance, that our anxiety might awe us, hanging over our heads like the sword of Damocles? On what circumstances is so important a key to the wealth of the island made to depend? May not the mere signature of a secretary of state, in an evil hour, rob the Cubans of their wealth, the commercial world of a market, and the Spanish family of a country? That Mr. Saco should be the one to qualify, as imaginary, the fear of the emancipation of the slaves, after the recent attack on the institution in other European colonies, is a matter of wonder; that he should think a war possible between Great Britain and the United States, evinces how little he has given his attention to the events herein noticed, and to the conciliatory policy of the latter government, or else that he sees every thing with the eyes of an abolitionist.

It would seem as if the ancient editor of the Cuban Review, precisely in the manner in which he appears unacquainted with the present backward political condition of the island, as contrasted with the remote period when the press was permitted to publish his writings, is equally unconscious of the influence and mighty power which the army and navy of the United States have acquired in this hemisphere—particularly on these seas, in sight, if I may be allowed so to speak, of their navy yard. In speaking of open war between England and the American Union, he says, " England, commanding the seas with her formidable fleets, will blockade our ports, will prevent the aid which we might expect from the confederacy; our produce would then not be exported, and as the climax to our misfortune, she would throw upon our coast an army of negroes."

Is not this a picture drawn to the taste of the painter? Are the results of the last war between those countries, and England's anxiety to terminate it, forgotten? Is no account to be taken of the subsequently acquired greatness of the American people? And with regard to the suggestion of employing negroes in the contest, the stain stamped on the British character, according to the powerful expression of Lord Chatham, by the enlistment of savages against their brothers, will not again be exhibited on the part of that great nation, who, after more than a half century of progress, is a model at this present day of whatsoever is noble and philanthropic.

It has been asserted before now, that the Anglo-Saxon family, divided as it now is into two great portions of American and English, from their own superiority and activity, are destined at some future day to come into conflict with one another in a most destructive manner; but experience, which often brings to nothing human foresight, is exhibiting on the contrary so many indications of the peaceful tendency of modern civilization, and particularly of those two nations, that I am really shocked at finding Mr. Saco anticipating hatred and war between them. At any rate, the care with which every subject of disagreement has been arranged among them during the past ten years, is an evidence that, at least during our generation, no change will take place in the harmony heretofore preserved for the weal of mankind.

Before closing this hurried, ill-concerted, and incomplete refutation, I must request the former advocate of Cuban rights to tell us, where lies the limit which should be marked to the forbearance and quiet submission to political degradation of his countrymen. I look around to the people of various countries, and I see none where, with so many interests, industry, and trade at stake, capital is so utterly without influence, direct or indirect, in the administration; I see that while despotism and its encroachments are disappearing elsewhere, we are pressed down with more tenacious grasp; I see the creoles put aside, oppressed, vexed, and personally and shamefully trampled upon as they never were before.

One only blessing—one only, but radiant, like the sun of Cuba—has come out of so much oppression and contempt: the consciousness of our dignity and self-respect. The Cubans have at least learned to suffer in silence, and to despise the tyrants who place themselves in the path of their rights. Spain will not find again the majority of the Cubans prostrated in an ingratiating attitude before their oppressors. If the rulers have the aid of an army of demoralized and constrained soldiers, the citizens may rely on the justice of their cause, on the moral support of the age, and on the democracy of the American Union. If the former are encouraged by the forebodings of an enlightened Cuban (Mr. Saco), the latter confide in the prophecy of a far-famed Spaniard, which is even now being fulfilled. "This federal republic," said the Count de Aranda, in his secret memoir of 1783, "is a pigmy at its cradle, if I am allowed so to speak; she has needed the support of two states powerful like France and

Spain to obtain her independence. The day will come when she will be a giant—a formidable colossus even in these parts. She will forget the services received from those countries, and will only think of her own aggrandizement. Freedom of conscience, facility in settling new emigration in vast territories, jointly with the advantage of a new government (he meant free) will draw to her the artisans and laborers of all nations, because men go after fortune; and in a few years we shall see the tyranny of this same colossus of which I speak."

It was ever the prerogative of minds of a high order to anticipate great events. Thus the Count de Aranda while judiciously estimating freedom of conscience and popular institutions in the United States, as causes for the future growth and annexation of neighboring states, and Chatham while recommending in the British parliament, notwithstanding the scant population of the incipient republic, that British power should not be enforced to oppose her—both acknowledged that moral influence superior to all other influences in this age, which Mr. Saco appears not to understand.

Would to God that this distinguished Cuban—disregarding the whisperings of his self-love, which may give bitter fruits to his country, should it keep him in the course he has chosen—would not battle against the march of the times, nor disavow the true progress which is being extended to the human race under the propitious flag of American Republicanism.

The United States increase in wealth, civilization, industry, and power, in a manner unknown in the annals of the world. Their population doubles every twenty-five years; and a progression so stupendous foils human calculation as to what will be their power and influence in times to come among the nations of the earth. What monarchy, what empire, what confederacy or league, can so much as raise their eyes to measure such boundless power? What arm is strengthening, and where, to subdue at some future day this proud and living expression of political and industrial freedom! Twenty millions of souls now, forty in 1873, and so successively on, till we come to 320,000,000 in one century. Make to this estimate, founded on the past experience, what reasonable deductions you please, and what splendid results may we not expect yet? Those are now in existence who will see this vast confederacy holding a population of 200,000,000! Where is the model, the precedent, the resemblance to this great spectacle, in the history of all the nations of the world?

In the presence of a standing reality like this, which strikes our eyes, which our hands touch, and which fills our hearts with raptures, because it is the triumph of humanity, how little must the reasonings, the views, the trivial and pompous declamations of the subdued press of Havana appear! Shall the great Mississippi, after mingling with its own the waters of the Missouri, the Ohio, and thousand other tributary streams—after impelling onward along its margin in majestic course, productions of all kinds, wealth, commerce, and population, so many signs of the mighty approach of a new, great, and enterprising civilization—shall the Mississippi, I say, while expanding its waters in the wide gulf, announce to the democracy of the world that the advantages and the glory of the American institutions will not pass forward—that the Queen of the Antilles, fertile, and great, and capable of presenting similar development of productions and well-being, will stand in the way as a check to the powerful impetus.

It is sufficient to look over the extensive valley of the Mississippi to understand that the natural direction of its growth, the point of connection of its prodigious European commerce, and of its rational defence, is Cuba. Situated as it were on the very path, in other hands, and with different institutions, Cuba is a wall that divides and interrupts their manifest growth; commanding as she does the narrow channels of Yucatan and Florida from Cape San Antonio and the Mayzi Point, were she to belong to a nation strong in the seas, what disaster and ruin would it not be in her power to inflict on the American Union in case of a war! The Americans know it, and the efforts of their government will multiply and become more energetic to obtain her annexation in proportion as their own greatness increases and approaches the extreme South with their settlements, their arts, their wealth, their wants, and their glory.

LEON FRAGUA DE CALVO.

THE END.

CONTENTS.

CHAPTER I.

CHAPTER II.

CHAPTER III.

CHAPTER IV.

CHAPTER V.

CHAPTER VI.

CHAPTER VII.

CHAPTER VIII.

CHAPTER IX.

THE KNICKERBOCKER MAGAZINE.

TERMS, FIVE DOLLARS PER ANNUM, IN ADVANCE.

THIS is pronounced, by the press of America and England, "the best Magazine in America." It has now completed its *thirty-fourth volume*, and in its list of *upward of a hundred contributors*, are found the names of every distinguished writer, male and female, in America, with several equally prominent of Great Britain, Turkey, Sweden, etc. A new volume commenced with the first of January, 1850. The following notices of the KNICKERBOCKER are from the American and English press, to which might be added hundreds of others.

"THE last KNICKERBOCKER is exceedingly good. Some of the articles are worthy of Blackwood's palmiest days. The *Editor's Table* is in Mr. Clark's happiest vein; varied and racy in a remarkable degree."—*New York Commercial Advertiser.*

"THE KNICKERBOCKER seems to increase in attraction as it advances in age. It exhibits a monthly variety of contributions unsurpassed in number or ability."—*National Intelligencer.*

"THE KNICKERBOCKER is one of the most valuable Magazines of the day, and outstrips all competitors in the higher walks of literature."—*Albany Argus.*

"THE KNICKERBOCKER MAGAZINE is now, beyond a question, *the* magazine of the country. Whoever wishes his money's worth, and something over, let him subscribe, now, to 'Old KNICK,' and our word for it, the Editor's Table alone will amply satisfy his expectations. It is not a periodical to be lightly glanced over and thrown by, but it forms a library book to be saved and re-read. A set of the KNICKERBOCKER, bound up in volumes, on the shelves of one of our popular libraries, is more consulted (so the librarian has often told us) than any other similar work."—*Boston Daily Transcript.*

"This very clever Magazine is the pleasantest periodical in the United States. Its articles, which are numerous and short, various and interesting, are well worthy of imitation by our Magazines on this side of the Atlantic."—*London Examiner.*

"Judging from the numbers before us, we are inclined to consider this the best of all the American literary periodicals. Its contents are highly interesting, instructive, and amusing."—*London Morning Chronicle.*

"The taste and talent which the KNICKERBOCKER displays are highly creditable to American writers, and very agreeable for English readers."—*London Literary Gazette.*

"We have read several numbers of this talented periodical, and rejoiced in them. They would do credit to any country, or to any state of civilization to which humanity has yet arrived."—*London Metropolitan Monthly Magazine.*

"The Knickerbocker.—The last number of this venerable and widely-popular periodical appears upon entirely new and beautiful type, in all its departments; and in its rich and diversified contents, continues to vindicate its reputation as the most agreeable and entertaining Magazine published in the United States. When we first started the old 'New-Yorker,' our friend Clark had preceded us, as editor of the Knickerbocker, about a twelvemonth; it has now reached an age greatly beyond that of any American monthly, a fact which literally 'speaks volumes' in praise of the manner in which the work has been conducted. No number of the K. has ever been issued under Clark's supervision that did not bear indubitable evidence of editorial care, and anxious thought, and well-directed labor enstamped upon its pages. We have known no monthly, of this country or Europe, so thoroughly *edited*, in the strictest sense of the term. With a corps of contributors embracing the most eminent writers of the country, with not a few from the other side of the water, it has been able to present articles of a high order of merit, and in rich variety; while, as if emulous of the contributed portions, the editorial department has regularly increased in variety and abundance."—*New York Daily Tribune.*

"Nothing is more remarkable than the unfailing promptitude of this old Monthly, except, perhaps, its constant, and constantly increasing excellence. Mathematicians tell us of certain curves called *asymptotes*, whose peculiarity is always to approach each other, and yet, even when infinitely extended, never to intersect. The Knickerbocker, which has reached an age for a Magazine much greater than a hundred years for a man, and only to be attained by a more marvelous miracle, has perpetually approached the highest possible point of interest and excellence; and yet it seems to have an *excelsior*, for each number seems better than that which went before. How it is done, our friend Clark may understand—but it is a sealed mystery to us. There is no publication in the United States that has so attractive or popular a feature as the *Editor's Table* of the Knickerbocker."—*New York Courier and Enquirer.*

OPINIONS OF DISTINGUISHED WRITERS.

"I peruse the Knickerbocker with high gratification. It seems to me of an order of merit quite above the average of the periodicals of this class, English or American."—*President Everett, of Harvard College, and late Minister to England.*

"The manner in which the Knickerbocker is conducted, and the great merit of its contributors, place it in the highest rank of periodicals."—*Hon. J. K. Paulding, late Secretary of the Navy.*

"The Knickerbocker stands high in this quarter. It is superior to most of the English magazines, and well deserves its large list of subscribers."—*Prof. Longfellow, Cambridge University.*

"The Knickerbocker is a work which requires no puffing; and I shall always feel that I am conferring a favor on those to whom I recommend it."—*Hon. Robert M. Charlton, Georgia.*

"I have long regarded the Knickerbocker as the best periodical in America, and it really seems second to none abroad."—*Mrs. L. H. Sigourney.*

"The Knickerbocker is the best American periodical I have yet seen. I take pleasure in inclosing you an article which was penned expressly for your work."—*Sir Edward Bulwer Lytton.*

I read the KNICKERBOCKER with very great pleasure; it is indeed a most varied and entertaining periodical. It affords me pleasure to contribute to the pages of a work which numbers among its regular correspondents such writers as Mr. Irving."—*Charles Dickens, Esq.*

"I have read a good many of the articles in the few numbers of the KNICKERBOCKER which you sent me, and find them to possess great merit. Some of its papers, it is true, were too light for my serious turn of mind, yet the whole appears well calculated to gratify the tastes of the mass of readers."—*Rev. Dr. Dick, Scotland.*

"You make an excellent Magazine—spirited, various, and original. I hope my '*Moonshine*' will reflect no discredit upon the good company in which it will find itself."—*Capt. F. Marryat.*

REDUCTION IN PRICE TO CLUBS.

The publisher has determined to do every thing in his power to bring the Knickerbocker within the means of all, and invites the attention of those who feel an interest in circulating the *best American literature*, to the following terms to clubs, viz.:

For five copies sent to one address, the price will be	$20 00
" ten " " " "	35 00
" twenty " " " "	60 00

Post Masters throughout the Unites States are invited and requested to act as agents. To all those who may interest themselves in getting up clubs, we will send a copy *free* so long as they keep up, and remit, regularly, the yearly payment.

GREAT INDUCEMENT TO SUBSCRIBE FOR THE KNICKERBOCKER

FOUR YEARS FOR TEN DOLLARS.

The undersigned will give the volumes of the Knickerbocker for the years 1847, '48, '49, and '50, to all persons who will remit to him *ten dollars*, in funds current in this city, *post paid.*

AGENTS WANTED FOR THE KNICKERBOCKER MAGAZINE.

Enterprising, active agents are wanted in every town and city in the United States, to procure subscribers for the Knickerbocker. To competent, active persons, with satisfactory references, the most liberal terms will be allowed. Apply, *post paid*, to SAMUEL HUESTON, 139 Nassau street.

☞ Back Volumes or Numbers supplied, and a complete set for sale.

Specimen numbers sent free of charge on application, *post paid.*

TERMS—$5 per annum, in advance. All remittances must be made to

SAMUEL HUESTON, Publisher,
139 Nassau-st., New York.

Just Published,

SAINT LEGER;

OR,

The Threads of Life.

"Quicquid agunt homines, votum, timor, ira, voluptas,
Gaudia, discursus, nostri farrago libelli."

NEW YORK: GEO. P. PUTNAM.
LONDON: RICHARD BENTLEY.

FROM THE AMERICAN JOURNALS.

"The author is entitled to the gratitude of all thinking and serious minds, for the very plan and leading idea of his book. A young soul anxious, agitated, and distressed with the mighty problem of our present human life as connected with our future destiny; a thoughtful spirit on the shore of the great ocean of existence, *dubitans, circumspectans, hesitans—tamquam in mari immenso vecturus, multa adversa secunda revolvens*—seeking rest, yet finding none, because unsatisfied with respect to the ultimate, and perfect, and absolute rest of the human spirit—extracting no substantial enjoyment from the 'seen and temporal,' while in darkness with regard to the 'unseen and eternal'—finding, in short, no happiness in any lower good while the great question remains unanswered—who, or what will show us *the* good, the *absolute good*, that *summum bonum* for which 'a man should straightway sell all that he hath;' that good which humanity lost in Adam, and which it hopes to find again in Christ?

"A religious weekly periodical,* of high standing, says of Saint Leger: 'It is a book we cannot recommend. Its want of definite moral purpose is the more noticeable in consequence of the manifest power of the writer.' With all deference we would say that, such a definite presentation of such a definite moral purpose, in the outset, would have entirely defeated any true moral purpose the author may have had in view........The author is evidently one familiar with his Bible. This, in these days, is not commonly true of any man, unless he really loves it, and it reveals the secret of much of his power. It is this which reveals to him a chapter in the human heart unknown to such writers as Dickens and Bulwer, for it is evident that, in the delineation of certain traits, and the power of certain emotions, he strikes a chord which never thus vibrates to their touch."—'*The Inner Life, a review of Saint Leger, by Tayler Lewis, LL.D.*'—*Literary World.*

"St. Leger is without a prototype in English literature. It is not to be read for the interest of its story, but as an accurate and subtile delineation of the workings of a deep, inner experience, and the rich blossoming out of character in a skeptical and fermenting age. In this point of view it is a work of originality and undeniable power. The style is exquisitely adapted to its subject. There are passages of rythmical, melodious sweetness, which belong to the best days of English prose, and reveal both the ear and the hand of a true artist."—*New York Tribune.*

* New York Observer.

"No man who has ever asked himself the three startling questions—where am I? what am I? whither go I? can fail to sympathize with the hero of our author's story. Our chief interest in the hero lies in tracing the progress of his individual mind from its consciousness to maturity, and in noting the effects which are produced on his moral and intellectual nature by a life full of passion and adventure. We see all passing circumstances from the centre of his spiritual being. We seldom feel like lending him an arm to protect him from outward troubles, but often like dropping into his mind a thought to save him from the evil influence of doubts engendered by the workings of such troubles on his inner nature. This manner of telling a story is, certainly, a bold and novel one; but, at the same time, one which rivets our closest attention, and attaches our warmest sympathy.

"In the darkest part of the hero's career, the profoundest point of the whole lesson is taught through the partial instrumentality of one of the most beautiful womanly creations in the whole range of English fiction. Theresa, the embodiment of the spirit of intuitive and simple faith—a type of uncorrupted humanity—and Wolfgang Hegewisch, the embodiment of desperate philosophy, and hopeless skepticism—a type of humanity suffering through its own sins, and through the sins of others—are the two opposite agents of St. Leger's salvation...

"Around the central character of Saint Leger, during his mental struggles, there is continually passing a series of rapid and startling events, which seem to arise, like the chain of circumstances in the doctrines of the Necessitarians, for the purpose of hurrying the hero to some fated end. The manner in which Saint Leger's inner nature, and the course of outward events, act and re-act on each other, is managed with a masterly hand.

"So subtile and intimate is the union of the two states of existence, and yet so distinct is the preservation of each, that the reader turns from one to the other with equal pleasure, never becoming so absorbed in the hero's mental movements as to lose sight of the story, nor so carried away by the story as to forget his sympathy with the silent workings of Saint Leger's mind.........Its strong good sense, its firm sentiment, its deep, subtile, metaphysical reasoning, its healthfúl morality, can only be passingly noticed."—*Sartain's Magazine.*

"There is a vein of deep sentiment pervading the book, which raises it far above the level of ordinary works of entertainment. The author is both poetical and philosophical; he writes with perspicuity, grace, and elegance; and the minute revelations of feeling, faith, mental processes, sensation, and superstition; the peculiar picture of the inward life of the chief personage, combined with the incidents and descriptions interspersed, render it one of the most attractive books of the season."—*Home Journal.*

"Saint Leger has many touching points; sometimes it touches us by its simplicity, sometimes by its eloquence, at all times by its truthfulness The poetry of young life is portrayed with enthusiam, and the cares with which its future is shadowed the author does not turn away from, with irresolution of judgment."—*New Orleans Bulletin.*

"A novel *sui generis* in the annals of American literature. Saint Leger solves the problem of human life, while it accurately sets forth the sufferings and strivings of an acute philosophical mind, and presents to the perplexed and wearied in the search of truth, the simple panacea of faith."—*Philadelphia Drawing-Room Journal.*

"Full of thought and sentiment, and of a thoroughly original cast, it will make a permanent impression on the public mind. It bears the marks, too, of scholarship, and fine taste, and of an eclectic cast of mind."—*New York Commercial Advertiser.*

"One of the very best books that has fallen under our notice, for a long time."—*Scott's Philadelphia. Weekly.*

"Abounding in the most thrilling interest, in narrative, and in maxim."—*Metropolitan.*

"The truth is, it is a peculiar production........ There are not many men in this country, known as authors, from whom it could have come....... A young Englishman, of a noble Warwickshire family, with a devout and gentle mother (he says of her, finely, 'Morning and evening did I lisp my infantile prayers to her, and it seemed as if she sent them up for me to God"), and with a high-principled, stern, and taciturn father, goes out, early, into the world, to see it, to taste of it, to master it, or to be mastered by it. The story runs in the first person singular; the hero is the narrator, and, *mirabile dictu*, he does not once fall in love, ride horseback, kill his man, nor commend himself to women as a rake. Perhaps these defects ought to take him out of the category of romantic personages. But he has his adventures, nevertheless........ He is educated, at home, by a private tutor—a cold-blooded, stoical, intellectual Pantheist—who drives an entering wedge for infinite mischief into the young man's faith. Saint Leger contends, all along, with a traditionary superstition, suffers from it, has his existence shadowed by it, and illustrates the wicked folly of dark predictions........ Instigated by his speculative preceptor, Saint Leger travels to the Continent, and takes up his abode at Leipsic........ To give the true termination to his unhappy internal struggle, we cannot but hope the author of Saint Leger will run the "Threads" of his "Life" a little farther."—*Boston Christian Register.*

"The author appeals only to the moral sensibilities. He is a thinker, and has not only the power to set others a thinking, but of uttering for others the thoughts for which they have never found a tongue. Many will find in this book the history of their own mental struggles."—*Newark Daily Advertiser.*

"A mystical, metaphysical novel, written with great power and beauty; original in its character, and deeply interesting. By the thoughtful and reflecting reader, it will be regarded as a work of rare merit."—*Washington Union.*

"This work, which has attracted so much attention, is in the form of an autobiography, and abounds in the most beautiful ideas of life and happiness, while a vein of elevated morality runs through the volume."—*Providence Journal.*

"The book is a strange one—neither a romance, a biography, or a love story, but rather a blending of them. Yet the occurrences are a part of the great book of eventful life. No one can read the first chapter without wishing to go on, and the interest is heightened at every step."—*Philadelphia City Item.*

"The author is one who has looked beneath the surface of things, and to whom the heart of man, in all its windings, seems familiar."—*Middletown Oasis.*

"A book of great strength, containing vivid and artistic limnings of human nature in its darkness, and in its spiritual brightness."—*New York Evening Post.*

"Under the drapery of fiction, the author inculcates the purest morals, and the highest, and most ennobling of Christian faith. The language is polished, and even elegant, and it abounds with passages of great fervor and beauty. The work has a peculiar fascination about it."—*New York Journal of Commerce.*

"Who is the author of this powerfully written work? We have read it with more absorbed interest than has been awakened by any work of fiction that has come within our notice for a long time."—*Philadelphia Evening Bulletin.*

"It may be called a diary of the human heart, its purposes, and its impulses; yet it inculcates a true Christian philosophy. No one can rise from its perusal without a satisfied feeling that his destiny is wisely ordered, and that the pursuit of truth is the surest path to happiness."—*Philadelphia Sun.*

"It is a book of power. Its author has genius; genius for description, for character, and for dialogue."—*Boston Post.*

"The book is of the highest order of English literature."—*The Metropolis.*

There is thought enough, learning enough, invention, passion, power enough, in Saint Leger, for the best half-dozen fashionable romances of the time. It is perhaps wanting in continuity of interest; but its very deficiency in this respect makes it but more true to the general experience........It is altogether profoundly philosophical, and must be classed among the finest of those fictions which illustrate the development and establishment of whatever is beautiful and true in human character.—"*Review of Saint Leger, by R. W. Griswold.*"

"A very singular production, written with great power, and unusual ability."—*Germantown Telegraph.*

"A book exhibiting great power and genius."—*Boston Times.*

"A brilliant book, full of suggestions of wisdom."—*Tribune.*

FROM THE ENGLISH JOURNALS.

"A very extraordinary book. It is the 'Tremaine' and 'De Vere' of the metaphysical student. There is the same force, the same knowledge, the same originality of thought and expression; and we shall be disappointed if Saint Leger does not rival the fame of those two justly celebrated works."—*Morning Post.*

"The moral purpose of Saint Leger is to warn against vague and dreamy apprehensions in childhood; the substitution of Rationalistic and Pantheistic notions for Christianity later in life, and their concealment—in the case of the hero from his mother. The first point is illustrated by the peculiar disposition of William Henry Saint Leger, his peculiar training at the family country-seat, and an old prophecy touching the Saint Leger race, which the rest of the family wisely disregard, but which the hero nourishes in secret, and which causes him to regard himself as a doomed mortal, or child of destiny.

"The heresy is produced by a German tutor, who is himself infected with the singular ideas of religion at that time (toward the close of the last century) springing up in this country..........The descriptions have force and picturesqueness; the reflections strength and rhetoric."—*Spectator.*

A powerfully written work, which unveils the baseness that underlies the loftiest pride, the doubt that ever haunts the struggling faith, the impetuous folly that mingles with wisdom's high resolves, the ignorance and blindness that lurk, ill-disguised, beneath the free-thinker's boldest speculations, and the emptiness and deadness of heart which succeed the satiety of a self-gratified life.........

"The variety of characters introduced, all sharply chiseled, their varied fortunes and destinies, all contribute to impart to Saint Leger a character of originality, and high moral and intellectual interest."—*John Bull.*

"Here, there, and every where, the author of Saint Leger gives exhibitions of passionate and romantic power."—*Athenæum.*

GEO. P. PUTNAM, Publisher,
155 Broadway.

www.ingramcontent.com/pod-product-compliance
Lightning Source LLC
LaVergne TN
LVHW010244110826
845151LV00004B/1388

* 9 7 8 1 4 2 5 5 2 3 4 1 1 *